SICKERT *in Venice*

CW01673931

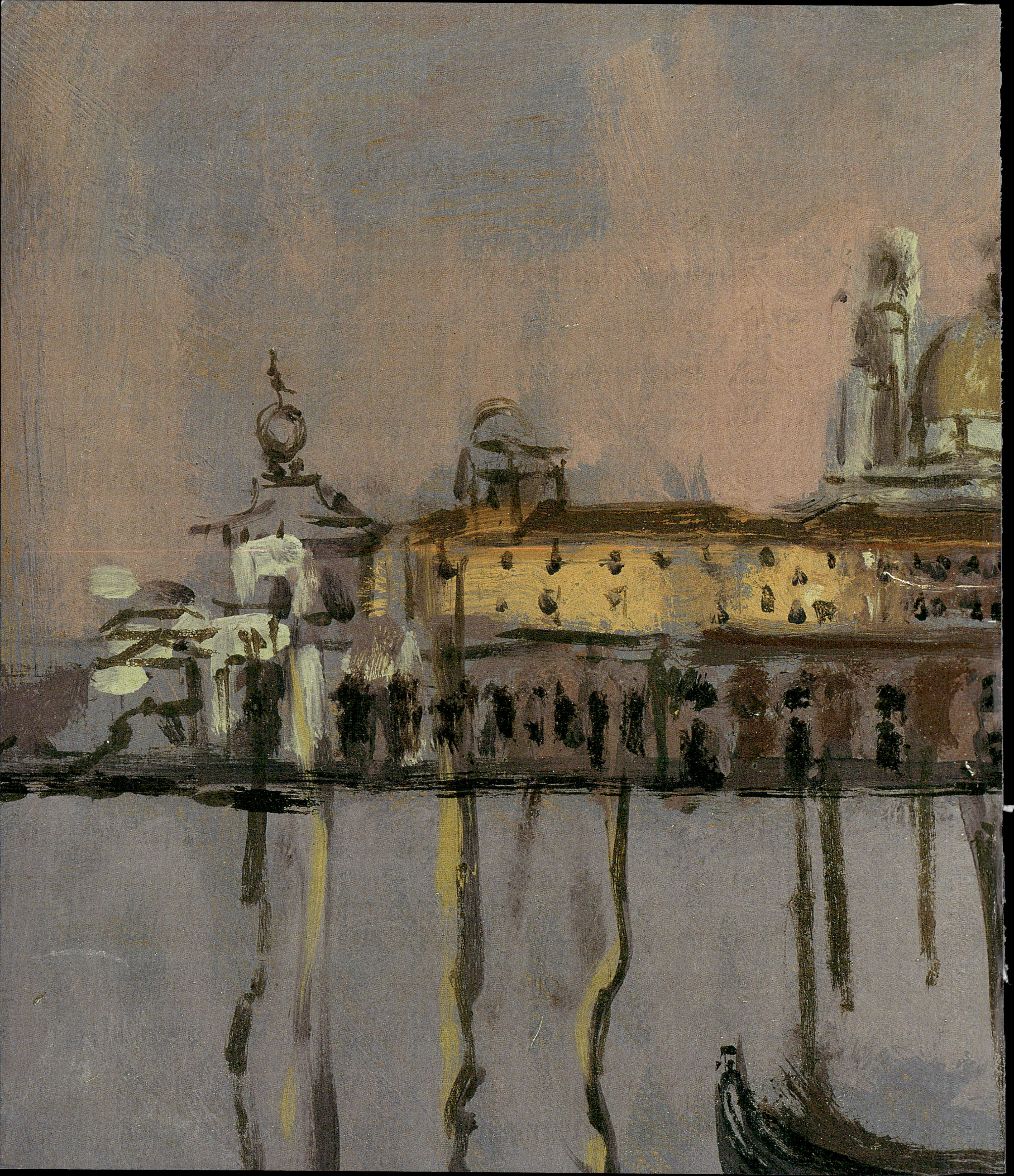

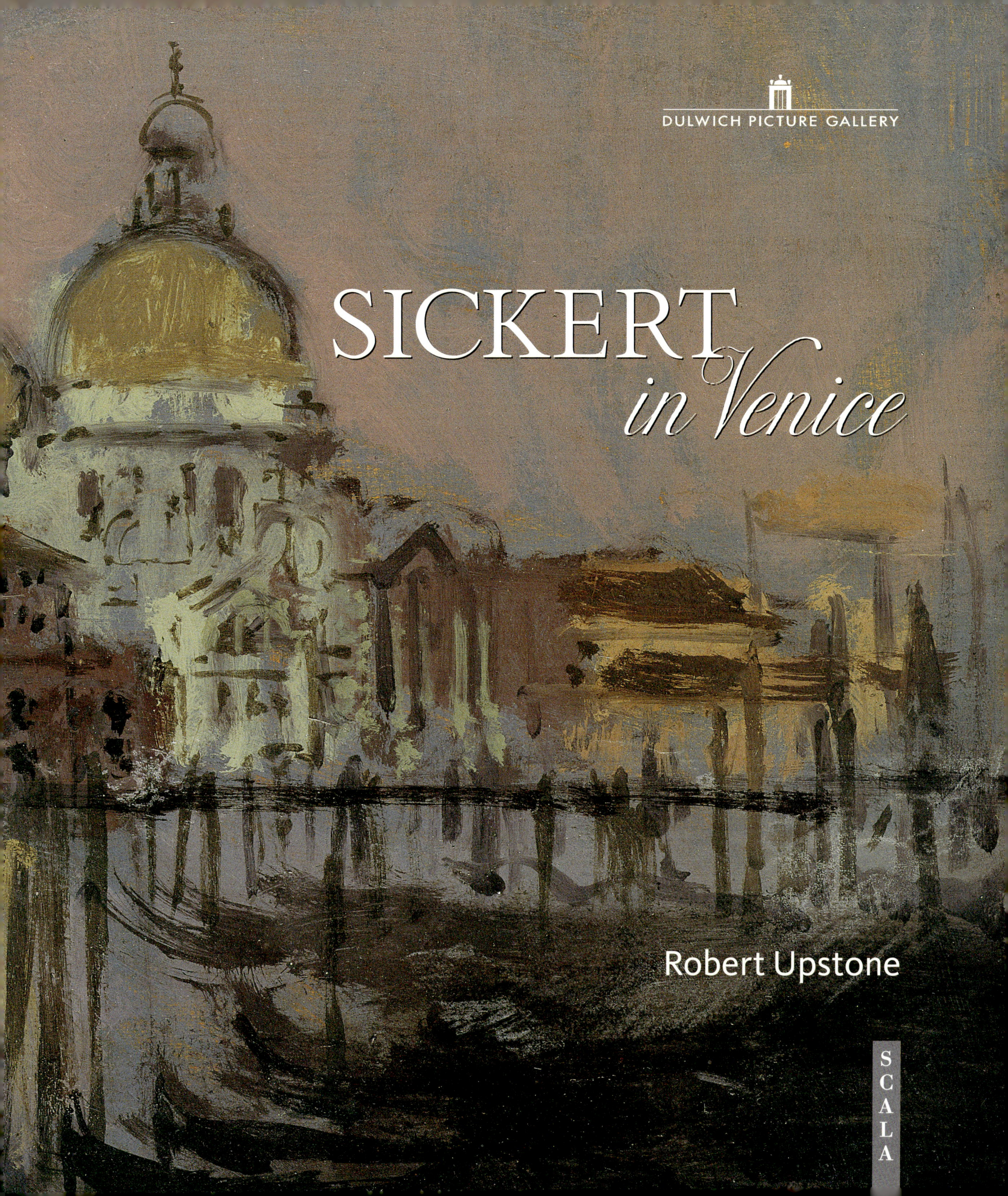

DULWICH PICTURE GALLERY

SICKERT *in Venice*

Robert Upstone

SCALA

This edition © Scala Publishers Ltd 2009
Text © Dulwich Picture Gallery 2009

First published in 2009 by
Scala Publishers Ltd
Northburgh House
10 Northburgh Street
London EC1V 0AT, UK
www.scalapublishers.com

In association with
Dulwich Picture Gallery
Gallery Road, London SE21 7AD
www.dulwichpicturegallery.org.uk

ISBN: 978-1-85759-583-3

Designer: Nigel Soper
Editor: Oliver Craske
Production Director: Tim Clarke
Printed in Spain

10 9 8 7 6 5 4 3 2 1

All rights reserved. No part of this book may be reproduced, stored in a retrieval system or transmitted in any form or by any means electronic, mechanical, photocopying, recording or otherwise, without the written permission of Scala Publishers Ltd.

Every effort has been made to acknowledge correct copyright of images where applicable. Any errors or omissions are unintentional and should be notified to the Publisher, who will arrange for corrections to appear in any reprints.

Pages 2–3: Walter Sickert, *The Dogana and Santa Maria della Salute*, *c.*1896 (cat. 24, detail)
Page 6: Walter Sickert, *Study in Rose*, 1903–04 (cat. 46, detail)

Contents

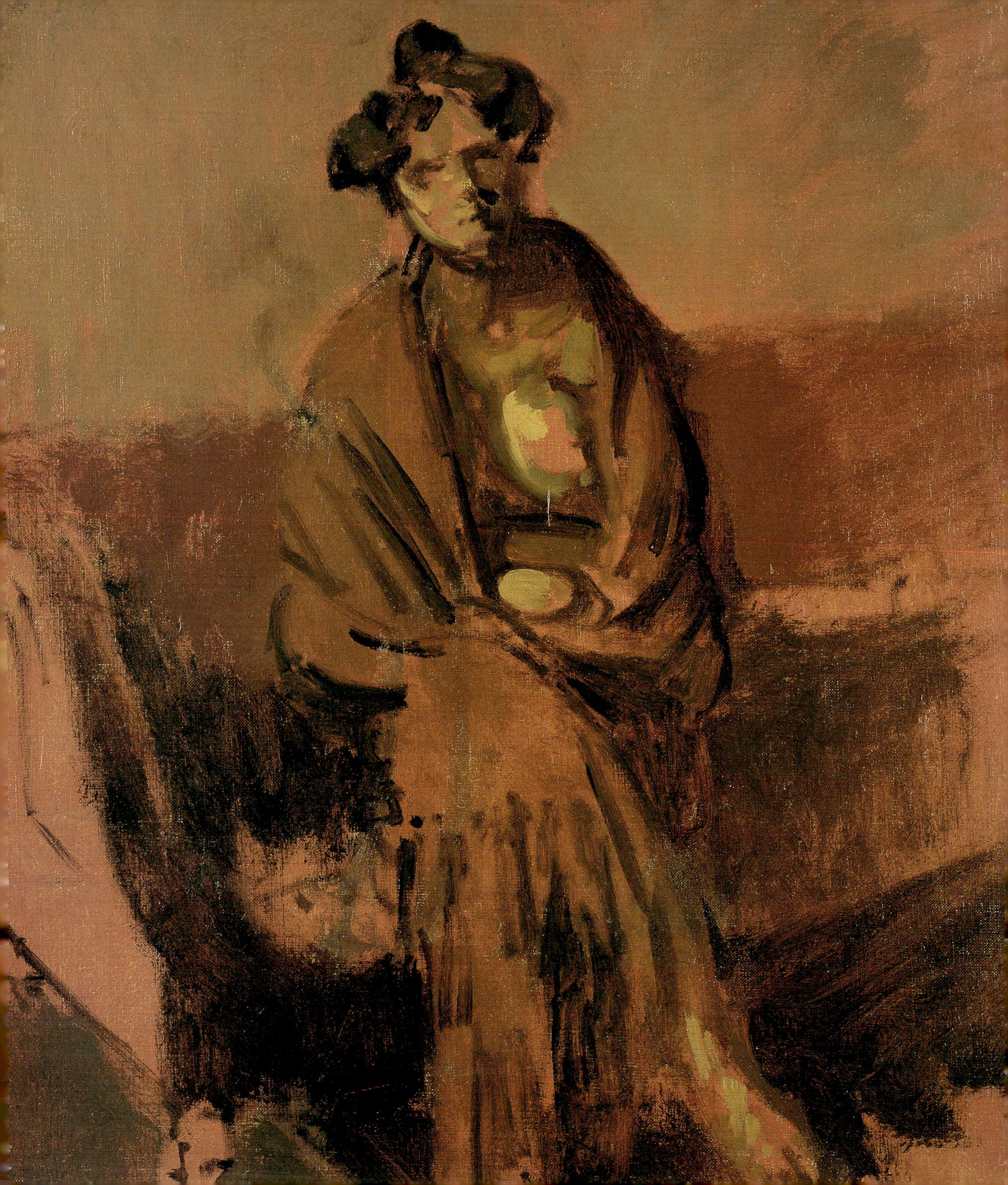

Foreword

IN 2007, DULWICH PICTURE GALLERY hosted a phenomenally successful exhibition entitled *Canaletto in England*. The Venetian master of the picturesque cityscape spent ten years in England, and that exhibition bore witness to the energising effect that London, the great 'boom' city of the age, had on his art. *Sickert in Venice* returns the compliment, but whereas Canaletto came to England in pursuit of the market and at the height of his powers, the influence of Venice on Walter Sickert was more personal and formative.

Sickert's relationship with the city of Venice may have been forged out of the bitterness of a personal tragedy – the failure of his marriage – but that seems only to have intensified his feeling for the place. Starting with ravishing 'tourist' views of St Mark's and the Bridge of Sighs, rendered partly in homage to Monet but always in his own remarkable palette, Sickert gradually moved his gaze away from the stones of Venice and focussed instead on its people, in particular his two favourite models, Giuseppina and Carolina; gradually he moved indoors, and into a more complex frame of mind. Ultimately, virtually every aspect of Sickert's later output – certainly all that we know him best for – was to be adumbrated in his Venetian work.

I am extremely grateful to Robert Upstone, Curator of Modern British Art at Tate Britain and curator of this show, who first pointed out that an exhibition that focussed on Sickert's Venetian output in fact contained the whole within the part; and that here, therefore, was the perfect 'chamber' exhibition for Dulwich Picture Gallery. Robert has done this great artist full justice.

I would also like to thank Sanne Klinge, Exhibitions Officer, for so expertly managing this project, with the support of Acting Head of Exhibitions Mella Shaw, and Exhibitions Assistant Matthew Cowpe.

This catalogue has been another happy collaboration with Scala Publishers: my thanks go especially to Oliver Craske, Editorial Director; and to Nigel Soper for yet another beautiful design. Our sincere thanks also go to the Design and Artists Copyright Society for granting copyright permission.

The show would not have been possible without the support of The Hon Elizabeth Cayzer, the Robinson Bequest, the Edith Callam Bequest, and – again proving their exceptional support to the Gallery – the remarkable Friends of Dulwich Picture Gallery.

IAN A. C. DEJARDIN
Director, Dulwich Picture Gallery

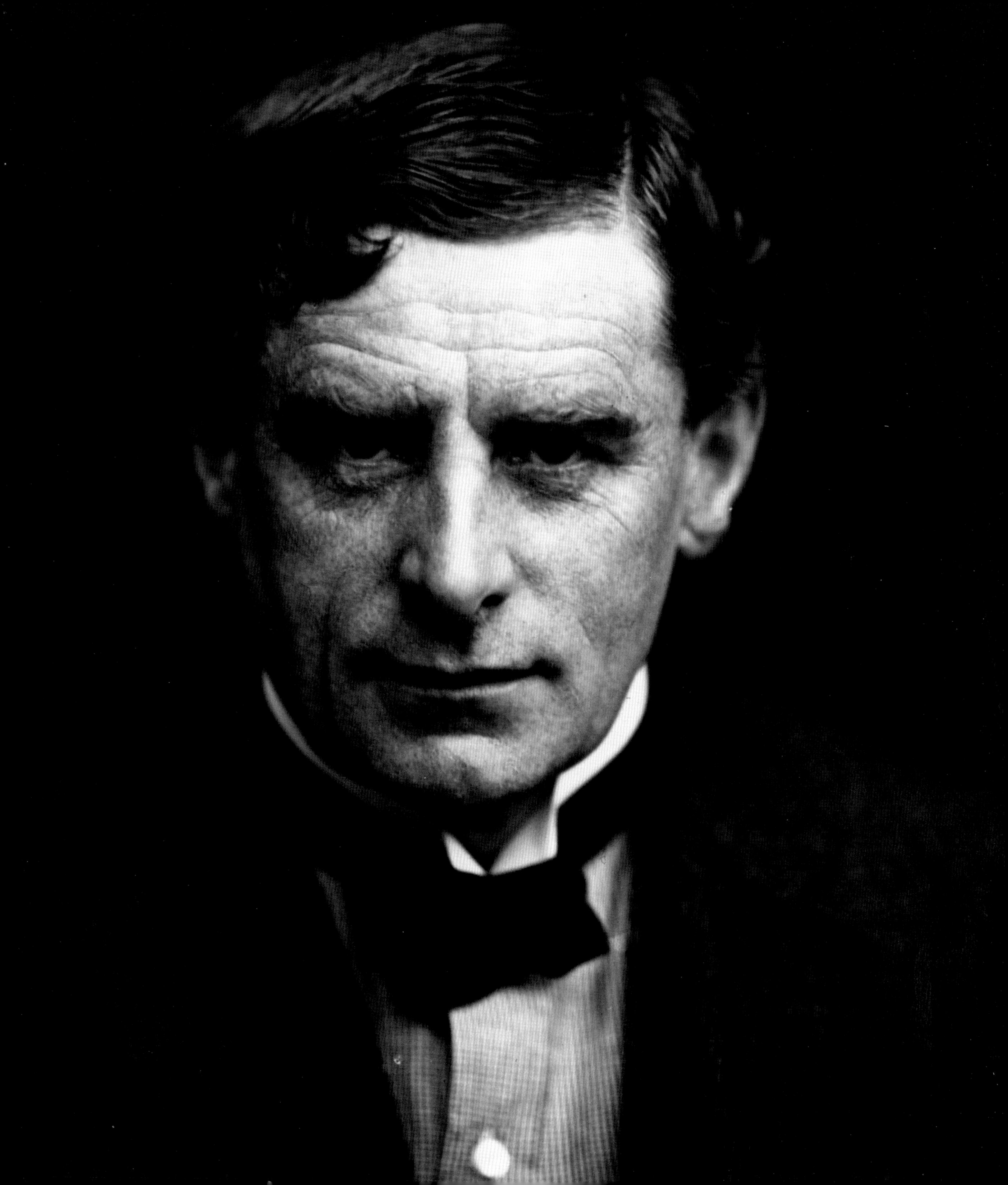

Sickert *in Venice*

A MAN OF SPARKLING WIT and forceful personality, Walter Sickert (1860–1942) was one of the most important British artists of the late nineteenth and early twentieth centuries (fig. 1). Pupil of Whistler, friend of Degas, Renoir and Pissarro, he introduced modern French painting to a younger generation of British artists, 'sent from heaven to finish all your educations', as he once put it.[1] Nevertheless, we tend to think of Sickert as a painter inextricably identified with London, whether it be the boisterous badinage of the music halls in his pictures of the 1880s, or the cheap bedsits of Camden Town and the working Londoners who inhabited them in the early years of the twentieth century. But the formation of Sickert's artistic identity between these two phases, and the route he travelled to become the painter of working-class pathos or torpor, was altogether international in its origins. It was in a city very different from London that Sickert developed his distinctive and highly original approach to the figure – it was in Venice (fig. 2).

Venice was, Sickert wrote, 'the loveliest city in the world'.[2] It was a place about which he was passionate, and it drew him back repeatedly. He first visited in October 1894 with his wife Ellen, making a relatively brief trip that was essentially a holiday and did not apparently inspire any pictures. But after this first foray, Sickert made a succession of much longer visits, in 1895–96, 1900, 1901 and 1903–04. Each one of these lasted several months and was characterised by intensive work which produced finished oil paintings in large numbers. Returning to London and his studio in Dieppe in between, Sickert continued to create pictures of Venice away from the city, using his archive of drawings on which to base fully developed oils. For nearly a decade Venice formed the dominant subject in his art and the city inspired him to discover new modes of expression. Through hard work and experimentation in Venice, Sickert became the painter who was to be recognised as the most significant figure in early Modern British art. In short, Venice was the crucible in which Sickert's mature work was formed. It was where Sickert remade his artistic identity, and where he worked through ideas that would prepare him as the godfather of Modern British art in the new century.

Between 1895 and 1903 Sickert focussed only on painting Venice's grand vistas and buildings. These were the mainstay of the pictures that he sent for sale in Paris, where they enjoyed commercial and critical success. The first pictures Sickert made in Venice were highly impressive views of St Mark's and the Rialto, treated in his own distinctive version of impressionism. Painting the city's architecture, he sometimes adopted Degas's practice of cropping compositions to make them visually more exciting. And he also painted a number of nocturnes, showing the city at dusk or in darkness.

But on his final painting expedition of 1903–04 the poor weather drove Sickert indoors, and he moved in a wholly new direction. Using a pair of Venetian prostitutes as models – La Giuseppina and Carolina del'Acqua – he began to experiment with

Fig. 1
George Charles Beresford
Walter Richard Sickert
1911
Half-plate glass negative
National Portrait Gallery, London

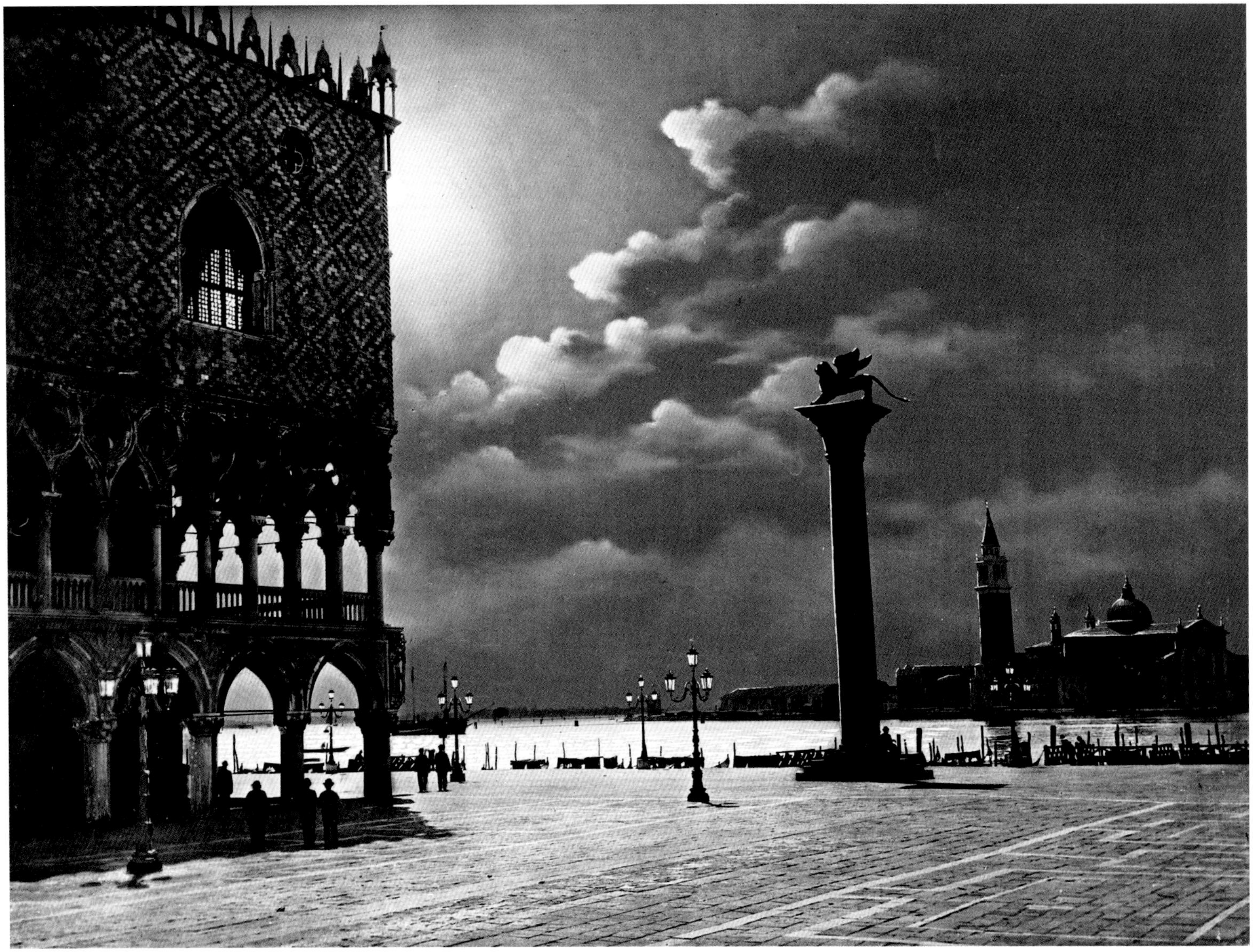

Fig. 2
Tomaso Filippi
St Mark's Square
*c.*1894–1903
Photograph

Venice photographed during the period Sickert visited the city.

approaches to painting the figure. The two women appear in pictures in which any narrative or commentary is wholly abandoned, and instead replaced by a subtle invocation of mood or atmosphere. The suppression of any story drives us to speculate on the pictures' status or meanings, and their indefinite titles compel us to contemplate the nature of what we are looking at. Witnessing the private moments of these paintings forces the viewer into the role of voyeur, searching for significance amid reflections of their own lives. This new hunger for naturalism might be linked to the theatrical realism of Ibsen and Strindberg, whose plays utilised silence, stillness and atmospherics to create dramatic tension instead of simple action and dialogue. Himself an ex-actor, Walter Sickert arranged figures in his Venetian interiors like people on a stage.

Sickert's study of the figure also explored placing the nude in naturalistic poses and surroundings, a development partly inspired by Degas. Until then, British artists had rarely dared portray the nude except as an element of classical myth. In Venice Sickert originated his own wholly distinctive approach to the nude which, unlike Degas, sought to emphasise the psychological impact of what was shown in the pictures. By mixing clothed and naked figures together he established a certain indefinite dialogue between them, and also implied uncertain relationships of ease or unease. These were the subjects that would become predominant in Sickert's art when he returned permanently to London. In Camden Town he continued his exploration of the potential of the figure, painting working-class women in dingy bedrooms. Surprisingly, the subjects of Camden Town painting, so British in their gloom and grime, were actually first evolved in Venice.

The backdrop to Sickert's artistic discoveries in Venice was a period of significant personal setback and hardship. His marriage collapsed, sending him into a period of despondency and self-examination. He was struggling with his career too, in need of new material and a new approach to reinvigorate his flagging fortunes. He had very little money and, leaving aside its artistic potential, Sickert found Venice an agreeable location because it was a cheap place to live. Slowly, there came the beginnings of a modest commercial viability for his art, which was starting to be admired and sold in Paris. Venice was where he reclaimed himself. With the success of his Venetian experiments, by the time Sickert returned permanently to London in 1905 he was in a position to extend the career gains he had carved from his long absence in Italy and France, and to lead a group of younger painters who together ushered modern painting into Britain.

Venice – 'The Loveliest City in the World'

Sickert's first meaningful experience of Venice was indirect, through the medium of James McNeill Whistler. As his studio assistant, Sickert helped Whistler print his series of Venetian etchings in London from around 1882 onwards. Much of Sickert's initial knowledge of Venice must have been absorbed through these images and Whistler's description of Venetian life. Most of Whistler's etchings and pastels were not of famous sites or views, but of locations away from the throng, evocative scenes in narrow walkways and canals. Sickert was evidently impressed by Whistler's Venetian prints, and he was inspired to make a copy of one of them, *The Little Lagoon* (fig. 3). He followed Whistler's design with scrupulous detail, even reproducing the master's butterfly signature. But, fascinatingly, there is a fundamental difference between original and copy: Sickert's etching is reversed. This may imply Sickert traced it in some way onto his own plate, but there may be a more complicated origin. Whistler's own practice was to draw directly onto his etching plate, thus producing a final print that was the mirror-image of what he had seen. This meant that architectural relationships were reversed, a fact that is known to have greatly irritated Sickert. In later life he wrote that Whistler's etchings should be reprinted in a book the right way round:

> Let us enjoy, *for the first time*, without having to reverse them in a looking-glass, the witty comments of the hand that flew like a swallow over the surface of the copper in lyrical appreciation of the loveliest city in the world. I do not want to think I am looking along the Riva towards the Via Garibaldi when I am really looking towards the Ducal Palace. It worries me, and spoils my pleasure to see the Salute on the Giudecca and San Giorgio on the Zattere. Whistler is great – but so is Venice.[3]

Sickert's first visit to Venice is often thought to be the trip that he made in 1895. But in fact he went there a year earlier, an intention he signalled in a letter to the publisher Rudolf Dircks in September 1894. His first experience of the city was early the following month, when he joined his wife Ellen who was staying at the Hôtel Beaurivage on the Riva della Schiavone.[4] This was one of the smarter hotels, similar in price to the Danieli, with rooms costing between three and seven Italian francs. Dinner was five francs, or full board could be had for between nine and sixteen francs.[5] The visit lasted until November, when Sickert was recorded as being back in London, while Ellen had travelled on to Florence. There are no details of this first trip and no dated drawings that derived from it. The visit may have had the character of a holiday rather than an opportunity for serious work, but it seems unthinkable that Sickert did not at least make some sketches or pocket-sized oil studies, and there must be the possibility that some works usually dated to 1895–96 might come from this slightly earlier phase.

When Sickert returned to Venice in May 1895 there was a strong sense that both his life and his art were at a crossroads. It was an opportunity for a new beginning in the face of setbacks and failures, both artistic and personal. At this early stage of his career Sickert struggled to sell his pictures, and his ability to continue was based solely on having the support of his wife Ellen's allowance. Ellen was the daughter of the wealthy Member of Parliament and free trade crusader Richard Cobden, and the income from her deceased parents' estate effectively supported the couple. The year had started badly. In January 1895 Sickert had gained the significant opportunity of an exhibition with his brother Bernhard at Van Wisselingh's Dutch Gallery at 14 Brook Street in London. It was the first opening Sickert had ever had to gather his work in force and he exhibited a total of 49 oils, drawings and etchings, while Bernhard showed 26 landscape studies. It gave Sickert the chance to present an overview of the work he had made over the past ten years. But when the show opened, it was greeted with little enthusiasm. Even supportive critics such as D. S. MacColl were lukewarm, complaining that Sickert did not possess Degas's innate sense of design and that his pictures were so dark as to be outshone by their frames.[6] And other usually hostile critics, who could at least be relied upon to make Sickert's work a talking point, failed to find anything to raise their ire. Instead they viewed Sickert's retrospective with indifference. Among the pictures exhibited were important music hall subjects such as *Minnie Cunningham* (1892)[7] and *Little Dot Hetherington at the Bedford Music Hall* (*c.*1888–89),[8] exhibited along with her classic song title 'The boy I love is up in the gallery'. These were pictures that had defined Sickert's originality and innovation in the late 1880s and earlier 1890s. Now they were met with little emotion other than something approaching boredom. The overall feeling was that Sickert had delivered nothing new, and that for an artist who had become known for pushing the boundaries of accepted taste in art, this was greatly disappointing. Roger Fry summarised this reaction when he wrote to his wife after seeing the exhibition that it seemed 'less than it would have done some years ago'.[9] Sickert later declared himself crestfallen.[10] If his work was not to slip from attention, he would need new subject matter, and shortly after the Van Wisselingh exhibition he aban-

Fig. 3
Walter Sickert
Venice, the Little Lagoon after Whistler
*c.*1884
Drypoint, 10.1 x 6.9 cm
Fitzwilliam Museum, Cambridge

doned the music hall. Venice would provide the new impetus, direction and focus for his art.

Sickert was left out of pocket by the exhibition, with a significant bill for framing. His financial situation worsened in the autumn of 1895 when *The Studio* and *The Idler* both stopped reproducing his drawings, their small fees having formed the major part of Sickert's meagre income. There was tension too in his studio. Whistler returned to London in the winter of 1894–95 and Sickert generously offered to let him share his studio in Robert Street in Cumberland Market. Whistler's personality made him an amusing but often tiresome guest, and there was also a very real sense that Sickert was unwilling to allow his former master to resurrect his formerly dominant status over him. The two men resumed their friendship and socialised intensively, but William Rothenstein perceived a new coolness between them.[11] The following year they would fall out and characteristically Whistler would regard Sickert with total enmity.

There were additional pressures on Sickert. His personal life had become a source of complexity. Ellen was travelling extensively on the Continent and Sickert used this as an opportunity in early 1895 to begin a passionate affair. The identity of the woman is likely to have been Ada Leverson, also married, and one of Oscar Wilde's closest supporters. Ellen's sisters urged Sickert to come to stay in their house, perhaps indicating some suspicion, but he appears to have resisted.[12] Wilde's trial dominated the news in April and May, and after it came a reaction against experimental artistic expression outside the established order. But in fact, Sickert was producing almost no work. He had been overtaken by lassitude and all his energies were spent conducting his affair with Mrs Leverson, and his creativity had stalled.

These various events and tensions formed the background to Sickert's departure for Venice in May 1895, travelling by train.[13] Leaving London behind, with its complications, he must have hoped Venice would offer new material for his art and potentially reanimate his career. It would be a new start. Reunited with Ellen, Sickert entered the well-connected and enjoyable expatriate social scene. His wife had already been in Venice long enough to make numerous social contacts, and she was staying in a flat at Canal San Gregorio 222.[14] But disaster soon struck. An incriminating letter signed 'Ada' was discovered by Ellen that indicated Sickert's affair, and their marriage reached a crisis. Ellen decided to forgive Sickert and together they decided that this moment would mark a new beginning. Perhaps fatally, in July 1895 they parted again, with Sickert returning to London and Ellen heading north to Germany. Back home Sickert reverted to type and began another affair, this time with Max Beerbohm's sister Aggie.

Sickert and Ellen arranged to meet in Milan in October 1895, and from there they travelled back to Venice together. Here they stayed in some style at 788 Zattere, although not without the occasional surprise. Sickert wrote to Philip Wilson Steer:

> A friend – you know Mrs Leigh Smith – well, Miss Leigh Smith her sister-in-law has lent us a 'very nice flat', as George Moore would say... with a south aspect over the Zattere... Good food, good wine, good cook (nearly sat on a *scorpion* in the W.C. Thought of you at once: of what you would say.)[15]

Sited close to the Gesuati church, Sickert could look across at the Giudecca, and he was only a short walk away from the Accademia gallery and its wealth of Old Master paintings. In the Gesuati was Titian's altarpiece of *The Martyrdom of St Lawrence*, and also works by Tintoretto and Palma Giovane. Sickert began to work well, and respond to what he saw around him, whilst keeping in mind his commitment to impressionist experiment. He wrote to Steer:

> Venice is really first-rate for work… and I am getting some things done. It is mostly sunny and warmish and on cold days I do interiors in St Mark's.[16]

He made a visit to London in January 1896, returning in February to Venice where he remained until October. But in May, when the tenancy of Miss Leigh Smith's apartment ended, Ellen took rooms in Calle San Zaccaria and Sickert moved elsewhere to live. Their relationship was now in near collapse. When Ellen left for England on 1 June, Sickert did not accompany her, and stayed on in Venice. His repeated infidelity and refusal to moderate his behaviour left Ellen few options, and their marriage was effectively over. It was dissolved in London in 1899. In a lengthy article about the divorce trial, *The Times* reported that in September 1896 Sickert had admitted to Ellen that 'he had been living an adulterous life ever since they had married'. In an exchange of letters in 1898, Sickert informed her bluntly, 'As I told you long ago, I cannot continue a life of dissimulation; I have chosen my mode of life and I am unable to alter it. An undertaking to do so on my part would be misleading.'[17] Ellen's hurt and dismay, and Sickert's unremitting mixture of charm and selfishness, found expression in a thinly disguised novel that she wrote, *Wistons*, published in 1902. The fictional couple visit Venice together, but the wife is constantly neglected, while the husband makes new friends. Looking back at their visit with sadness and longing she recalls 'how often she had wanted him to be with her, on the piazza at night… to be with her in the gondola, to hold her hand and tell her prettier things than anyone else could think or say.'[18]

In early May 1896, just at the moment he and Ellen began to live apart, Sickert took as his studio a flat at 940 Calle dei Frati. It was here that he would complete his paintings during all his subsequent time in Venice, and in retrospect it is tempting to see its occupation as the beginning of a new phase in his life and career, and a break with the past. The flat is in a building that still stands. In Sickert's time the bottom floor was occupied by a bar, and he was on the top floor. This was where he would go to work, living elsewhere, and so separating the seriousness of painting from other aspects of his life. Calle dei Frati runs north off the Zattere, close to the Rio di San Trovaso. It was extremely close to the flat Miss Leigh Smith lent him and Ellen, and was a walk of perhaps three minutes to the Accademia and Grand Canal. But the area was not on the tourist trail, and was popular with artists, perhaps attracted by cheap accommodation.[19] Horatio Brown, the expatriate British writer about Venice, whose guides and histories were standard travel books for visitors, was on friendly terms with Sickert and lived a short distance away up the Zattere, on Ca'Torresella. Returning in September 1903, Sickert took new rooms in which to live at 1057 Rio Terà di San Silvestro, preferring the working-class bustle of this area. He had gone off the Zattere as a place to live because 'it smells of the British & the Church of England & of Ruskin'.[20] But he kept up the flat at Calle dei Frati in which to work, and even appears to have paid rent to retain it after his departure, believing he would return after 1904.

St Mark's Basilica

Sickert's remark to Steer about painting inside St Mark's Basilica relates to a significant oil on which he had been working, *Interior of St Mark's, Venice* (cat. 8). His comment suggests he made a number of paintings of the interior, but in fact only one other picture in oils is known, *Church Interior with a Figure in a Niche* (1895–96), which shows a smaller section of the same composition.[21] The loose painting and free handling of *Interior of St Mark's, Venice* bolsters the suggestion that Sickert painted it *in situ*. There are no suggestions of composition lines under the paint surface, or squaring up, and no surviving drawings of the composition, and the clear impli-

Walter Sickert
Interior of St Mark's, Venice
c.1895
(cat. 8, detail)

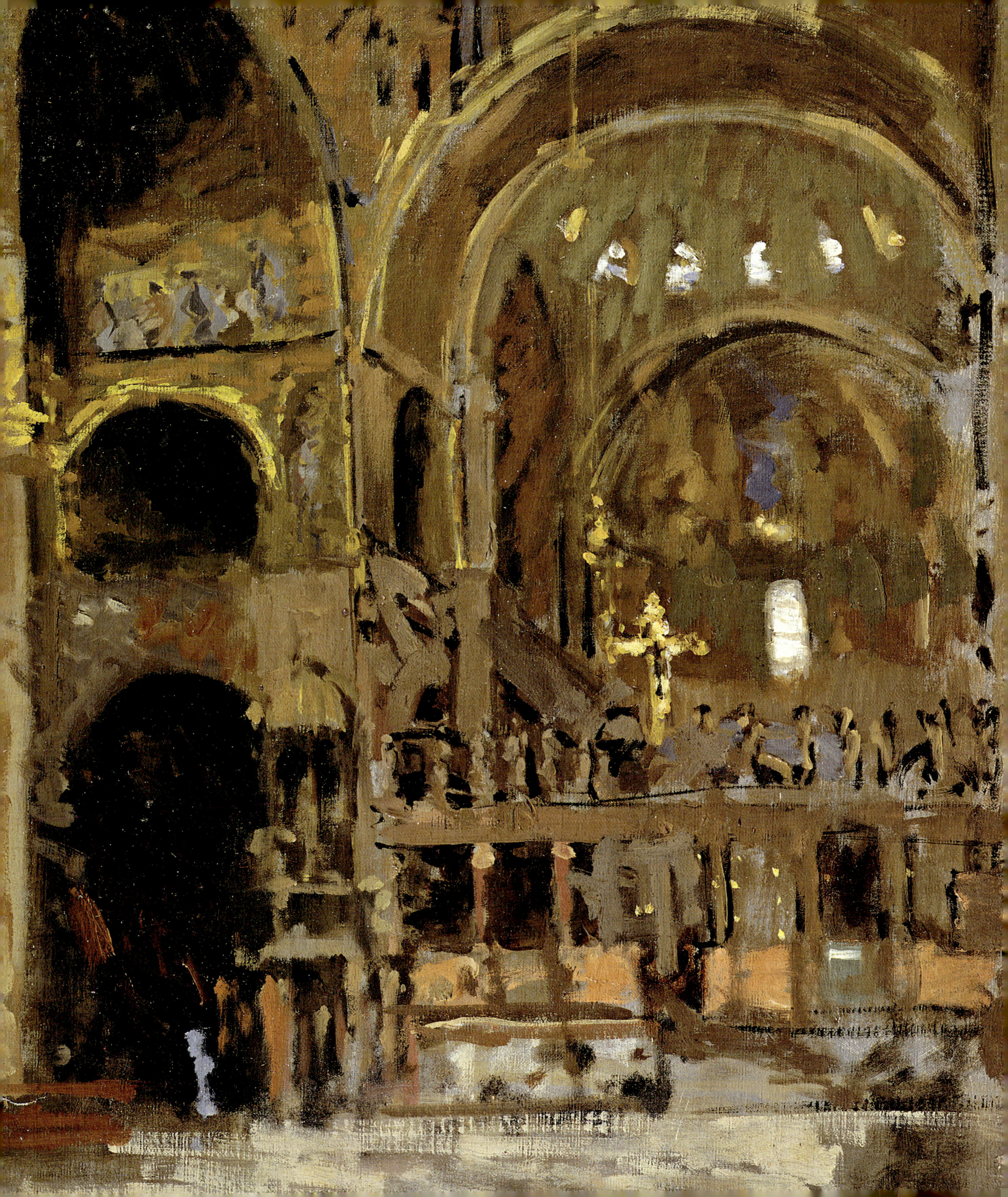

cation is that Sickert painted the interior from sight, a very considerable achievement on this scale. Its size meant that he would have required a large easel to support it. Sickert positioned himself halfway down the right side of the nave, looking towards the iconostasis and apse, but also allowing him to gain a dual perspective on the left up to the mosaics of the Chapel of St Isidore. It is a complicated and ambitious perspective that manages to include much of the interior and gives a sense of the complex vaulting of St Mark's. Wendy Baron has drawn comparison with the pictures of the balcony of the Old Bedford music hall Sickert made before leaving for Venice.[22] While *Interior of St Mark's, Venice* is more expansive in its composition, the viewpoint looking up, the handling of paint, rich colouring and extravagant architecture all hold strong resonance with the Old Bedford pictures. But there is an even more arresting similarity to the series of studies that J. M. W. Turner made in St Mark's (fig. 4).[23] Executed in gouache on brown paper, these hold strong resemblance to Sickert's oil in that they are painted in loose, fluid brush strokes, and have the same kind of low-key palette accented with highlights. Displays of Turner's works on paper were shown regularly at the National Gallery in a series of selections made by Ruskin in the closing decades of the nineteenth century and it is likely Sickert would have viewed them. Indeed, he later acquired a copy of A. J. Finberg's *Inventory of the Turner Bequest*, published in 1909, the detailed listing of Turner's sketchbooks, drawings and watercolours.[24]

For *Interior of St Mark's, Venice* Sickert's viewpoint is relatively low, indicating he was seated. Although painted in subdued, restricted colours, Sickert conveys the glitter of the Basilica's mosaics and gilding, and the lamps above, by using carefully controlled highlights. He was evidently preoccupied with conveying in touches of paint the contrasting effects of both natural and artificial light. Sickert applied a thin layer of grey paint over the white primer to function as an 'optical ground', brushing it on randomly in order to produce a texture independent of the final image. His initial drawing was made with the brush directly onto the canvas in black paint. The layers of paint applied subsequently suggest he worked on the picture over several sittings, allowing the paint to dry thoroughly in between. Sickert's paint was applied thinly in scumbles, so that the grey ground would harmonise its tonality, and the texture of the canvas has been allowed to break through to sustain a lively surface and sensation of spontaneity.[25] He evidently wished to experiment, and when it came to painting another church interior at this time, *Gli Scalzi: The Church of the Barefoot Friars* (cat. 9), his technique was quite different. Whereas for the St Mark's interior he allowed patches of brushed-on colour to define form, in *Gli Scalzi* he made a carefully detailed outline drawing and then meticulously filled in each individual sector with colour.

Sickert described his approach to *Interior of St Mark's, Venice* in detail to Philip Wilson Steer, summarising just what he was trying to create:

> It may be a poor compliment, but for all practical purposes the more experience I have, the more I find that the only things that seem to me to have direct bearing on the practical purpose of painting my pictures are the things that I have learnt from you. To see the thing all at once. To work open and loose, freely, with a full brush and full colour. And to understand that when, with that full colour, the drawing has been got, the picture is done. It sounds nothing put into words, but it *is* everything put into practice.[26]

St Mark's was easily the most famous building in Venice, and it is interesting that in this initial phase of Sickert's artistic exploration he stuck to very conventional architectural subjects. Unlike Whistler,

Fig. 4
J. M. W. Turner
Venice: The Interior of San Marco, looking into the North Transept
*c.*1840
Bodycolour and watercolour, 29.6 x 22.3 cm
Tate, London

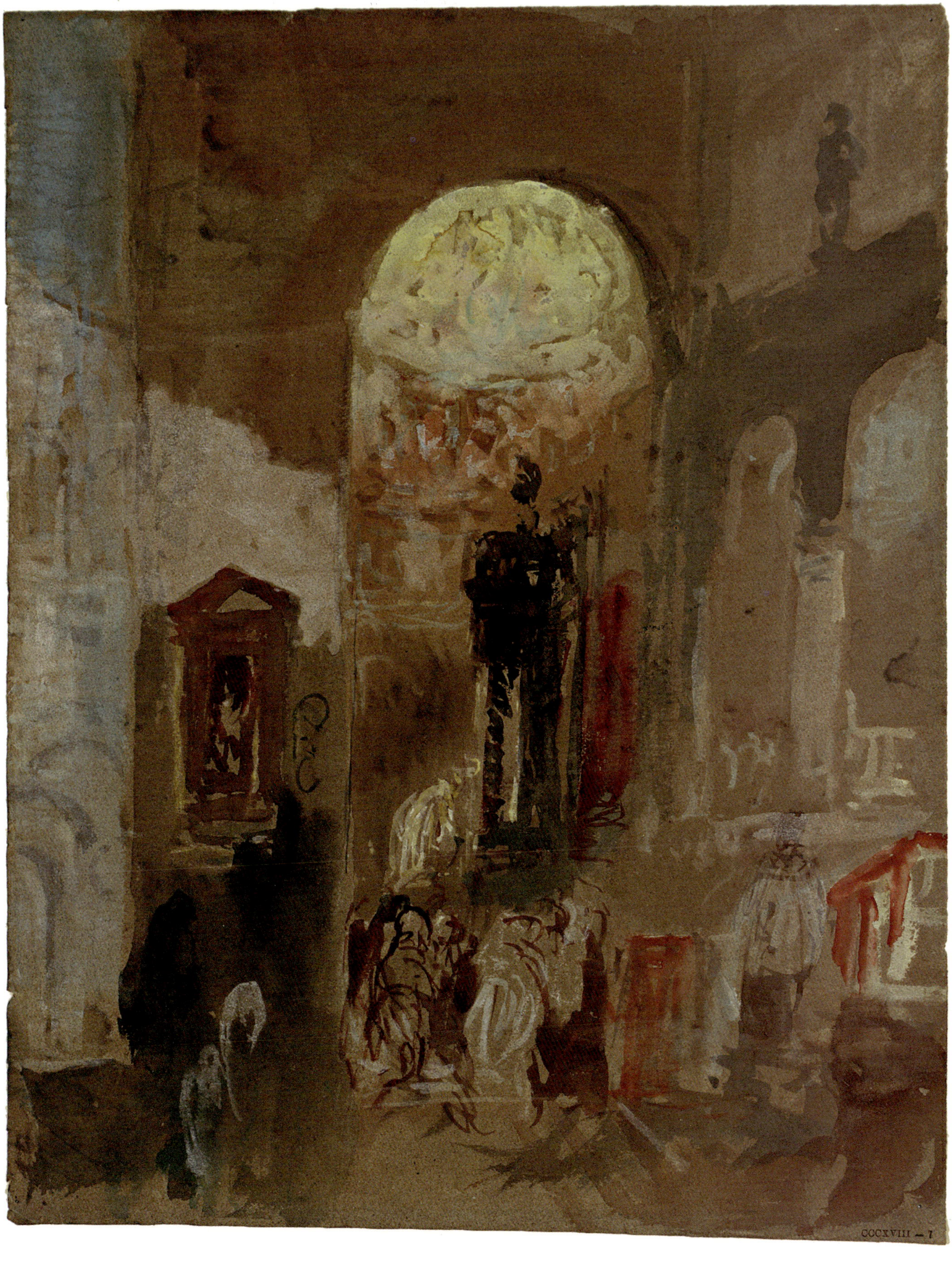
CCCXVIII – 7

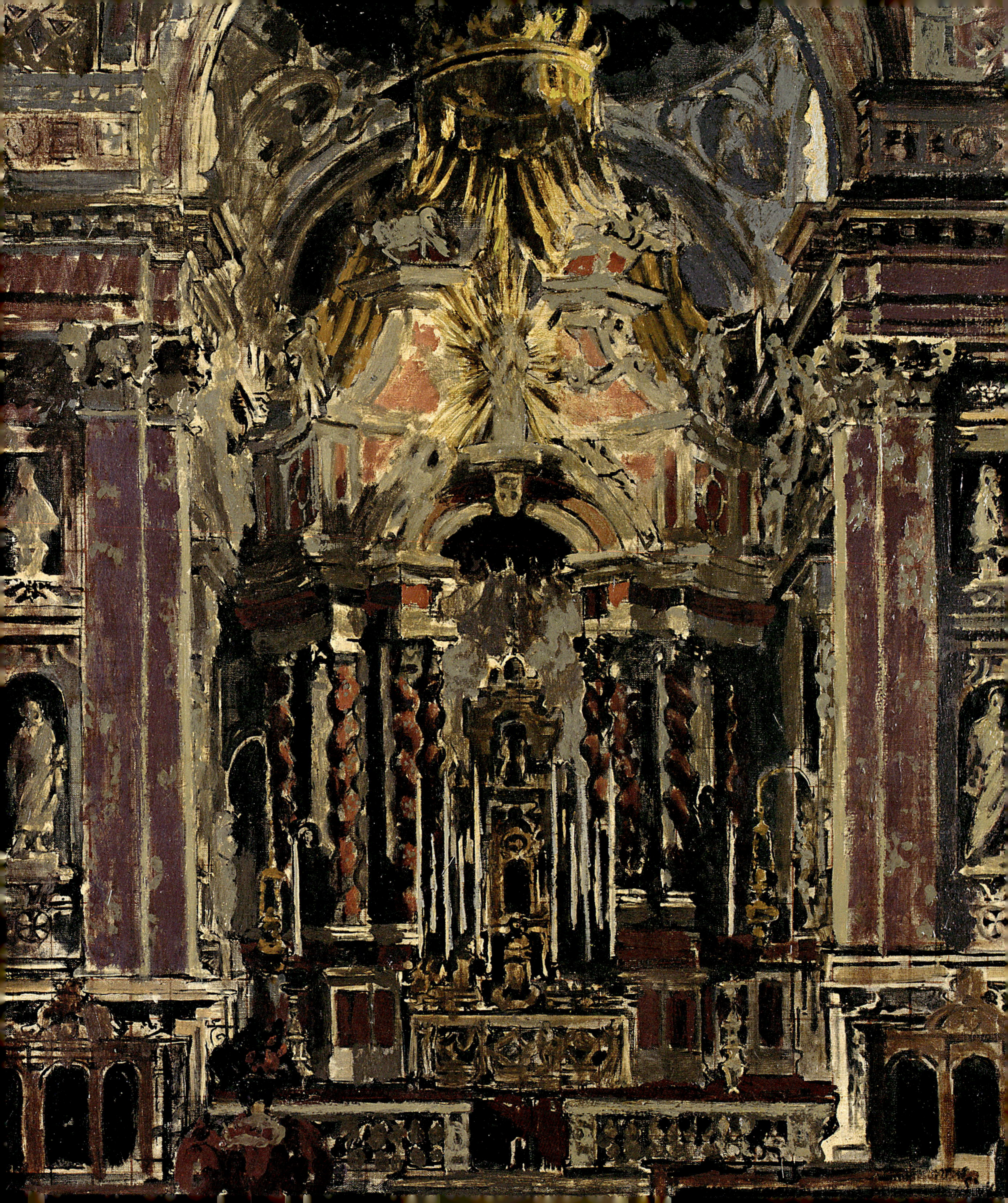

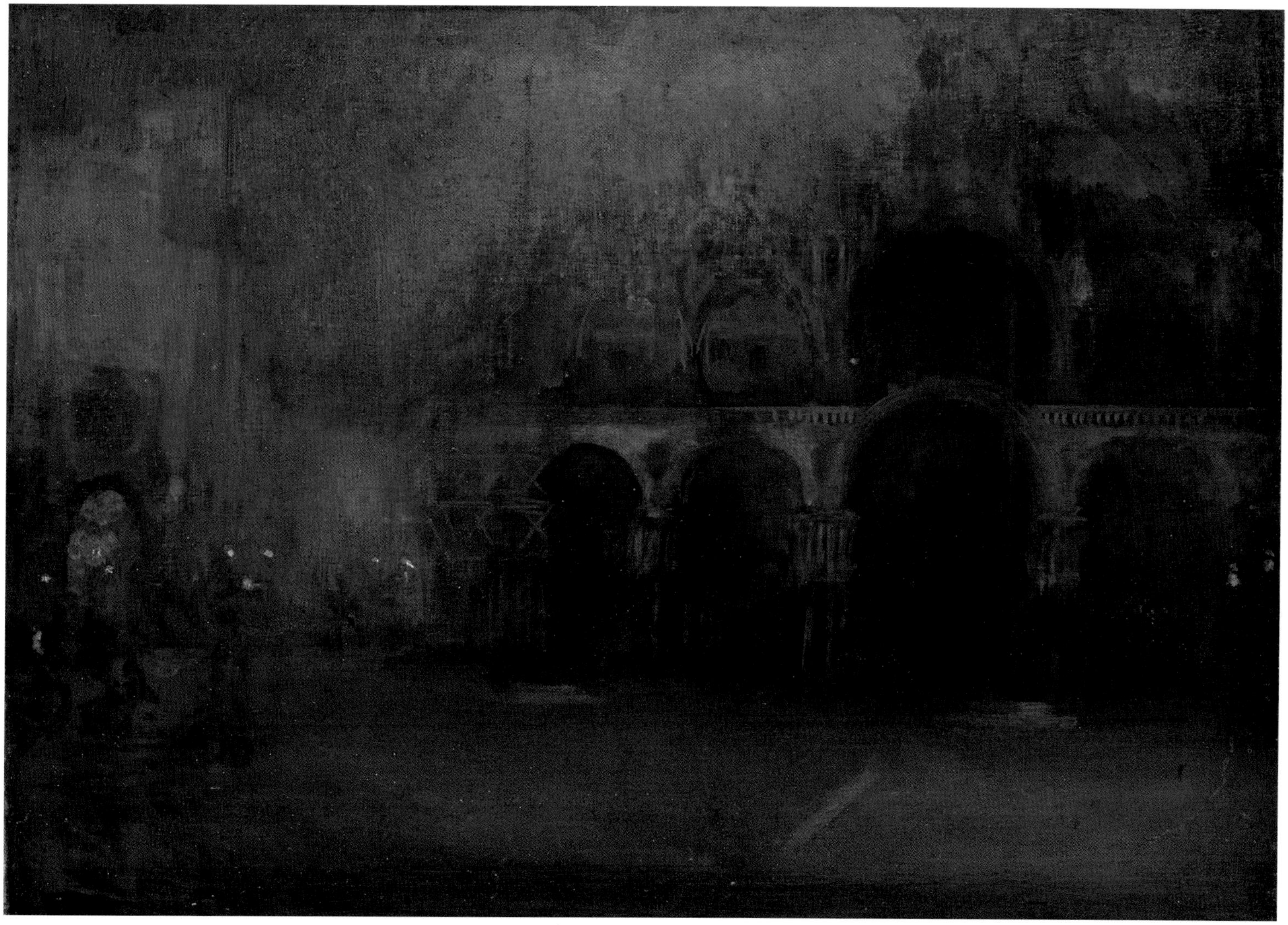

Fig. 5
James McNeill Whistler
Nocturne: Blue and Gold – St Mark's, Venice
1879–80
Oil on canvas, 44.5 x 59.7 cm
National Museum of Wales

Walter Sickert
Gli Scalzi: The Church of the Barefoot Friars
c.1895–96
(cat. 9, detail)

who focussed on lesser-known backwaters, Sickert concentrated on the principal tourist sites. As he wrote to Steer, 'St. Mark's is engrossing and the Ducal Palace and 2 or 3 Renaissance gems, the Miracoli and S. Zaccharia and the Scuola di San Marco.'[27] Perhaps Sickert was feeling his way, or possibly in his selection of what to paint he recognised that these modern *vedute* would be the easiest to sell. St Mark's, however, was evidently a source of genuine fascination and it formed the subject of a sequence of paintings that were the earliest oils that Sickert produced of Venice. Some inspiration could have come from Whistler. While Whistler generally selected obscurer corners of the city, one notable exception was the night view he painted in oils, *Nocturne: Blue and Gold – St Mark's, Venice* (fig. 5).[28] Sickert must have seen it, either in Whistler's studio in the 1880s or at its exhibition at the Society of British Artists in 1886–87 and at the Goupil Gallery in 1892. It is an atmospheric study of mood and darkness, the Basilica occupying only one half of the composition, and at odds with the concept of Sickert's St Mark's façade pictures except in being an evocation of a particular time of day and location. While Whistler was in Venice, Ruskin's disciple John Wharlton Bunney (1828–1882) was there painting his own meticulous record of the Basilica, *St Mark's as it Looks in the Early Morning of a Sirocco Day* (fig. 6).

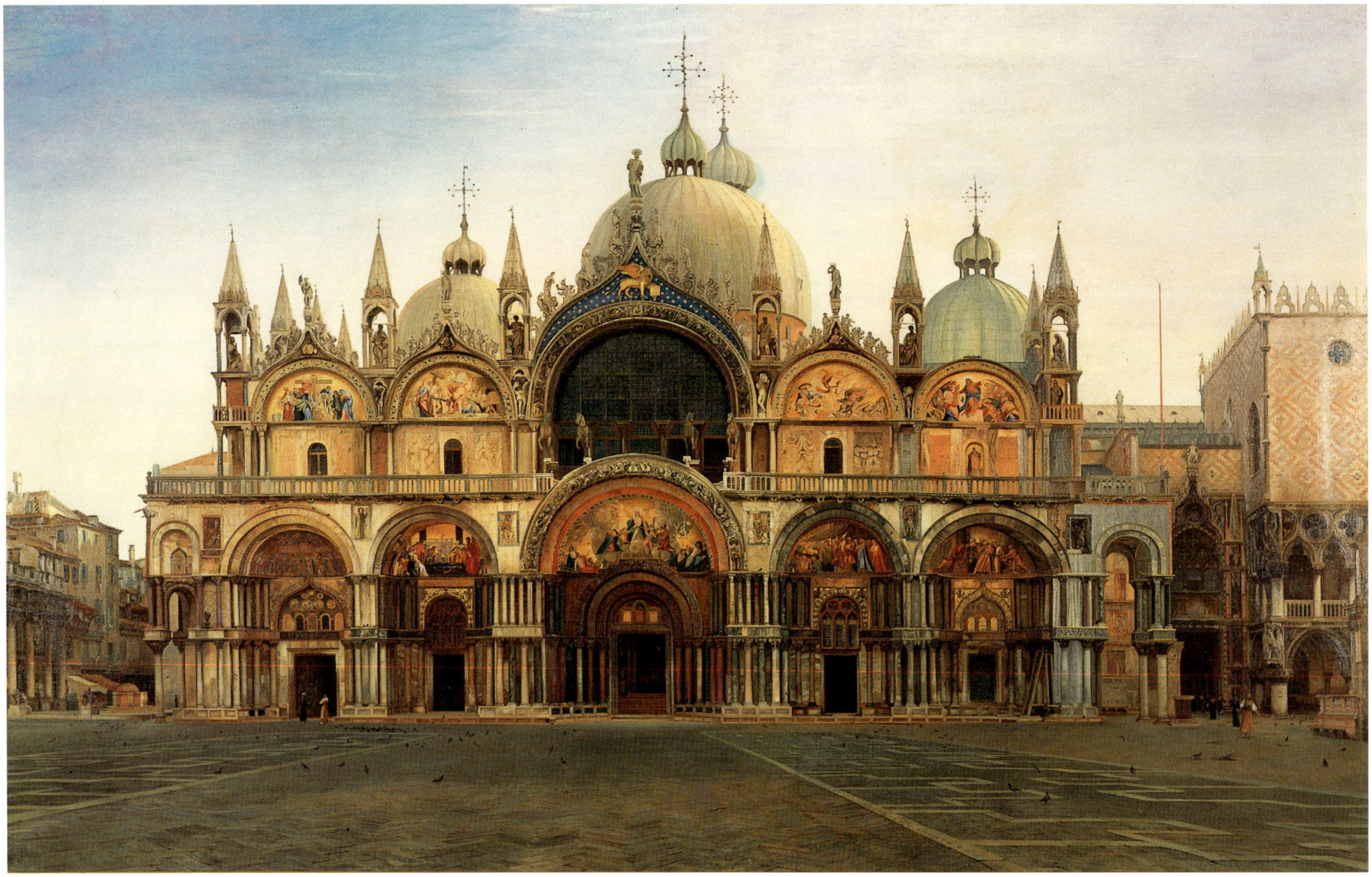

Fig. 6
John Wharlton Bunney
St Mark's as it Looks in the Early Morning of a Sirocco Day
1877–82
Oil on canvas, 114.8 x 226.1 cm
Collection of the Guild of St George, Museums Sheffield

Seated before his subject, Bunney spent years creating a 7 1/2 feet wide record of the building in obsessive and exacting architectural detail. Still smarting from losing his libel case against Ruskin, Whistler encountered Bunney in St Mark's Square and is said to have pinned a note to his back. It read, 'I am totally blind.'[29] Bunney's picture is a completely frontal composition in which – like Sickert's St Mark's façade series – the building fills almost all the available picture space. Sickert was no doubt aware of this work, which enjoyed great publicity when it was exhibited at the Fine Art Society in London in 1882, and there are striking similarities between the two artists' pictures – in their format and spatial composition and in their recording the lighting effects of a precise time of day.

But there were other more radical sources from which Sickert perhaps drew inspiration. On the way to Venice in May 1895 it is possible he stopped off in Paris and saw Monet's exhibition at Durand-Ruel's of 20 pictures of Rouen Cathedral. In these so-called series paintings, Monet repeated the same composition, but painted it under greatly varying lighting effects, at different times of day (fig. 7). Sickert would already have been familiar with Monet's work from the 20 pictures exhibited in London at the Goupil Gallery in 1889, and paintings were also shown at the Royal Society of British Artists and the New English Art Club. As Wendy Baron has noted, there are strong similarities to Monet in Sickert's delicately dabbed touches of paint in *The Lion of St Mark's* (fig. 8), a technique that creates a pulsating impressionist picture surface.[30] Writing in 1927, Sickert rejected the simplicity with which series paintings

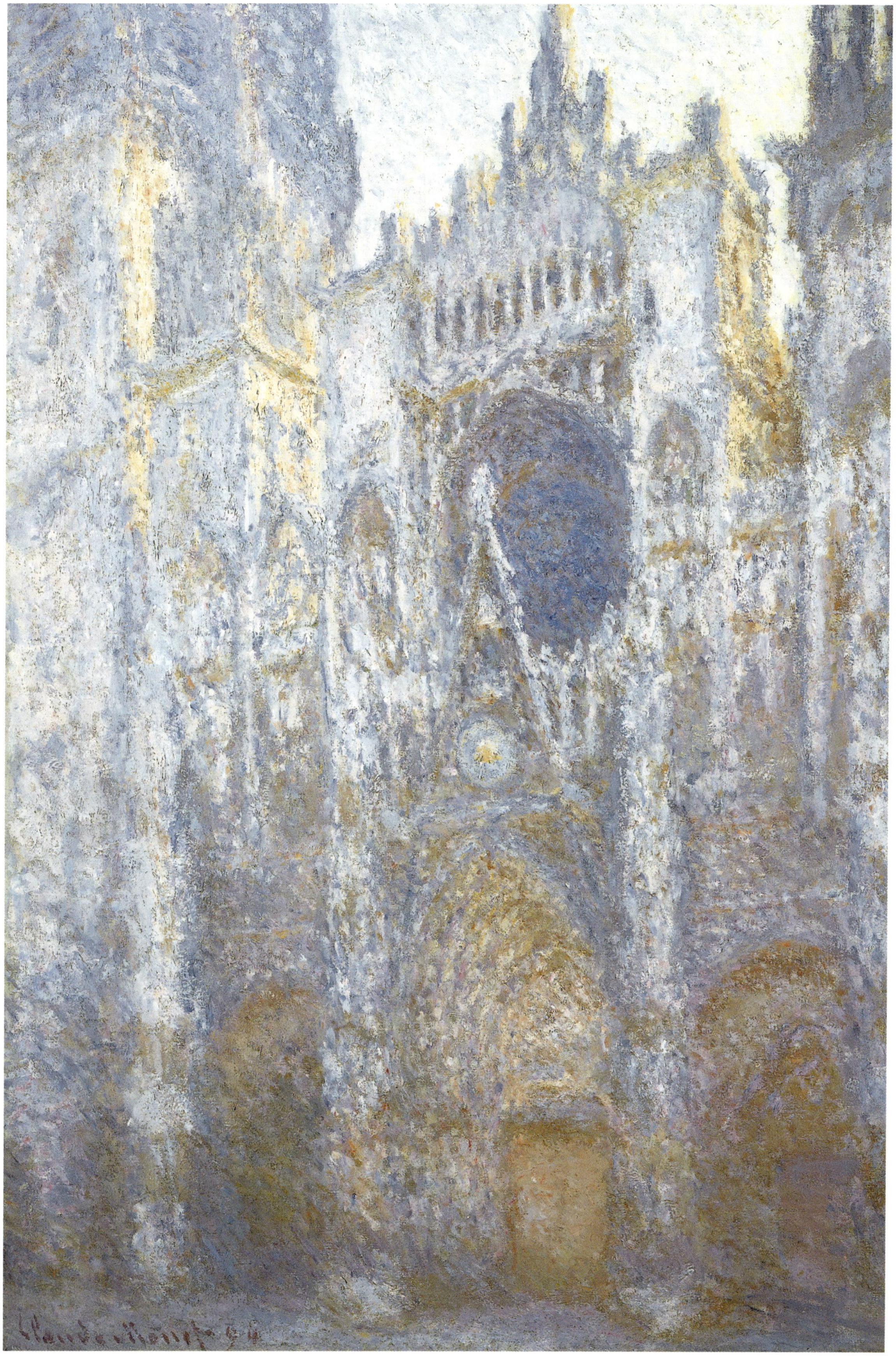

Fig. 7
Claude Monet
Rouen Cathedral, West Façade
1894
Oil on canvas, 100.1 x 65.9 cm
Chester Dale Collection,
National Gallery of Art,
Washington

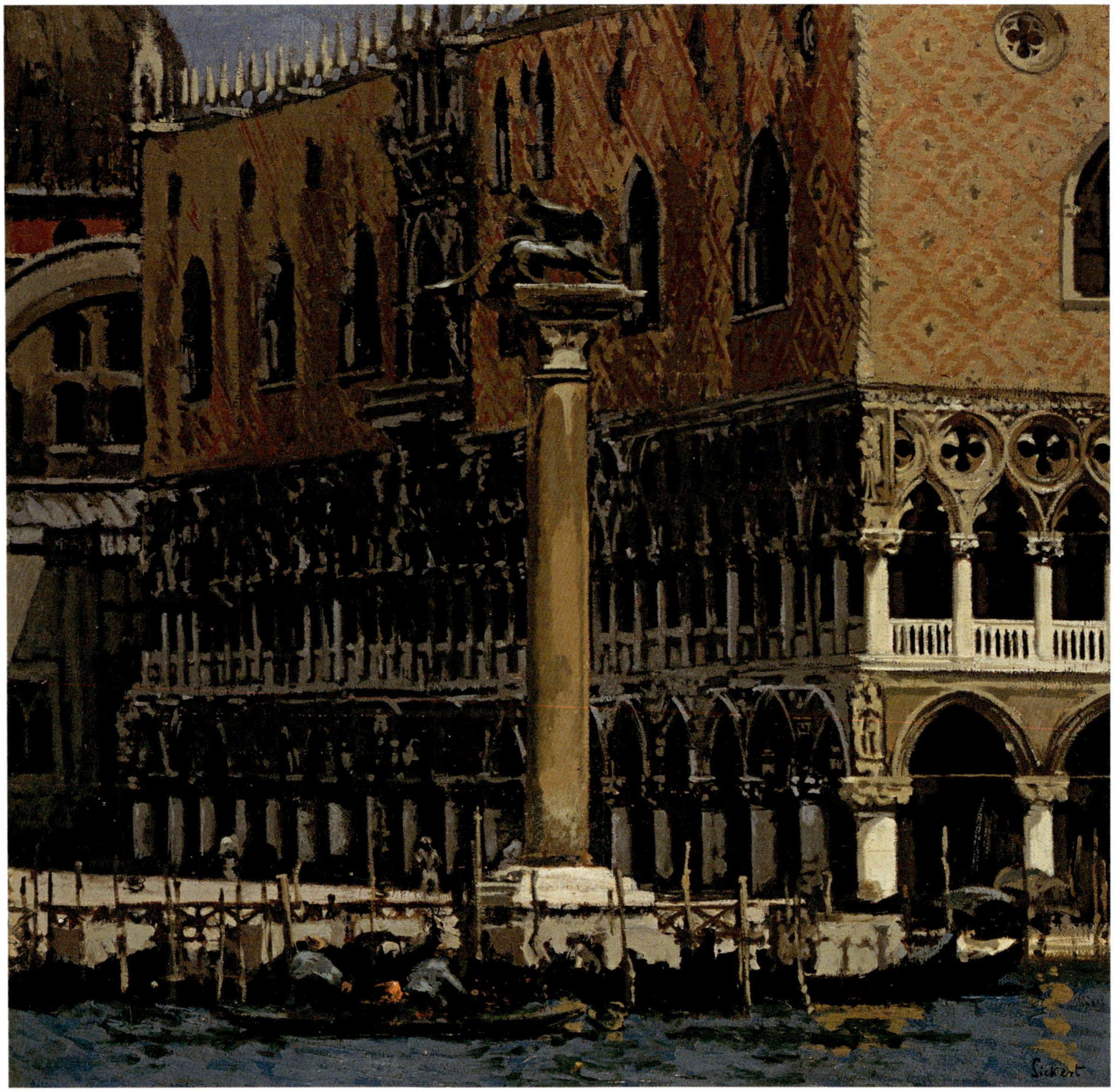

Fig. 8
Walter Sickert
The Lion of St Mark's
*c.*1895–96
Oil on canvas, 90.2 x 89.8 cm
Fitzwilliam Museum, Cambridge

were sometimes thought of, and offered instead a view that highlighted individual character, writing of Monet with reverence and praising his ability to circumvent repetitiveness:

> The theory that it is the main business of an artist to paint half a dozen views of one object in different lights cannot be seriously maintained. It would be nearer the truth to say that the artist existed to disentangle from nature the illumination that brings out most clearly the character of each scene. But an artist must be judged by his successes and Monet created a thing, the like of which had never been done before... Monet's large view of the Ducal Palace and the Piazzetta smouldering before their extinction in twilight must remain one of the masterpieces that have been wrung by the painter's art from the city in the sea. None of the painter's august predecessors have done just that, or indeed anything at all like it. It is neither the Venice of Canaletto nor that of Byron or Turner. It is very modern.[31]

To 'disentangle from nature the illumination that brings out most clearly the character of each scene' might well describe Sickert's approach to his first sequence of large paintings of St Mark's made in 1895–96 and after. Perhaps begun in Venice but certainly finished in London, this series shows what is essentially an identical composition at different times of day. In *The Façade of St Mark's: Red Sky at Night* (cat. 5), Sickert's title acknowledges this is evening, as the setting sun tints the sky crimson. The title also alludes to the popular saying, 'red sky at night, shepherd's delight', which anticipates good weather the following day. In *St Mark's, Venice (Pax Tibi Marce Evangelista Meus)* (cat. 4) the time is slightly earlier, perhaps the very end of the afternoon as it turns towards evening. The sun reflected on the mosaics and gold crosses on the Byzantine domes, and the gathering shadows at ground level, indicate that the sun is low in the sky. St Mark's Basilica faces west, and so the time represented is the end of the day, as the sun sinks. This was widely considered an ideal moment to capture the great Basilica. Writing in *The Studio* in 1894, the artist Frank Richards advised:

> The effect of St Mark's with the late afternoon sun shining upon it is too delicious for words; it is simply marvellous – the upper part and domes shine out, as it were, beset with diamonds and mosaics, all glittering in the unpolluted sunlight from a Venetian sky; the lower part of the Cathedral and Piazza being in shadow of the most lovely lilac hue, dotted here and there with the many-tinted costumes of the natives, and occasionally with the white dresses of nurses.[32]

So close to this is Sickert's painting that it might almost have been made following Richards's instructions. One of the picture's central characteristics is the contrast between the glow of reflected sunlight on the domes and the rich shadows below. And indeed, Sickert has also punctuated the linearity of the foreground with strokes of colour – and dashes of creamy off-white – to indicate passing figures. Creating balancing focus points for the eye to lead it into the shadow, this aspect of the composition is repeated in each of the painted versions. The figures are also present in the same position in the large monochrome squared drawing that Sickert produced of the composition (cat. 2). Squaring indicates the transfer to canvas, yet in *St Mark's, Venice (Pax Tibi Marce Evangelista Meus)* intriguingly there is no corresponding grid on the canvas. Nor is any graphite drawing visible, and Sickert has actually drawn in the composition in black paint directly with his brush, leaving brush marks that are clearly visible in the paint surface.[33] He did not, therefore, transfer the design from the drawing using a grid, and yet the scale of the architectural forms in the drawing are exactly half that of the finished oil. This suggests some complex relationship between the drawing and the painted versions and it must be a tantalising possibility that Sickert used some other method of transfer, perhaps from an already-painted and grid-transferred canvas. As we shall see, it is quite likely that at times Sickert used copy paper and experimented with drawing instruments in his work (see pages 60–61). Conversely, a further alternative is that, despite its size, the picture was actually painted before the subject. In a lecture to the students of the Manchester Painting School in 1925, Sickert recalled 'with regret… how he, too, had once set up Gargantuan canvases on the piazza before St Mark's'.[34]

In 1901 Sickert returned to the series painting concept, suggesting to the dealer Paul Durand-Ruel that he paint a new cycle of metre-wide views of St Mark's 'par effets différents', a concept that implicitly suggested Monet.[35] He appears to have had a precise interest in the lighting effects of different times of day. On a drawing on which he based *A Canal, Venice: Palazzo Montecuccioli* (cat. 15), Sickert carefully recorded the time and location: '2 to 3 P.M.

from Bridge'.[36] And when Mrs Donaldson Hudson in 1907 asked him when one of his Venetian pictures was painted, Sickert responded with great precision:

> About 7 o'clock in the evening I should say. San Giorgio gets the light of the setting sun. Your disputants are wrong about the water. Very few people spend their lives noting these things. Why should they? The water is in shadow. When a mirror is in shadow it reflects with great clearness & intensity. So it reflects the deep blue of the sky with great intensity at that hour.[37]

Pursuing his explorations of the effects of different times of day, Sickert's architectural pictures of Venice also include a small number of nocturnes. These include emotionally expressive pictures of deep darkness such as *Ponte della Guglie sul Cannaregio* (cat. 27) and a watercolour and oil of St Mark's (cats. 25–26), along with more conventionally lyrical sunset scenes as dusk gathers, including the beautiful *The Dogana and Santa Maria della Salute* (cat. 24). Sickert's former master Whistler had first attached the musical term nocturne to his pictures of the Thames at night, implying that, like music, these images should affect the viewer's senses directly without the need for narrative or subject. It was a recognition of the way that night summoned a particular mood or atmosphere, and heightened sensations of mystery. There was also the implication that individual creative forms, such as music, could find synaesthetic correspondence in wholly different media such as painting or poetry. These were theories explored among symbolist practitioners on the Continent, tying Whistler and in turn Sickert to a programme of avant-garde European cultural experimentation. Nor was Sickert alone in investigating the poetry of the night. Other artists, such as the Scottish watercolourist Arthur Melville, also made evocative pictures of Venice under darkness. Exhibited at the Royal Watercolour Society in 1898, his large, velvety watercolour *The Blue Night, Venice* (fig. 9) is strikingly similar to Sickert's *The Campanile, Venice* (cat. 28), probably made on or after his visit of 1901. Such close similarities illustrate the spread of aesthetic ideas, as well as the limited number of viewpoints artists might take in depicting Venice's landmarks. The introduction of street lighting to the city in this era caused ripples of protest among those who appreciated Venice's magical cloak of darkness.

Fig. 9
Arthur Melville
The Blue Night, Venice
1897
Watercolour and bodycolour on board, 86.4 x 61 cm
Tate, London

Walter Sickert
The Campanile, Venice
*c.*1901
(cat. 28, detail)

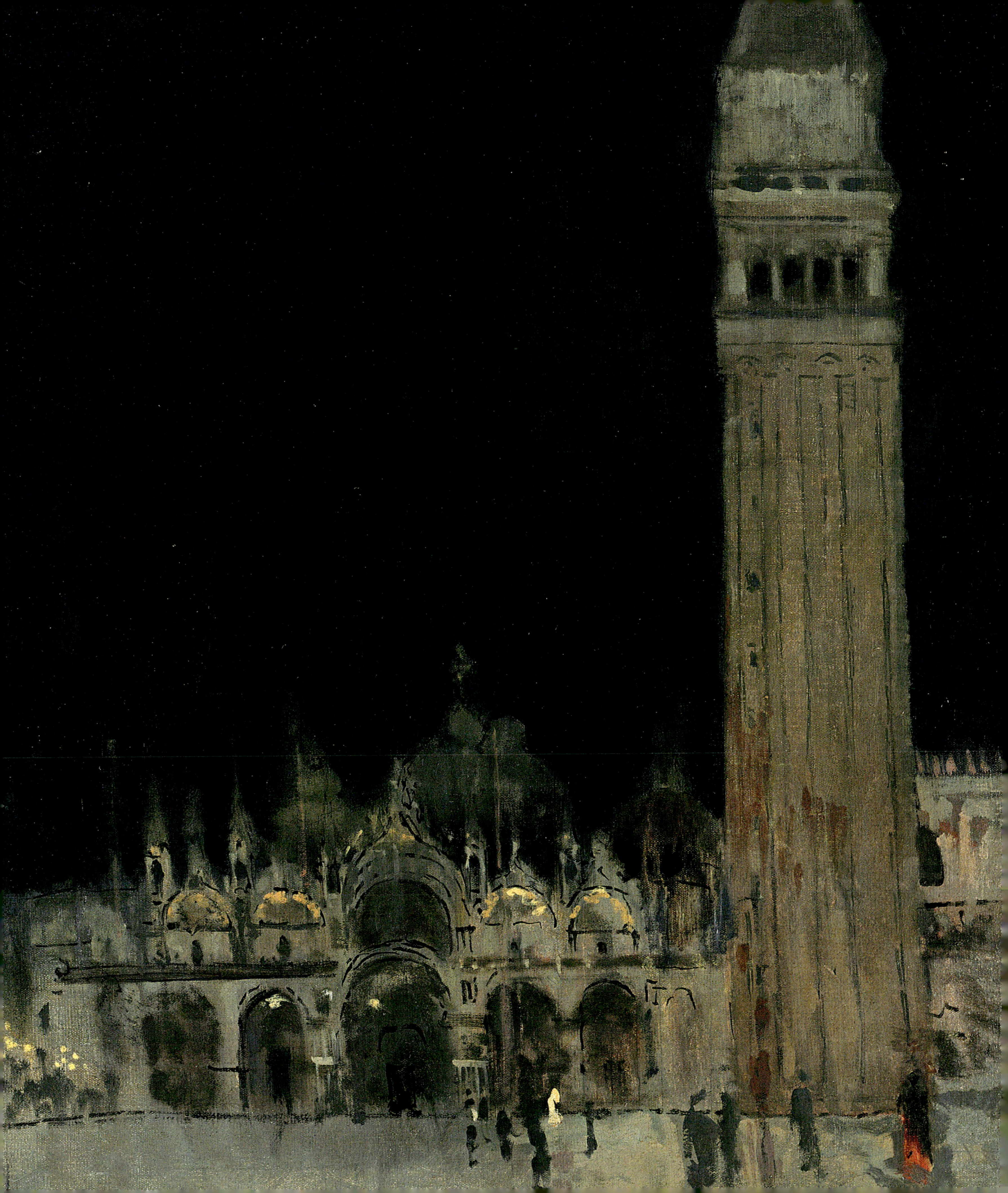

Sickert's connection with European innovation was in his blood. Born in Munich to a Danish painter father and an Anglo-Irish mother, Sickert was, as he liked to emphasise, wholly international in his heritage. He was instinctively against the petty nationalistic isolationism of late 1880s Britain that viewed with suspicion any aesthetic contagion of the national school by Continental practices.[38] Sickert pursued significant and intimate exposure to impressionist French painting through his friendships with Degas in the 1880s and 1890s, and with Camille Pissarro, with whom he came to be on easy terms in Dieppe in 1901. Pissarro pushed Sickert to consider a brightening of his colour and a lightening of tone,[39] advice that was to be echoed by Sickert's Paris dealers. Sickert considered himself intensely connected with French art in his own practice and began mentally to distance himself from identification with British painting. Writing from Dieppe to Mrs Constanzia Hulton, a friend he had made in Venice to whom he confided many of his thoughts and working practices at this time, Sickert pondered that although he was effectively an exile, he had absorbed an immense amount from exposure to art on the Continent:

> I have learnt here what I couldn't have learnt in a lifetime at home. So I suppose an all-wise Providence is interested in my technique, & exiles me from beef, & beer & music-halls, most of my friends, & all my mistresses so that I may leave behind an oeuvre.[40]

Sickert was extremely clear in how he analysed the way he fitted into the shared inheritance he had received by learning from other artists. He wrote to his friend Jacques-Émile Blanche, 'I am a *French* painter… As a pupil of Whistler I derive from the French school. Why not take my place in it?' So committed was Sickert to this idea that he investigated the practicalities of becoming a naturalised French citizen, even obtaining from the authorities reassurance against his anxieties that he might make himself eligible for military service. In all events, he told Blanche, he intended to submit work for international exhibitions in the French section, not 'the *English*, or *German*', the country of his birth.[41] While he did not in fact become a French citizen, the Ministère des Beaux-Arts did invite him to contribute to the French section at Munich in 1903; Sickert told Steer he was sending his large portrait of Hilda Spong and *Katie Lawrence at Gatti's Hungerford* to it.[42] He was also represented at the Venice Biennale of 1903, and was again in the French pavilion. This was a major breakthrough, and a highly prestigious opportunity. Initially he had wanted to submit a music hall scene, as he was wary of showing his Venetian work in the city that had inspired it. But in the event, he exhibited a picture of the cemetery island of San Michele.[43] This engagement and participation in the Continental art world was highly distinctive, and Sickert was virtually alone among his generation of British artists in holding this position. Surveying his standing, he considered it providence alone that had brought him to Dieppe and his involvement in French galleries and exhibitions. 'What a lucky chance,' he wrote to Steer, adding that, if he had stayed in London, 'I should have been art critic of the Licensed Victuallers' Gazette by now, and doing articles for them on Johns and Albert Rothensteins!'[44]

Symbolism versus Realism

The sheer bulk and brooding, looming presence of St Mark's has an insistence in claiming significance that is pressing but ambiguous. Instead of simply recording the architectural facts of the building, Sickert suggests a meaningful form of symbolist cityscape, of the type that is found in a number of European artists' work from this time. Fernand Khnopff was fascinated by the Flemish town of Bruges, and by presenting it as in some way express-

Fig. 10
Fernand Khnopff
Du Silence
1890
Pastel, 87.8 x 44.3 cm
Musée Royaux des Beaux-Arts de Belgique, Bruxelles

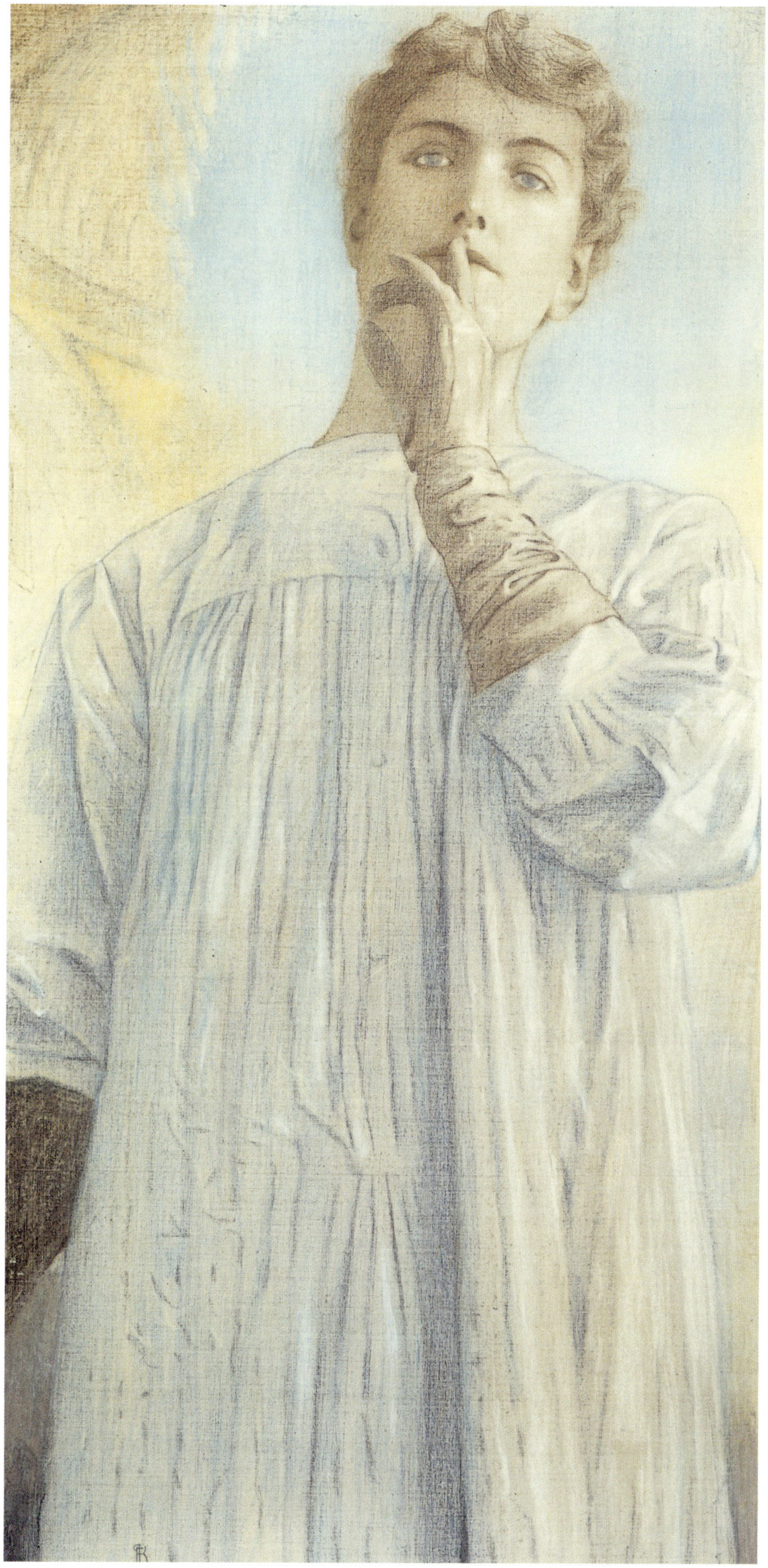

ing the sadness and mourning of a human existence aware of its own mortality (fig. 10). Khnopff's work was prominent in international exhibitions, and from 1889 he exhibited in London. Sickert had some familiarity with his pictures as early as 1890, when he made a reference to them in an article,[45] and certainly by 1897 when he praised Khnopff's contribution to the New Gallery – 'M. Khnopff shows what a stately decoration may be made of the simplest subject'.[46] There are later affinities with the gloomy, indefinable menace of the interiors and architectural studies of James Pryde, whose pictures, like Sickert's, are not simply about capturing the physical elements of buildings but instead their psychological effect. Sickert's St Mark's emphasises the smallness of man against his constructions, and, as much as this serves to emphasise mankind's achievements, it stresses too the insignificance of human life. Writing in 1897, Sickert noted how in cityscapes indefinable emotional messages could be conveyed by the relative scale of small details. He used as his example Whistler, but in the subjects he listed, it might equally be his own pictures that he had in mind:

> His knowledge of the justness in the proportion of small objects to the wide field on which they occur is unique. It is not, with him, that he copies a tiny hansom, creeping along the wide Embankment, or a slim gondola on the lagoon, or shifting figures on the Rialto steps, or the Dieppe beach. That is not the matter at all. The matter is, that he holds the key by which a certain rendering of these sights is able to exercise a powerful emotional effect. He can touch some secret spring that gives an immense significance – a deep emotional importance, to mere nothings. He knows the laws of what a very penetrating critic has called 'the music of spaces'.[47]

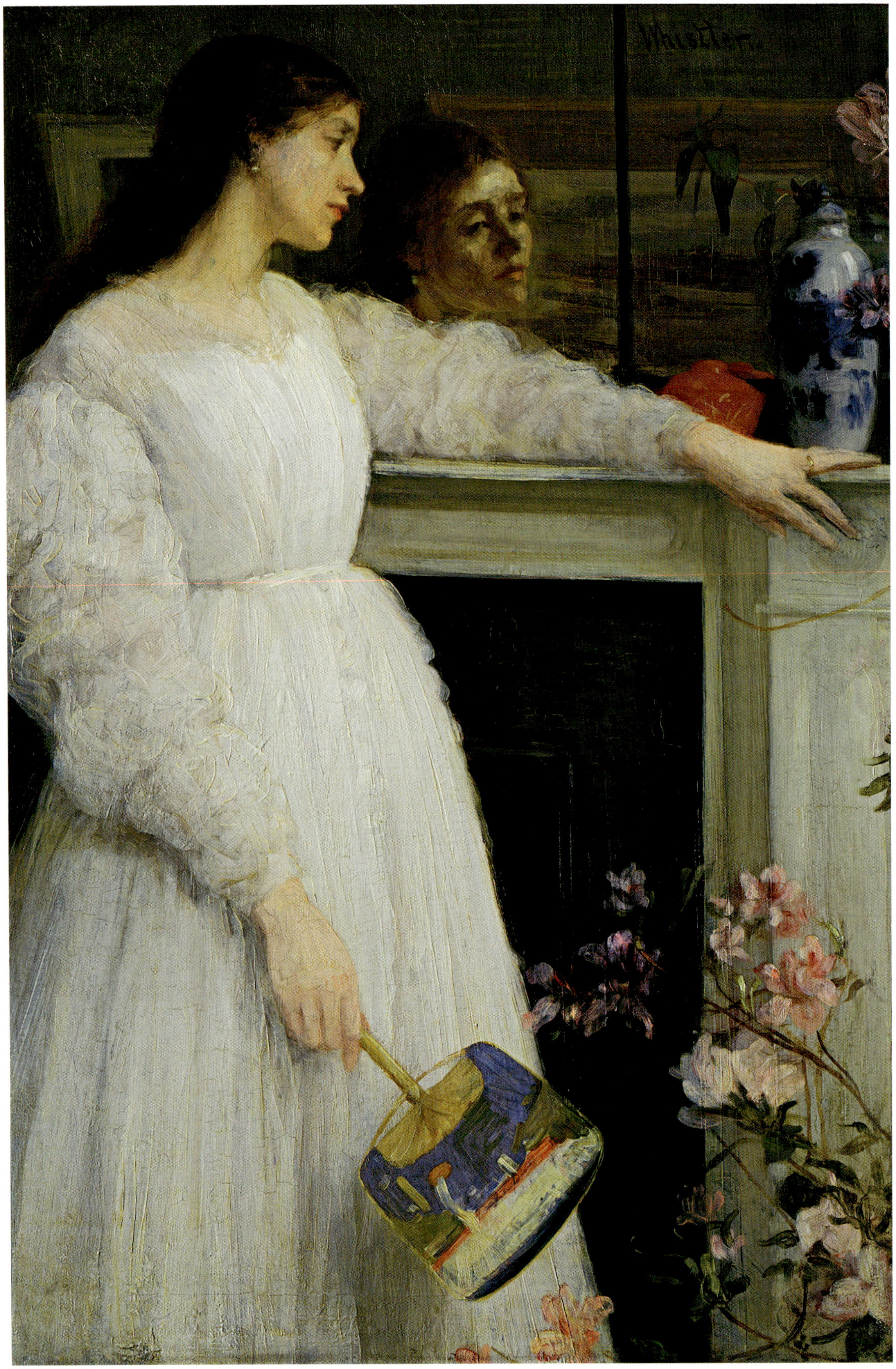

Fig. 11
James McNeill Whistler
Symphony in White No. 2: The Little White Girl
1864
Oil on canvas, 76.5 x 51.1 cm
Tate, London

There is a compelling case for us to view some of Sickert's pictures from this period as a knowing synthesis of realism and symbolism, bringing together the two strands that dominated later nineteenth-century European art.[48] Venice offered a rich source of symbolist allusion. It was a city of shadows and former glories, and rotting palaces. Henry James believed that 'the essential present character of the most melancholy of cities resides simply in its being the most beautiful of tombs'.[49] The crumbling physical decay of the city, and the dwindling of its fortunes from the heights of a once-great empire, offered a telling metaphor for the failure of human ambition. Similarly, Venice's centuries-old reputation for licentiousness, especially during the carnival, was linked by writers such as Ruskin to the inevitability of its declining political powers. Its decaying architecture perfectly symbolised Venice's moral degeneration and corruption, matching its physical decline. It is a theme found widely in literature from around this time. In Henry James's *The Aspern Papers* (1888) and *The Wings of the Dove* (1902), Venice is the location for a set of morally ambiguous relationships. Later, in Thomas Mann's *Death in Venice* (1912), the city acts as a cipher for the moral and physical deterioration of its central character, the writer Gustav von Aschenbach. In all these stories Venice becomes a stage on which telling questions of existence are played out. It is in these essentially symbolist contexts that Sickert's art might be considered.

While Sickert's suppression of narrative in his figure subjects in Venice may simply appear to be sound realist practice, the mood and atmosphere that is the principal focus of these intense and sometimes almost stifling paintings is not simply about naturalist observation. Instead such scenes seem to embody indefinable truths that express in some abstract manner the quality of human life. This is the essence of the symbolist strategy, that the world's external appearance is simply a surface that is a code for other things. In this schema, the mood that characterised the everyday might communicate some essence of the eternal dilemmas of human consciousness. The quality that pervades many of Sickert's pictures – whether of figures in gloomy interiors in London or Venice, or of the streets of Dieppe – is a sense of uncertainty and mystery. While seemingly pregnant with meaning, there is no story contained in what we are looking at, although Sickert's sometimes playfully obscure titles almost tauntingly invite us to try to create our own. In Venetian figure subjects such as *Le Tose* (cat. 56) or *La Carolina Standing in an Interior* (cat. 45), or famous Camden Town nudes like *La Hollandaise* (*c.*1906), the pictures are not even identifiable portraits, the women's faces treated only cursorily with broad dashes of paint. Abstractions from human life, such paintings might be identified simply as beautiful objects in themselves. But often the dark, sometimes grimy interiors seem to negate this, and suggest instead a ruminative contemplation of the indeterminacy of existence. There is some close correlation with Dutch seventeenth-century interiors, like those painted by Vermeer, or in the late nineteenth-century paintings of Vilhelm Hammershøi. In all these works our contemplation of the ostensible subject of a figure in a room prompts us to ponder deeper questions of human mortality. Frozen in time, Vermeer's stillness, perhaps like Sickert's, is a form of *vanitas* that alludes to the transience of human life. Vermeer would have been familiar to Sickert, his *Young Woman standing at a Virginal* (*c.*1670–72) having been acquired by the National Gallery in London in 1892. Yet a further, more contemporary source under which to consider Sickert's solitary figures in rooms is Whistler's famous *Symphony in White No. 2: The Little White Girl* (fig. 11). With this picture Whistler demonstrated the full expression of the Aesthetic project, substituting any easily read story with emotional tone and atmosphere. Like his nocturnes, Whistler's title suggested the picture should act on the senses in the same way as a piece of music, directly affecting the emotions without the intervention of extended intellectual analysis or textual reading. It was a showcasing of the primal, abstract ability of art to affect the viewer's feelings simply through the act of viewing. And the mood the picture suggested was highly ambiguous, mixing beauty with an intangible but insistent sense of sadness. Lost in thought and self-contemplation, the woman's melancholy acts as a mirror, in which the viewer's own emotions or concerns might find reflection. Sickert was evidently familiar with Whistler's painting, and shortly after his sequence of Venetian interiors in *c.*1906–07 he painted *The Mantelpiece*, which made explicit reference to the composition of *The Little White Girl*.[50]

An important document in considering the status of Sickert's Venetian figure painting is the portrait that he made of himself (fig. 12). It has a strong undercurrent of ineffable sadness or morbidity, Sickert's face looking gaunt and drawn. In the background a spectral Giuseppina hunches forward meaningfully, watching Sickert intently, but also creating the effect of them both observing the picture's viewer. The searching, unsettled quality of Sickert's expression gives it the character of an expressionist portrait, which hints not only at the uncertainty of the artist but appears a projection of some wider human anxiety about existence. The ruminative, interior gaze of Giuseppina in other pictures, such as the emotively-lit *La Callera* (cat. 42), seems similarly to allude to a deeper sense of contemplation, giving these works greater emotional significance and depth, and negating their reading as only uncomplicated observations of a model at rest. They make interesting comparisons again with the art of Fernand Khnopff, in whose symbolist pictures of androgynous female models narrative is suppressed in favour of a mysterious and unsettling mood (fig. 10). In the paintings Sickert made of *Mamma Mia Poveretta* (cats. 43–44), he again presents us with portraits whose intensity suggests wider existential concerns. The woman is in advanced old age, her waxy, thin skin drawn taught and her face holding the appearance of the skull that lies beneath. On one level they are a pendant to the portrayals of youth represented by her supposed daughter, Giuseppina, although the relative difference in their apparent ages must suggest it is more likely Giuseppina was her granddaughter. The contrasting of youth and age to symbolise mortality and the irrevocable destructive force of time was a juxtaposition featured in painting of the Venetian Renaissance. Mamma Mia gazes far into the distance, lost in thought and causing us to ponder the effect time has wrought on her physical form. The word 'poveretta' in the title means 'poor thing' rather than implying poverty, and presents her therefore as an object of pity. Representing extreme old age – and implicitly the nearness of death – had appeared as a subject in European symbolist painting, but it was also treated in the sculpture of Alfred Gilbert. His *Study (Head of a Capri Fisherman)* (fig. 13) was the focus of great critical admiration and discussion when it was shown at the Royal Academy in 1884 and similarly was admired for its powerful study of the effects of age on the body and the symbolism of human corporeality and transience. Sickert's own portrayal of Mamma Mia has the quality of a death's head, and Wendy Baron has noted the passing similarity to Edvard Munch's *Scream* (1893–1910), versions of which Sickert might easily have seen at any of the international exhibitions in which they were included. Each of the trio of paintings he made of Mamma Mia show her from a different angle, as if surveying her features sequentially and methodically like a specimen under scientific or philosophical scrutiny.

A further slightly spectral treatment of Giuseppina's features is presented in *Piazzetta di San Marco* (cat. 23). Here she is portrayed crossing the Piazzetta at dusk. Sickert has emphasised her high cheekbones and sharp facial features, and she is cut off by the picture space, her truncated form occupying the

Fig. 12
Walter Sickert
Self Portrait with La Giuseppina
1903–04
Oil on canvas, 25.4 x 20.32 cm
Harvard Art Museum, Fogg Art Museum

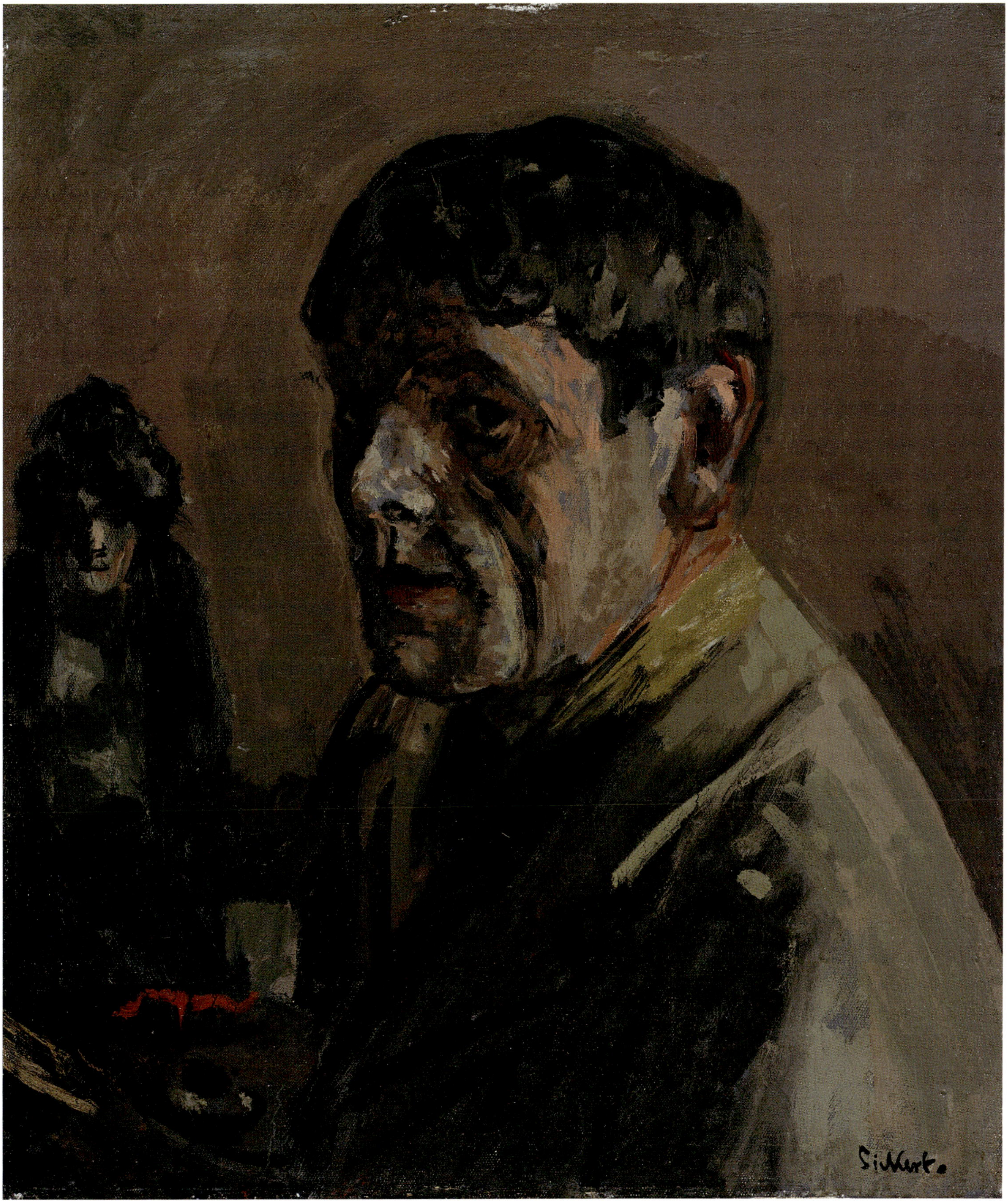
Sickert.

foreground. Giuseppina's passage gives the picture a sense of gliding movement. The sky is streaked with beautiful colours from the setting sun, but there is some odd sense of disjunction to the scene. The bilious strength of the colouring, Giuseppina's strangely skull-like face and the open manner in which the picture is painted all create a highly individual and troubling mood. In this it seems somewhat akin to Picasso's *Le Moulin de la Galette* (fig. 14), a Paris café scene where the revellers' faces become transformed into disquieting masks. Sickert's picture is quite different in recording the architecture of a highly specific place, but it goes much further than being a merely topographical record, or of being a study of a Venetian woman. It is the mood that is most insistent and gives the picture its status and, while it is ambiguous, there is some sense of it being laden with more meaning than the sum of the scene's physical components. This too, it might be argued, takes it into the realm of symbolism rather than simply realism.

Sickert's originality and the subtly symbolist quality with which he imbued his figure studies are made even more apparent by comparison with what his contemporaries were producing in Venice. Like Sickert, John Singer Sargent incorporated certain elements of modern French technique into his paintings but escaped critical censure by fitting into and reviving the traditions of the Grand Manner in his society portraits. Sargent was not a painter Sickert particularly cared for, and the differences between the creative vision of each of them is apparent when comparing the figure paintings they made in Venice. Both utilised working-class women and both relished the delicate fall of diffused interior light on the figure. But Sargent's pictures such as *Venetian Bead Stringers* (fig. 15) seem emotionally aloof by comparison, observing their subject with probity and distance. There is no sense of the psychological impact or suggestion of suppressed meaning found in Sickert. Nor is there any of his tangible sense of engagement, and the evident relish with which Sickert suggests the exciting baseness and vitality of his subject's lives and surroundings. La Giuseppina and Carolina often look out to challenge our gaze, while Sargent's women always lower their eyes.

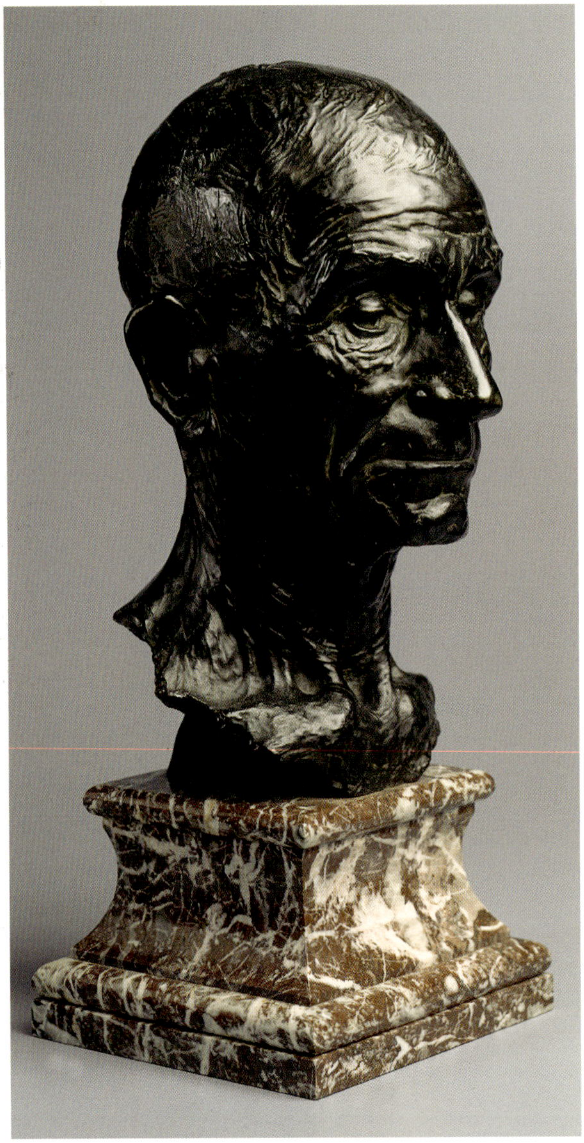

Fig. 13
Alfred Gilbert
Study (Head of a Capri Fisherman)
1884
Bronze, 36.8 x 22.8 x 24.1 cm
National Gallery of Victoria, Melbourne, Australia

Venice in the 1890s

By the time Sickert arrived in Venice in 1895 there had been a fascination for the city among the British public for some decades. The sensuous lyricism of Byron's *Childe Harold's Pilgrimage* (1812–18) enjoyed continuing admiration and mass appreciation. Its

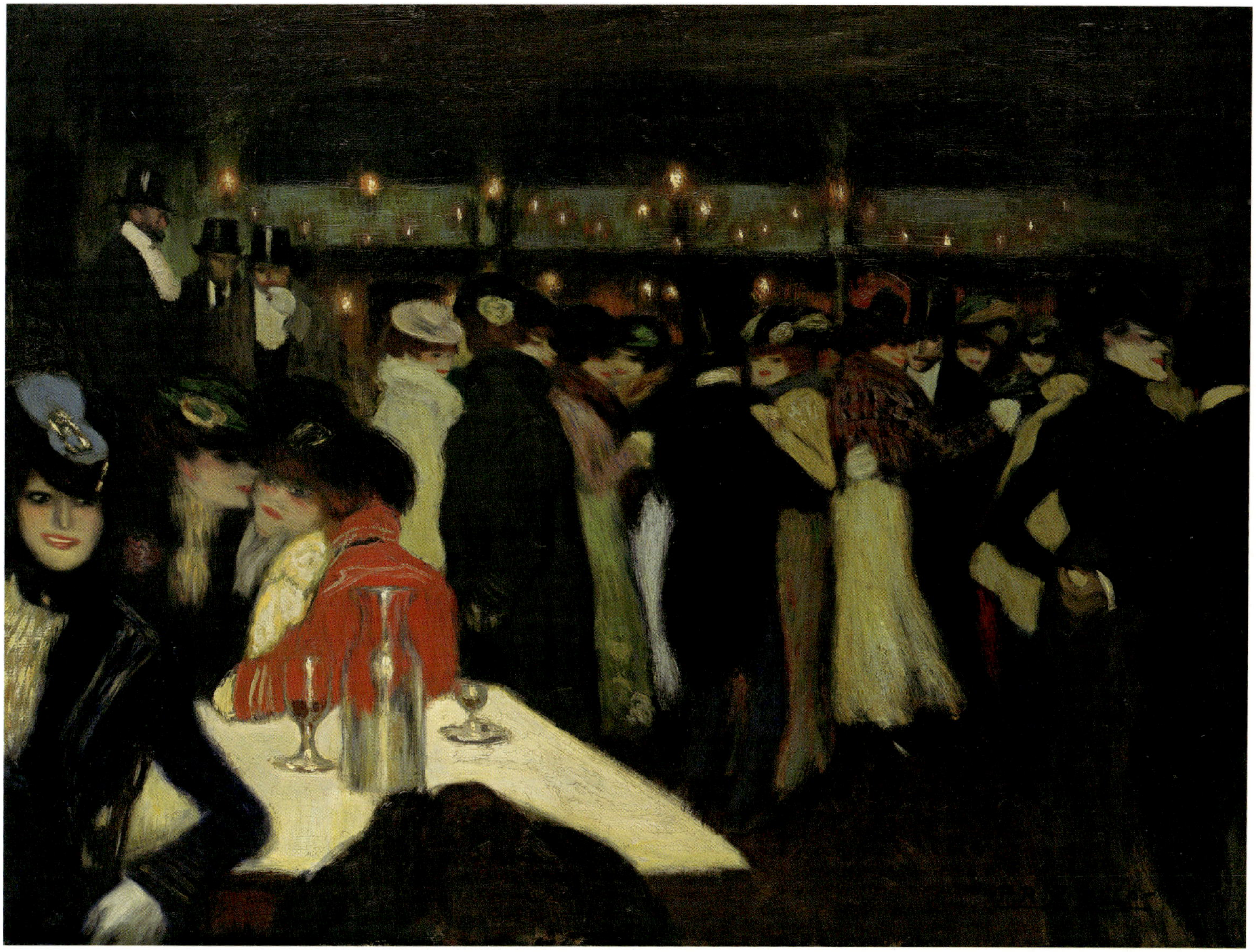

Fig. 14
Pablo Picasso
Le Moulin de la Galette
1900
Oil on canvas, 88.2 x 115.5 cm
Solomon R. Guggenheim Museum, New York

essence seemed to find visual manifestation in the paintings and watercolours J. M. W. Turner made of Venice in the 1830s and 1840s. These works enjoyed new exposure in the National Gallery from the 1870s after Turner's bequest of his pictures to the nation began to be revealed there in a sequence of displays selected by John Ruskin. But it was the appearance of Ruskin's *Stones of Venice* that most strongly fuelled public taste for pictures of Venice. Published between 1851 and 1853, Ruskin's extraordinary, passionate description in mesmeric prose of Venice's Byzantine and Gothic splendour sold in vast numbers and was a staple of all educated people's reading. It was part guide book and part impassioned argument for the primacy of these previously maligned architectural styles, and their simplicity and spiritual honesty. Indeed, in his third volume, Ruskin heaped scorn on what he viewed as the weaknesses of Renaissance design and decoration and the moral culpability of the age in which it flourished. In effect, his book was an architectural recapitulation of the arguments of the Pre-Raphaelites, whom Ruskin had also championed, and who similarly rejected the mannerism of High Renaissance art in favour of the simple purity of the Italian Primitives. Ruskin highlighted the creative,

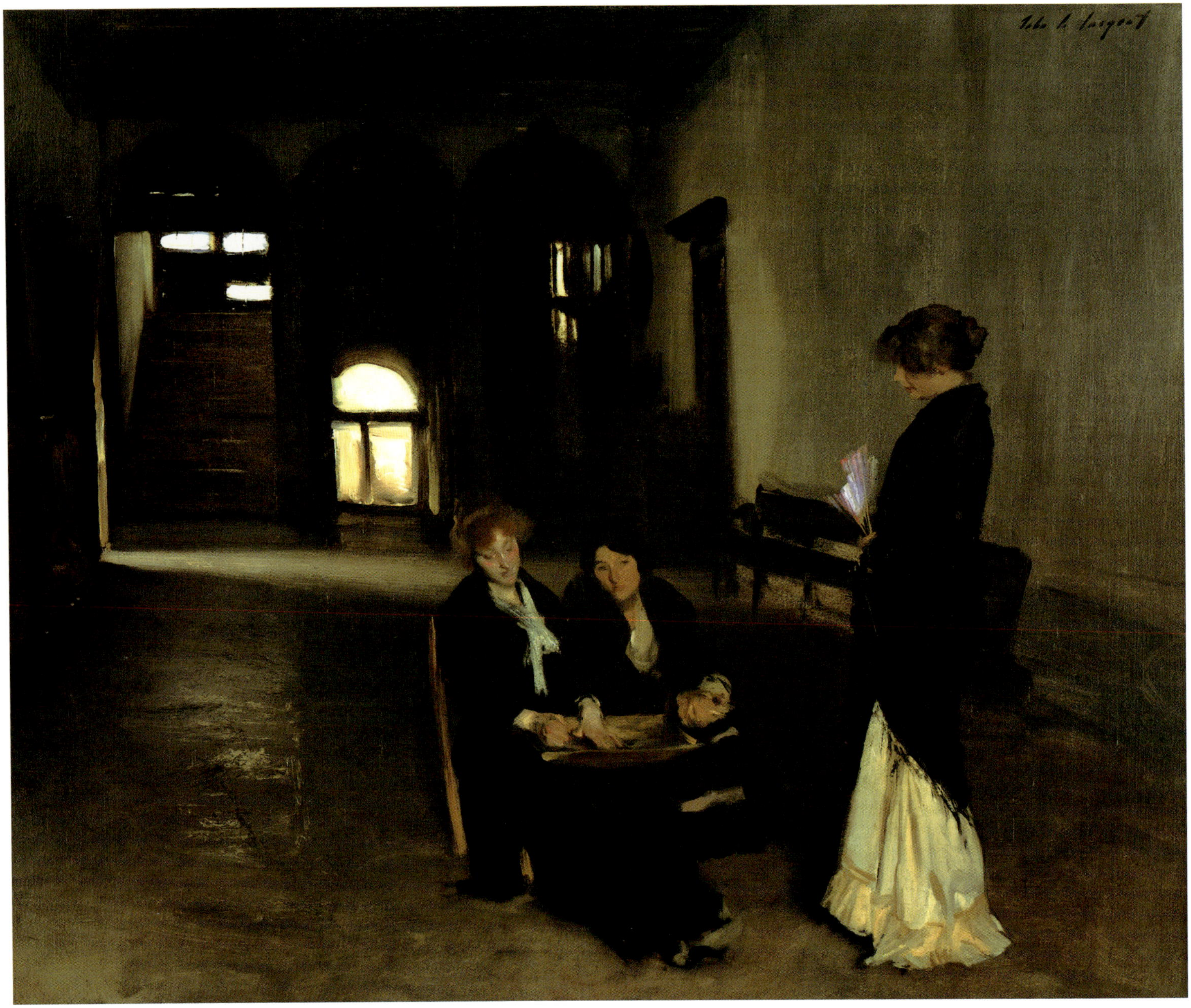

individual craftsmanship of the Venetian masons, who unlike the slaves of previous empires were free to put personal expression into their craft because Christianity recognised their individual personal value. He drew negative comparison with the conditions of Victorian factory workers, most notably condemning the requirement for uniformity and perfection in the production line for inhibiting individual expression.

Ruskin stimulated concern for Venice's crumbling vulnerability. In 1879 the Society for the Protection of Ancient Buildings campaigned successfully to prevent demolition of part of St Mark's Basilica, with the support of both Gladstone and Disraeli. But evidence of Venice's fragile architectural inheritance came in 1902 when the Campanile collapsed (fig. 16). Ruskin's text also spawned a passionate readership and an unforeseen imitation of the Venetian Gothic style throughout the new buildings of London. Suburban terraces and corner pubs now

Fig. 15
John Singer Sargent
Venetian Bead Stringers
1880–82
Oil on canvas, 66.9 x 78.1 cm
Albright-Knox Art Gallery, Buffalo, New York

habitually incorporated debased Gothic architectural references, a phenomenon that later in life reputedly disgusted Ruskin.

This passion for Venice encouraged tourists to visit the city themselves, and by the 1890s travel agent Thomas Cook was offering ready-made package tours. And it was an enthusiasm which was by no means a solely British phenomenon. Artists from across Europe and America congregated in Venice, lured by a newfound source of the picturesque and the promise of a healthy market for their work at home. By 1882 paintings of the city had proliferated so much that Henry James could note:

> Venice has been painted and described many thousands of times, and of all the cities of the world it is the easiest to visit without going there. Open the first book and you will find a rhapsody about it; step into the first picture-dealer's and you will find three or four high-colored 'views' of it.[51]

When Sickert arrived in Venice, pictures of *La Serenissima* remained a popular and profitable component of both the annual Royal Academy exhibition and the Paris Salon. Paintings of the city had of course been bought intermittently by British collectors since the time of Canaletto and Guardi, but a renewed enthusiasm peaked in the 1880s and 1890s. Large numbers of artists from many countries went to work in Venice at this time to portray its picturesque canals and, most commonly, senti-

Fig. 16
Collapsed Campanile
1902
Photograph

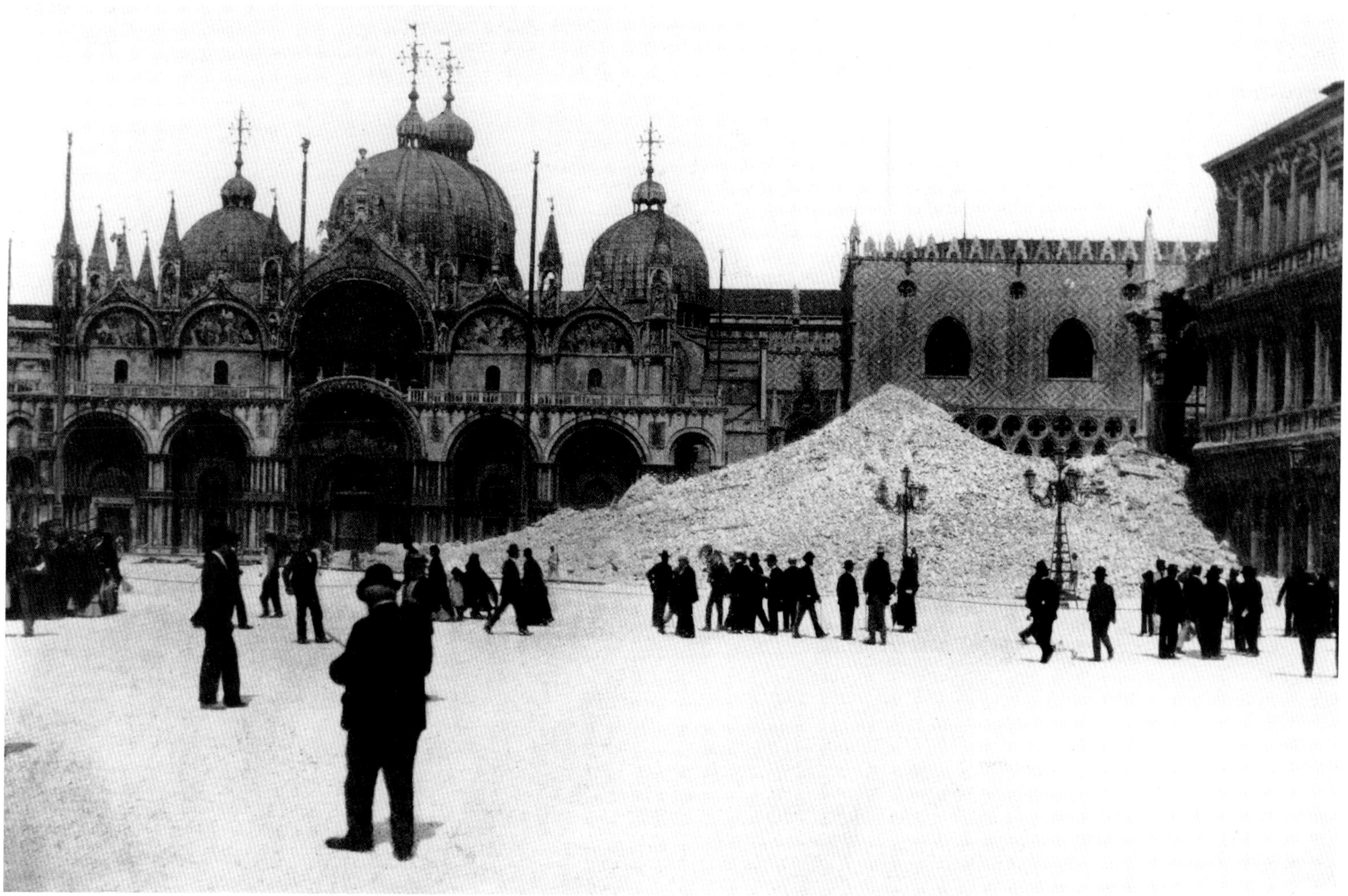

mental genre scenes of the inhabitants. The leading Continental exponents of this type of picture were two Austrian painters, Cecil van Haanen (1844–1914) and Eugene von Blaas (1843–1932), whose style and choice of subject exerted a strong influence on the work of British painters, most notably Henry Woods (1846–1921), who made his whole career out of Venetian genre scenes. By 1886 the *Art Journal* was able to identify a 'modern Venetian school' whose foremost members were Woods, Luke Fildes (1844–1927; fig. 17) and William Logsdail (1859–1944; fig. 18), noting that:

> Home-staying Englishmen, if they were years ago contented with such indistinct impressions of Venice as they received from Turner's pictures or the stanzas in 'Childe Harold', are now familiar with another Venice, quite as poetic, quite as suggestive of romance, the Venice of today. Following the best of modern Art, which makes the real its aim and end, this clever Venetian school has carried us beyond Venice the romantic to Venice the actual, and has created our present interest in the delightful comedy of her streets and people… yet they are not content merely to reproduce the noble beauty of her architecture or the lustrous hues of her landscape. They use these, yes; but as a background against which to set some scene of human interest, trivial at times, but always true.[52]

Interest in Venetian subjects in art, music and literature was so widespread and mainstream by the late 1880s that they formed the focus of a plethora of romantic historical novels and popular songs. This permeation of British culture by Venetian themes, first started lyrically by Byron, was now both embodied and to some extent parodied by Gilbert and Sullivan's operetta *The Gondoliers*, which opened to acclaim at the Savoy Theatre in 1899.

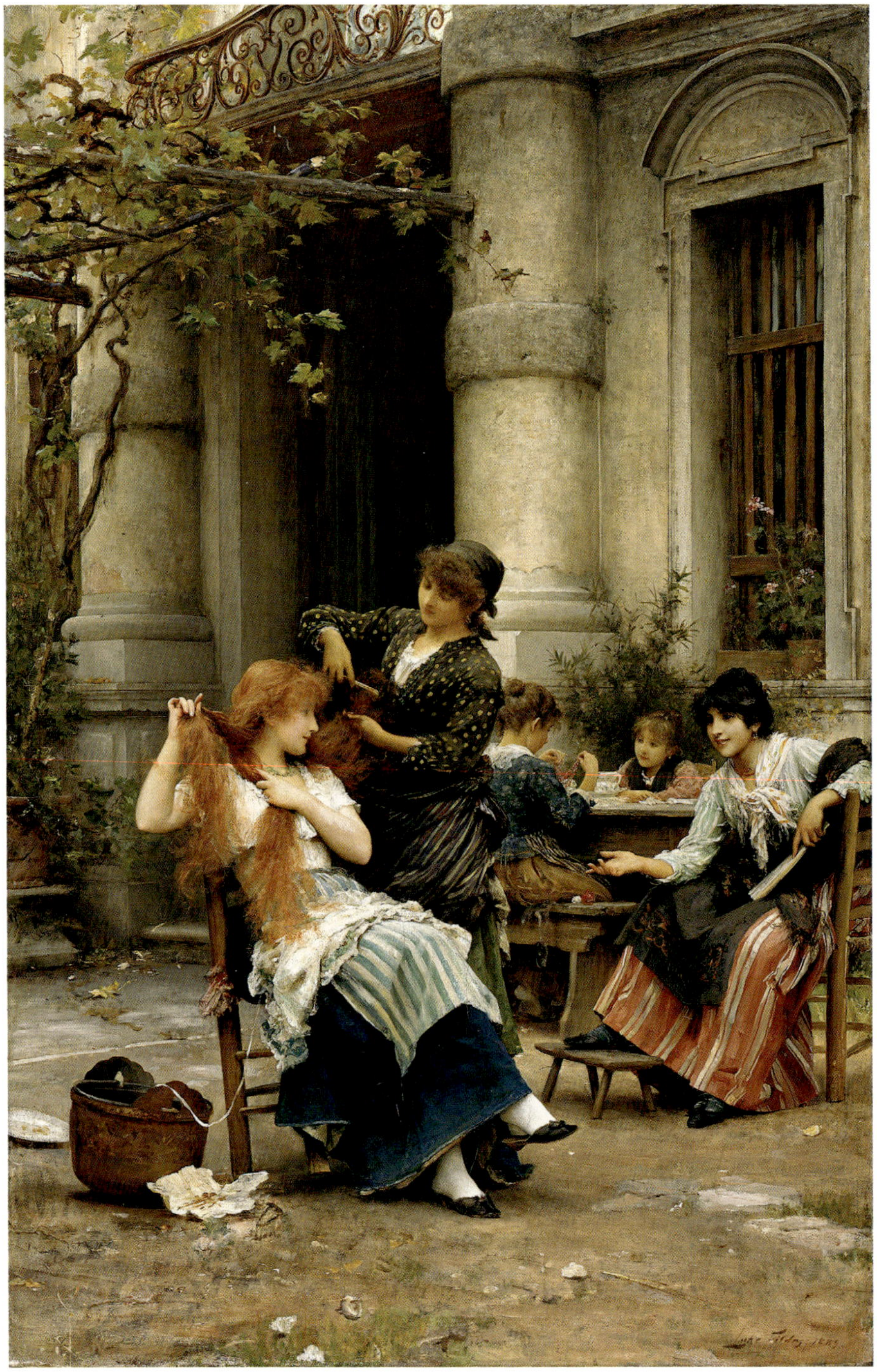

Fig. 17
Luke Fildes
An Al-fresco Toilette
1889
Oil on canvas, 173 x 108 cm
National Museums Liverpool, Lady Lever Gallery

The Artist as Ethnographer

In the 1890s there existed in Europe a kind of artistic ethnographic tourism – a pursuit of unusual and unspoilt folk societies apparently unaffected by the modern. It was what drew people, and especially artists, to Pont-Aven with its folk customs and distinctive Breton dress. It was what took them to Newlyn in Cornwall to paint the fishermen and to establish an artists' colony. And it was partly a similar motivation that took Gauguin to Tahiti. This same impetus to study local inhabitants also took painters to Venice, and there are links of motive between what was considered the 'exoticism' of authentic fisher folk as suitable subjects for painting in the west of England and those of Venice (fig. 19). This was a period of newfound ease of travel, when people could sample these rural or maritime societies away from the experience of large cities where – in Britain – the majority of people now lived. By 1901 in Britain almost 80 per cent of people lived in towns or cities. At the beginning of the new century Cecil Sharp and Ralph Vaughan Williams began collecting English folk songs in the realisation that, with urbanisation and industrialisation, these cultures were untenable and might soon disappear. Mostly written between the 1870s and the 1890s, Thomas Hardy's novels were further evidence of this concern or interest, and also represented the commercial viability of material connected with a supposedly authentic rural experience.

But there was a powerful element of fantasy in all these artistic interests – that the people of these distinctive societies led romantic lives, governed by custom and superstition, at one with the sea or the land, and in some vital way more attuned to the natural world than metropolitan existence permitted. Yet, paradoxically, it was the coming of tourism that most destroyed the homogeneity and integrity of these areas. In the way such people were considered by outsiders there was also a strong element of per-

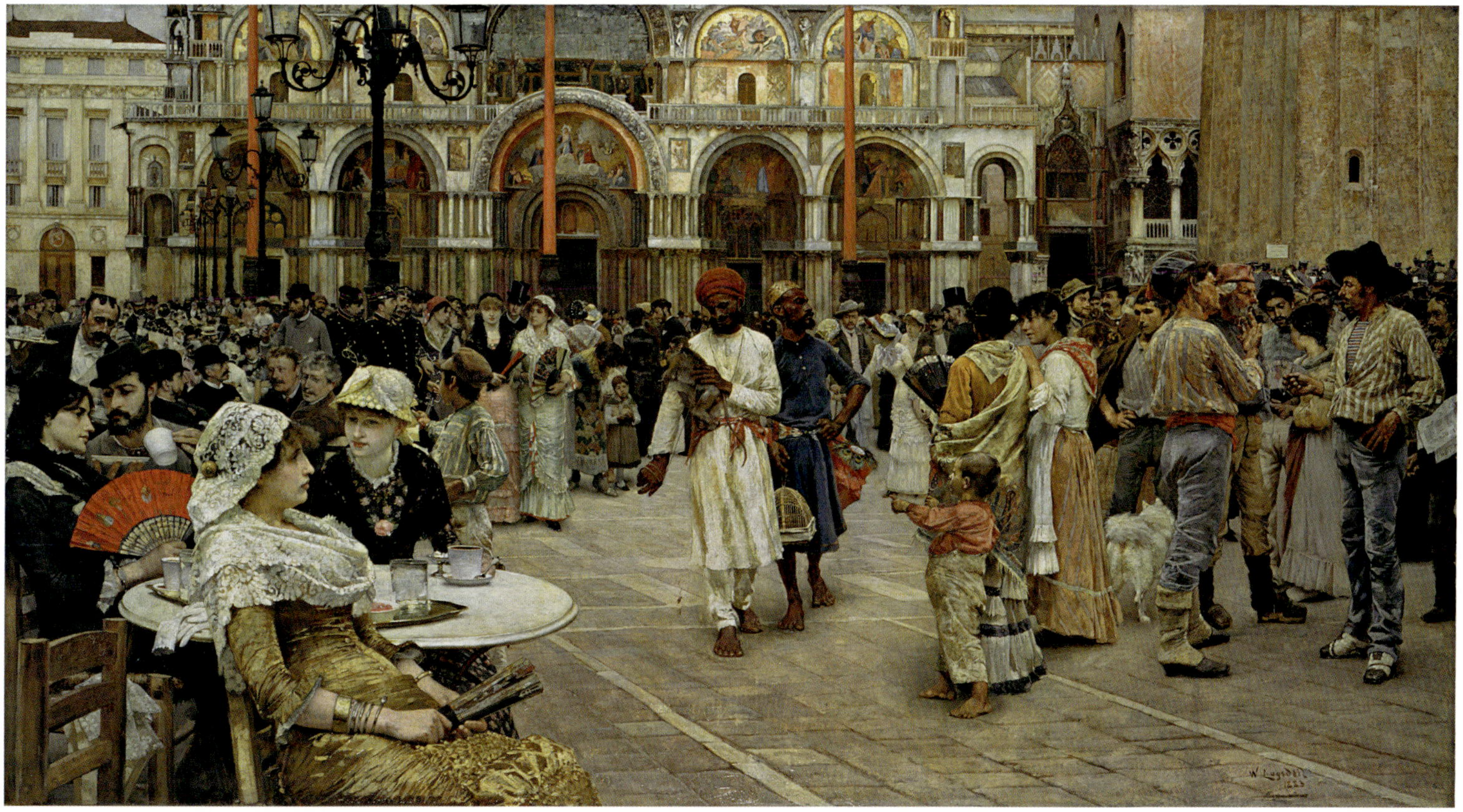

Fig. 18
William Logsdail
The Piazza of Saint Mark's
1883
Oil on canvas, 126.2 x 222.3 cm
Birmingham Museums & Art Gallery

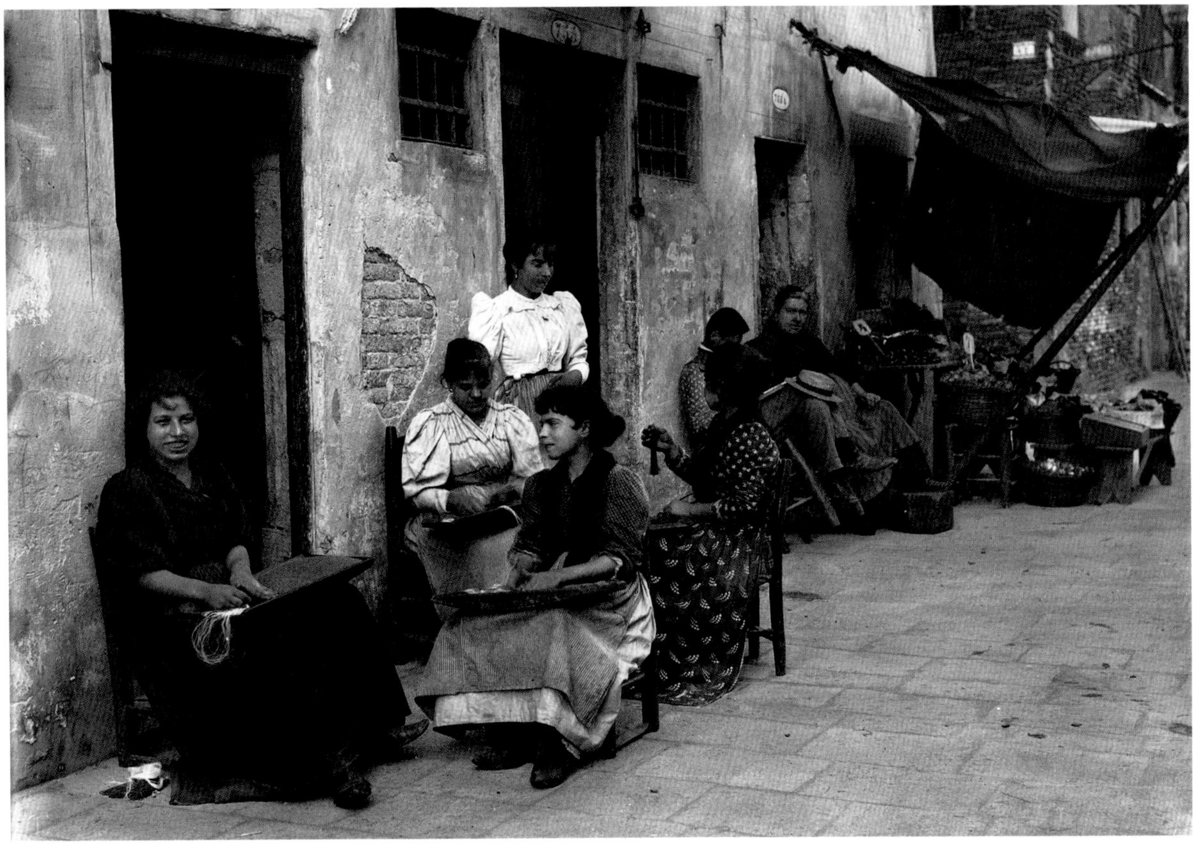

Fig. 19
Tomaso Filippi
Venice – Street Scene
*c.*1894–1903
Photograph

Filippi photographed Venice extensively during this period, documenting the appearance and lives of working Venetian women.

ceived 'otherness' – they dressed differently, had distinct dialects or accents, and there were supposed racial or physical characteristics. Such peoples were the object of a fascination with what were perceived as exotic ethnic types. Selectively painted depictions of them reinforced this characterisation and bolstered the mental creation of an exotic type. There was in this construct some democratising ideal – an interest in ordinary working people, rather than bourgeois society. But there is also the patronising stereotype that such people were less fettered in their emotions or behaviour, acting outside of bourgeois conventions and restrictions. And there was the belief that, in their 'simplicity', such people were unselfconscious in their behaviour.

In painting images of Venetian fisher girls, or the inhabitants of Newlyn, late nineteenth-century British artists can be seen partly acting as ethnographers, recording and reproducing information about these distinct societies. In all these pictures the subject's costume was an important element, their dress very different from the modern prototypes of urban style. There was a wider European interest in studying, recording and preserving these folk cultures, partly illustrated by the formation of ethnographic museums. In 1888 a museum opened in Haslemere that was devoted to illustrating ethnic cultural diversity, while in 1891 the Skansen Museum was founded in Stockholm to show the way of life in different parts of Sweden before industrialisation.

Sickert's Venetian figure studies can be seen as fitting into this matrix of ethnic interest, and it was a process he continued when he returned to London in 1905 and began his programme of painting the coster girls of Camden Town. Renowned for their flamboyant dress and smart backchat, they occupied a particular position in the Edwardian mind and were a distinctive urban type. Sickert was greatly excited by what he believed was the drama of their lives, and the casual violence they encountered, writing to Nan Hudson and Ethel Sands:

> They *always* wearing for every day [not] dirty, old, worn clothes but Sunday clothes… Extra-ordinary lives. Men, who thrive on them, now & again hitting them with hammers, putting poisonous powders on cakes, trying to cut their throats, drugging their whisky etc.[53]

What Sickert was doing in London was almost a revival in paint of the questing spirit of Henry Mayhew. Published in its entirety in 1861–62, Mayhew's *London Labour and the London Poor* had been the first detailed study, presented in first-person interviews, of the capital's working classes, the most numerous section of the population. Mayhew had divided his study by occupation or mode by which his subjects scraped a meagre living in the streets. Sickert's choices of the coster girl and Venetian fisher girl were of identifiable 'types'. His viewers would have been familiar with the coster girl from the streets of London, while Venetian women would have been almost equally recognisable from their recurrence in paintings and popular illustrations. Perhaps more than the architecture of the city, it was the people who interested Sickert, and, as much as the buildings, it was they who defined a sense of place. It is partly this realisation that underlies Sickert's championing of the city as a suitable and compelling source for the study of nature, pronounced in 1889 in his introduction to the first exhibition of the London impressionists. In Sickert's mind impressionism

> does not admit the narrow interpretation of the word 'Nature' which would stop short outside the four-mile radius [i.e. the boundary of London and the countryside]. It is, on the contrary, strong in the belief that for those who live in the most wonderful and complex city in the world, the most fruitful course of study lies in a persistent effort to render the magic and poetry which they daily see around them.[54]

Sickert had a predisposition to take studios in working-class districts of London, such as Cumberland Market in the 1890s and Camden Town in 1905. It was only partly for economic reasons, and a major factor was an interest and delight in working-class culture. In Robert Street in Cumberland Market Sickert's studio was reached via a tenement building passage, 'reeking of cats and cabbage', and he delighted in taking the dandified Max Beerbohm to a rough local pub nearby.[55] This kind of transgressive class interaction, breaking out of accepted boundaries of social sphere, was as much an expedition to investigate and experience working-class life, like an anthropologist of native culture in far-flung parts of the globe. There is a strain of egalitarianism about it, but a more pressing motive of seeking out the exotic, the quirky and the vulgar that is somewhat condescending and has more to do with the rejection of bourgeois strictures and the bolstering of bohemian credibility than with sincere empathy with working-class people. It revolves around the frisson of excitement at social exchange with people not usually encountered as social equals. Sickert went further and slept with his working-class models – Mme Villain, his mistress in Dieppe, was an illiterate fisherwoman whose sharp wit and vulgarity Sickert greatly enjoyed. In Venice, Giuseppina and Carolina were also reputedly sexual partners and Giuseppina's way of making money is made harshly clear in a portrait of her Sickert titled *Putana Veneziana*. Sickert does not meet them as equals, but there is very evident – and genuine – delight in the conversation and character of these models. He wrote to Jacques-Émile Blanche how:

> From 9 to 4 it is the uninterrupted joy of these kind, obliging little models who laugh, to amuse me with smutty talk while posing

like angels. They are happy to be there, and are not hurried. By four I am ready only to close the shutters, lie on my bed and sleep the sleep of the just until seven.[56]

In the British mind, the Venetians conformed to a distinct stereotype, one that blended passion, quaintness and romance, reinforced by the belief that they were less restrained in the way they led their lives. This particularly extended to the realm of love, where romances were pursued without the strictures of northern European bourgeois restraint. Writing in 1895 Henry Perl described how:

> Young couples wander hand in hand, looking with southern warmth into each other's eyes… A girl of fifteen, born on the shores of the lagoons, accounts it the greatest disgrace if she possess no *amoroso*, for a girl must be made much of and petted; in the language of this country it is called *far a l'amore*. This leads to no light conduct, the love-making being strictly overlooked by the relatives on either side, and almost without exception ending in marriage. Oh, Venetian girls are cunning and calculating little maidens![57]

That there was a view among northern Europeans that Venetian women were more relaxed in their morals concerning love or sex was confirmed by Horatio Brown, who, in his own account of the lives of Venice's people, was keen to dismiss it as a fallacy. 'I do not know why,' Brown wrote, 'the women of the Venetian *popolo* have acquired a reputation for a certain elasticity of morals; unless it has been given them by those who wish to find it so. The reputation is not deserved nor fairly based.'[58]

Salacious enthusiasm for the fantasy of relaxed sexual morals sat alongside other prejudicial and highly negative stereotypes of Venetian or Italian behaviour. Baedeker's guide book warned tourists to check their change, and Henry James set out plainly what he believed distinguished the Venetians:

> In the Venetian manner there is something peculiarly ingratiating. One feels that the race is old, that it has a long and rich civilization in its blood, and that if it has not been blessed by fortune, it has, at least, been polished by time. It has not a genius for morality, and, indeed, makes few pretensions in that direction. It scruples not to represent the false as the true, and is liable to confusion in the assignment of property. It is peculiarly susceptible to the tender sentiment, which it cultivates with a graceful disregard for the more rigid formalities. I am not sure that it is very brave and was not struck with its being very industrious.[59]

James sets out what is essentially a highly negative racial stereotype, while writing that he finds it 'ingratiating'. He wrote fondly of the beauty of the women of the Venetian islands. In Burano you could:

> admire the wonderful fisher-folk, whose good looks – and bad manners, I am sorry to say – can scarcely be exaggerated. Burano is celebrated for the beauty of its women and the rapacity of its children, and it is a fact that though some of the ladies are rather bold about it, every one of them shows you a handsome face.[60]

Further away in Chioggia, he directed his readers, could be sought out:

> young girls with faces a delicate shape and a susceptible expression, with splendid heads of hair, and complexions smeared with powder, faded yellow shawls that hang like Greek draperies, and little wooden shoes … [and]

> brown-cheeked matrons with lustrous tresses and high tempers, massive throats encased with gold beads, and eyes that meet yours with a certain defiance.[61]

In Venice, James noted, the people themselves 'were to a certain extent the objects on exhibition'.[62] His long article on the Grand Canal published in 1892 was accompanied by illustrations of Venice's inhabitants, presented like specimens – 'A Girl of the People', 'Type of Gondolier', 'Fishmongers'.[63] Some of Sickert's titles for his figure pictures similarly specify the type or origin of the sitter. A portrait of one of Sickert's Venetian models known as La Inez, in a beautiful yellow blouse, is titled *La Chiozzotta* (cat. 51) – 'the woman from Chioggia', the place James noted was associated with feminine beauty. Another of La Giuseppina is titled *La Callera* (cat. 42) – 'the woman of the streets'. And Sickert was keen to display his knowledge of Venetian dialect and slang in his titles, further attesting to the genuineness of his pictures and their distinctive regional origins. His double-figure picture *A Marengo* (cat. 53), for instance, is a transposition of the Venetian phrase 'a remengo', meaning 'to hell with it' which perfectly fits the scene of the women gossiping.[64] Sickert always liked to immerse himself in the everyday life of where he lived and quickly become part of the local scene rather than an outsider or foreigner. In Venice he relished performances of the comic plays of Carlo Goldoni featuring unsophisticated, down-to-earth characters whose vulgarity is an essential component of their humanity. Sickert's selection of his models seems to have followed similar lines, and he deliberately chose people with highly distinctive characters from among the *popolo*, the ordinary street people of Venice.

Painting the Figure

Up until he arrived in Venice in 1903, Sickert had confined himself almost exclusively to painting the city's architecture. Very few figure subjects are known from his earlier visits, and all are portraits: an oil of Signor de Rossi (cat. 31), a watercolour of Mrs Hulton in fancy dress, and his portrait of his friend Israel Zangwill, which, while it may have been started in Venice, was likely to have been partly completed back in London (cat. 30).[65] But in the early winter of 1903 Sickert began an extensive sequence of figure studies of models he set in natural poses in the flat he used as a studio in Calle dei Frati. It proved to be the breakthrough he had been seeking, and these ambiguous, atmospheric studies of local working-class women would serve as the material that would dominate Sickert's art for many years after. It was subject matter that would be transferred to his paintings in Camden Town when he returned permanently to London. Surprisingly, the move indoors to paint figures which transformed Sickert's later work was entirely coincidental. The winter of 1903–04 was one of the wettest on record in Venice, and Sickert was forced to abandon his pursuit of landscape subjects. He wrote to Blanche:

> I am only waiting for a sign of spring… it just isn't worth battling with all the elements. First of all it would make me ill, and then I wouldn't do anything worth while, and what is more Venice itself is like a tomb until the summer comes, high summer when everything is bathed in opal and sapphire. That's the reason, not unbridled ambition, why I have only done figure pictures for Bernheims.[66]

'Meanwhile this studio is a change,' he wrote elsewhere to Blanche, '[and] prevents me wasting my time worrying for spring so I am sure of working every day.' The models, he emphasised, 'are charming,' but the switch to figures presented certain challenges compared to architectural painting, and, 'alas I haven't the aplomb in drawing a hand that I have putting in a square window.'[67]

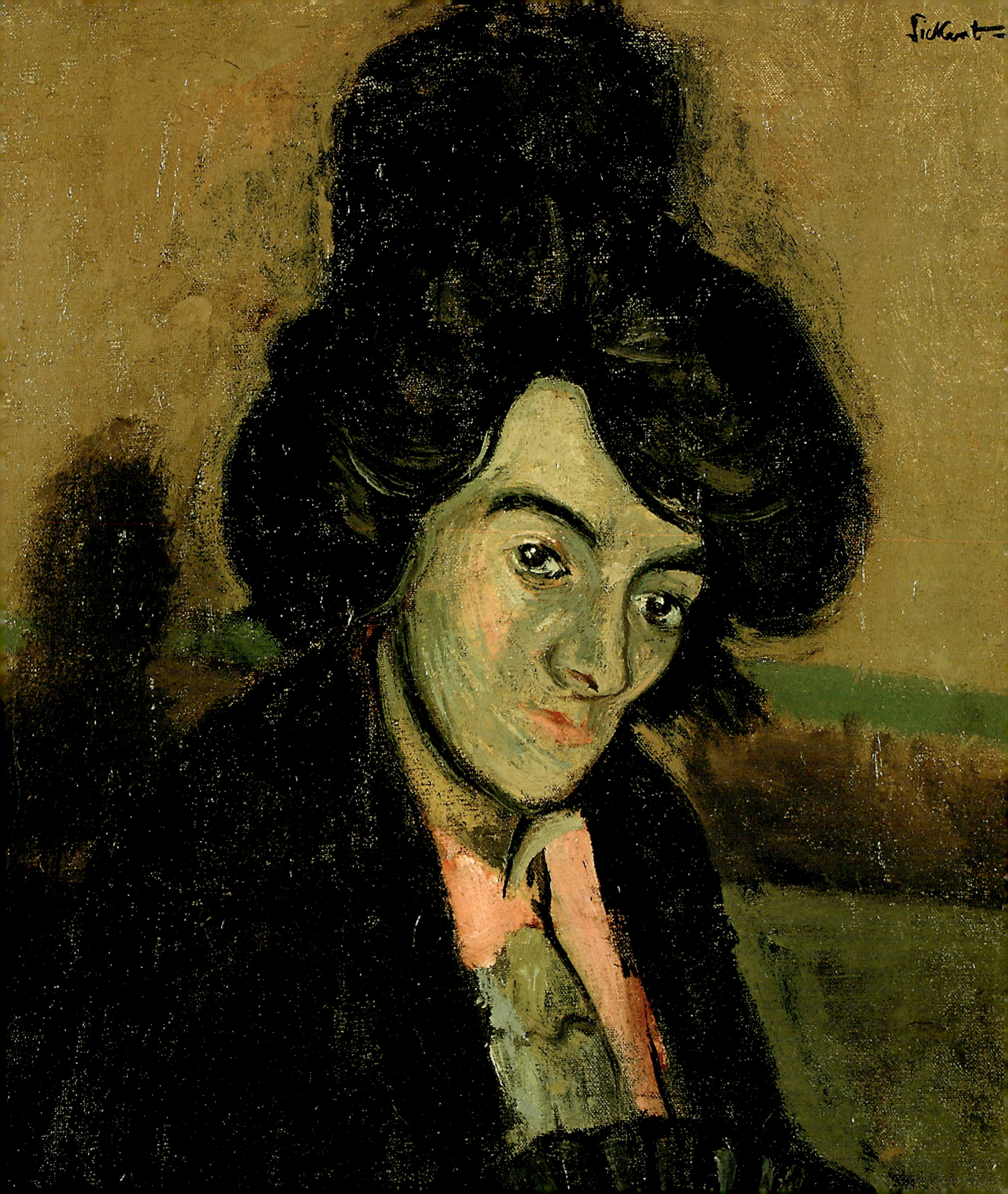
Sickert

The illustrator Frank Richards noted in 1894 how professional models were less desirable than casual ones:

> It is very difficult to get really good models, unless one is thoroughly accustomed to the place – the regular professional sitters being as a rule fat, coarse-looking women. We employed none of them, but used instead to go about with our gondolier and engage models as we came across them... We always found it most satisfactory to arrange terms beforehand, not commencing work until that was settled, which saved a lot of inconvenience and misunderstanding... Many one engages in the streets whose paintable appearances are suitable for good character studies, who are yet as a rule very bad sitters, expect the same pay as a first-class model would receive.[68]

Sickert got most of his models from the local trattoria where he generally had his lunch, the Giorgione di San Silvestro. Here he sketched some of the other patrons and also made the painting *Ladies' Bar* (cat. 39) which shows the restaurant's interior. He would chat with the proprietor Signor de Rossi, and it was he who reputedly provided Sickert with his two models, La Giuseppina and La Carolina. Writing to Mrs Hulton on New Year's Day 1901, Sickert reported delightedly:

> I have got hold of some splendid models. A very old woman with a fazzoletto [handkerchief], black, with peacock's feathers on her head, & some very pretty young ones. A Chiozotto with a Louis XI felt hat. A blind man & [his] leader. I got most of them from the Giorgione.[69]

The old woman was Mamma Mia Poveretta (cats. 43–44), supposedly Giuseppina's mother. De Rossi himself was the subject of an oil portrait painted in 1901, which was dedicated 'Al simpaticissimo e geniale Sig. de Rossi – l'amico Sickert' (cat. 31).[70] Supposedly a wholesale importer of vegetables to the city as well as a restaurateur, De Rossi has the slightly stringy appearance of a lean 50- or 60-year-old. The painting is delicately highlighted, with touches of grey-cream paint over the sitter's face and body animating the paint surface. Sickert presented it to his friend and considered it his best portrait. In 1927 Sickert asked Mrs Hulton to buy back the picture from De Rossi's widow, as he was anxious it should not be lost to his *oeuvre*.

The models Sickert described as 'pretty young ones' were Giuseppina and Carolina del'Acqua, the latter's nickname deriving from her antipathy to water. Both were reputedly local prostitutes. The popularity in London of paintings of anecdotal genre scenes from Venetian life adds an important context to Sickert's decision to paint the series of indoor studies of these two women on his 1903–04 visit. Another framework in which to see them, and which the genre scenes also engage with, is the interest in physical type, in particular the specific attributes of Venetian women. Various books appeared in the second half of the nineteenth century which adopted an openly ethnographic approach to the women of Venice. There was interest in the possibility that the voluptuous physical type which had once fascinated Titian was still to be found in the city.[71] Published in London in 1895, the German critic Henry Perl's book *Venezia* records and comments extensively on different female types, even down to their way of walking. Perl, who was in fact a woman writing under a male alias, drew comparison between what were claimed to be two discernible Venetian types:

> the rosy-fleshed Venus-like form rendered so familiar to us in the paintings of Giorgione

Walter Sickert
La Giuseppina: La Callera
1903–04
(cat. 42, detail)

> and Titian, and the slender yet muscular brunette, who has hitherto been too much neglected… The first has the light reddish-brown hair of the tint known as Venetian, with which are generally associated sea-green or azure-blue eyes and a snow-white bosom; a pathetic material beauty full of latent poetry. The second type varies more, but its usual characteristics are raven-black hair, great dark eyes with light-blue shadows beneath their lids, a finely arched nose, small lips, and a pale complexion with a soupcon of a greenish shade. If the owner of all these charms also has good teeth, the latter type of beauty is very fascinating, for there is an underlying fire about it, and it is greatly enhanced when it is animated by smiles, expressive glances and words. Moreover, there is about this loveliness a certain undercurrent of melancholy, of a resignation so unassumed and inherent as to take from passion all that could seem to connect it with sin.[72]

Perl argued that it was the people that gave Venice its distinction, and were the raw material for artists to utilise:

> These peculiar types are of very great importance to the general effect of any Venetian scene, and must therefore be taken fully into account in any study of the local colouring of the place. They do not exactly give the whole scheme of colour, but they do give the tone to every picture which can truly be styled Venetian, and in which the tints are properly blended.[73]

This distinctiveness or individuality was a quality also highlighted by Horatio Brown, the leading British historian of Venice, who wrote both serious and popular books about the city and its evolution. 'The home life of the Venetian people,' Brown wrote, in an extensive chapter devoted to the working classes, 'is as strongly characterized and as peculiar as everything else in that unique city. No race possesses a more distinctive set of customs, or clings to them with greater tenacity than the Venetian *popolo*'.[74]

Advances in the medium of photolithographic colour reproduction spawned a series of illustrated books about Venice in the early years of the new century. These almost invariably mixed portrayals of the city's architecture with plates which showed the appearance of Venice's inhabitants, particularly the women. One of the most successful was by Mortimer Menpes, who was to illustrate a sequence of travel books published by A & C Black with text by his daughter Dorothy. With a hundred plates, Menpes's *Venice* appeared in May 1904 and surveyed every aspect of the city. Many of his illustrations show women with dark hair and black shawls who bear close resemblance to those found in Sickert's paintings. Both Menpes and Sickert were illustrating a recognisable 'type' that their audiences would expect to see. Alongside Sickert, Menpes had also been Whistler's assistant, printing his Venetian etchings. The frontispiece to Menpes's book showed a Venetian girl crossing St Mark's Square (fig. 20). It immediately recalls Sickert's *Piazzetta di San Marco* (cat. 23) with Giuseppina, and it is evident that both painters were fulfilling similar aims when integrating working-class Venetian women into recognisable surroundings.

An important further context in which to consider Sickert's figure pictures was the widely held contemporary conviction that Venice was a place of moral degradation. One of the leitmotifs of Ruskin's *Stones of Venice* was his belief that the fall of Venice's power as a city-state was an inevitable effect of the moral decay of its populace.[75] In this scheme, the physical crumbling of Venice's architectural heritage

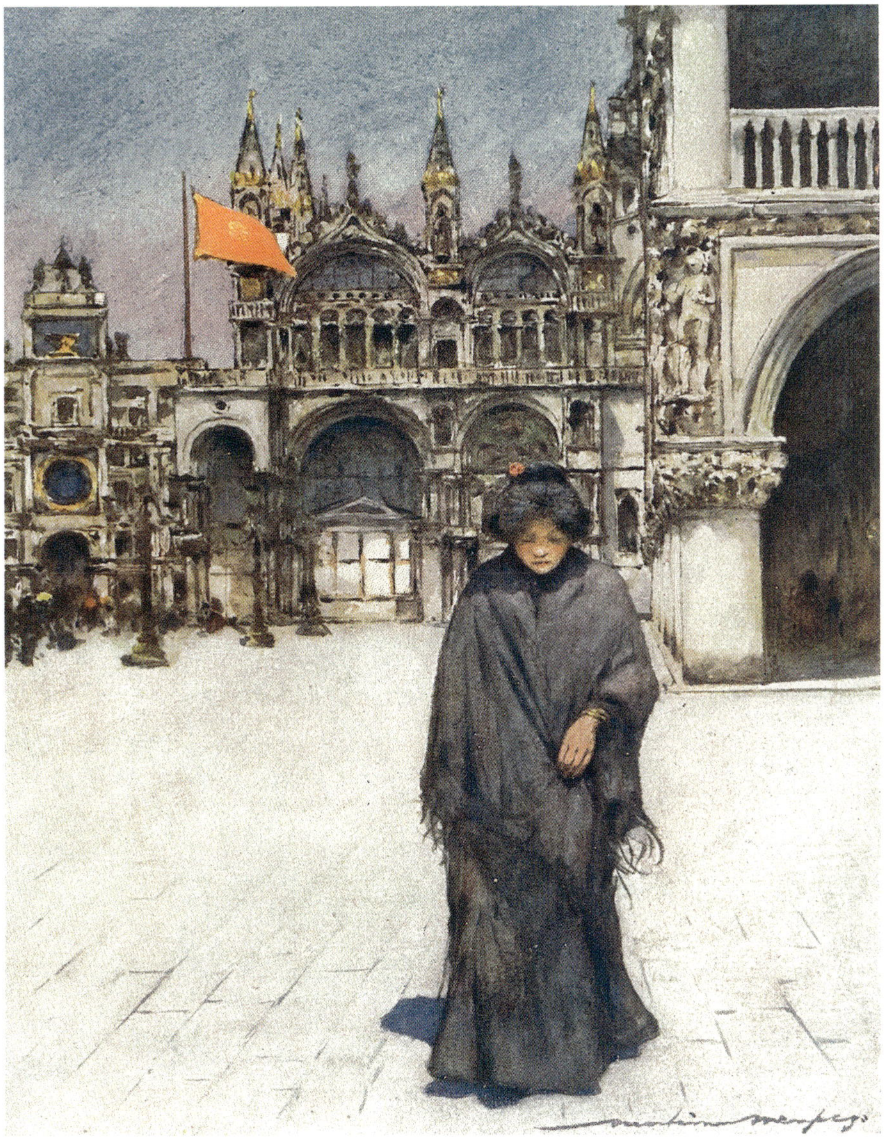

Fig. 20
Mortimer Menpes
Crossing the Piazza
1904
Frontispiece to Mortimer Menpes and Dorothy Menpes, *Venice* (London, 1904)

mirrored or expressed the moral collapse of the people. In *Pierrot and Woman Embracing* (cat. 38) Sickert showed a couple down an alleyway, the Campielo de la Sacrestia that runs along the side of the church of San Martino, close to the entrance to the Arsenal. The viewer is cast in the role of voyeur, glimpsing an erotically charged moment of intimacy. The costumes of the Pierrot and his companion suggest this is a scene during the Venetian carnival, a time notorious for some centuries as a period of revelry and, in particular, sexual intrigue and licence. The masks people wore for anonymity and the relaxation of social codes concerning sexual relations encouraged the proliferation of fleeting liaisons. Traditionally the carnival started on 2 February and ended the day before Ash Wednesday. By the time Sickert was in Venice, the carnival was reportedly somewhat in abeyance, although it had not completely died out. Dressed in his trademark white costume with black pompoms, Pierrot was a staple of the Italian Commedia dell'Arte. His hapless buffoonery was a rich source of comedy, but he was also a figure of sadness and longing who inspired sympathy. His frustrated amorous pursuit of Columbine allowed great pantomime potential. But Pierrot's disasters and humiliations, and his continuing desire for the unobtainable, became a metaphor for human existence.

When it came to his pictures of figures in interiors, Sickert was well aware of how setting could completely change the dynamics of the figure conjunctions. His shifting indoors of the traditional Venetian subject of a pair of fisher girls was slyly subversive. The pictorial convention for painting these women was to showcase them against a recognisable landmark or a picturesque backwater. But Sickert understood that the psychological impact of what we see is changed irrevocably when it is brought into the boudoir. Here the focus on the figure is heightened to an almost oppressive degree, which encourages a direct relationship with the subject. The reading of the picture is changed entirely by its location in a personal space, and there is, in the heightening of intimacy, a distinct undercurrent of sexual potential.

This was a particular feature of the double figure subjects Sickert painted of his two principal models Carolina del'Acqua and La Giuseppina. In *Le Tose* (cat. 56) – Venetian slang for 'the girls' – they sit on the Empire-style sofa that Sickert had in his painting room on the top floor of 940 Calle dei Frati. The constrained, planar composition forces attention onto the figures, although their faces are blurred and impossible to read, creating a sense of ambiguity. We can look only to the pose and set of their bodies to read meaning – they are evidently looking back at the painter, the figure on the left looking bored as she rests her head on her hand, the two women obviously on familiar terms as they sit together closely. The figure on the right is relaxed, her feet tucked up under her. There are affinities with Degas's pictures of resting prostitutes such as *Waiting* (*c*.1876–77). However, whereas in pictures by Degas and Toulouse-Lautrec there is no question of the calling of the women portrayed, or misunderstanding that the setting is a brothel, Sickert's are more ambiguous and less explicit,[76] inviting the viewer to speculate on the significance of the scene. However, while this level of innocent reading is possible with *Conversation*, *Caquetoeres* and *Le Tose* (cats. 52, 54 and 56), it is more difficult to sustain in other pictures in the series, especially those such as *Conversations* where the nudity of one of the women implies a clearly sexual interpretation.

The bed, and other items of furniture such as the Empire-style sofa in *Le Tose*, were essentially studio props, to complete the naturalism of his observations. Pictures such as *A Marengo* (cat. 53) are exercises in the concept that Sickert learned from Degas of life viewed through a keyhole. The two girls chat and gossip on the bed in relaxed attitudes that seem entirely natural, but are nevertheless poses that they held for an hour. Their unselfconscious positioning allows us to spectate on the intimacy of their friendship, and to observe them in their natural state, almost like a social anthropologist. In Venice Sickert developed the idea, derived from Degas, of the 'boudoir nude', showing a naked woman in the natural environment of the bedroom, and he applied

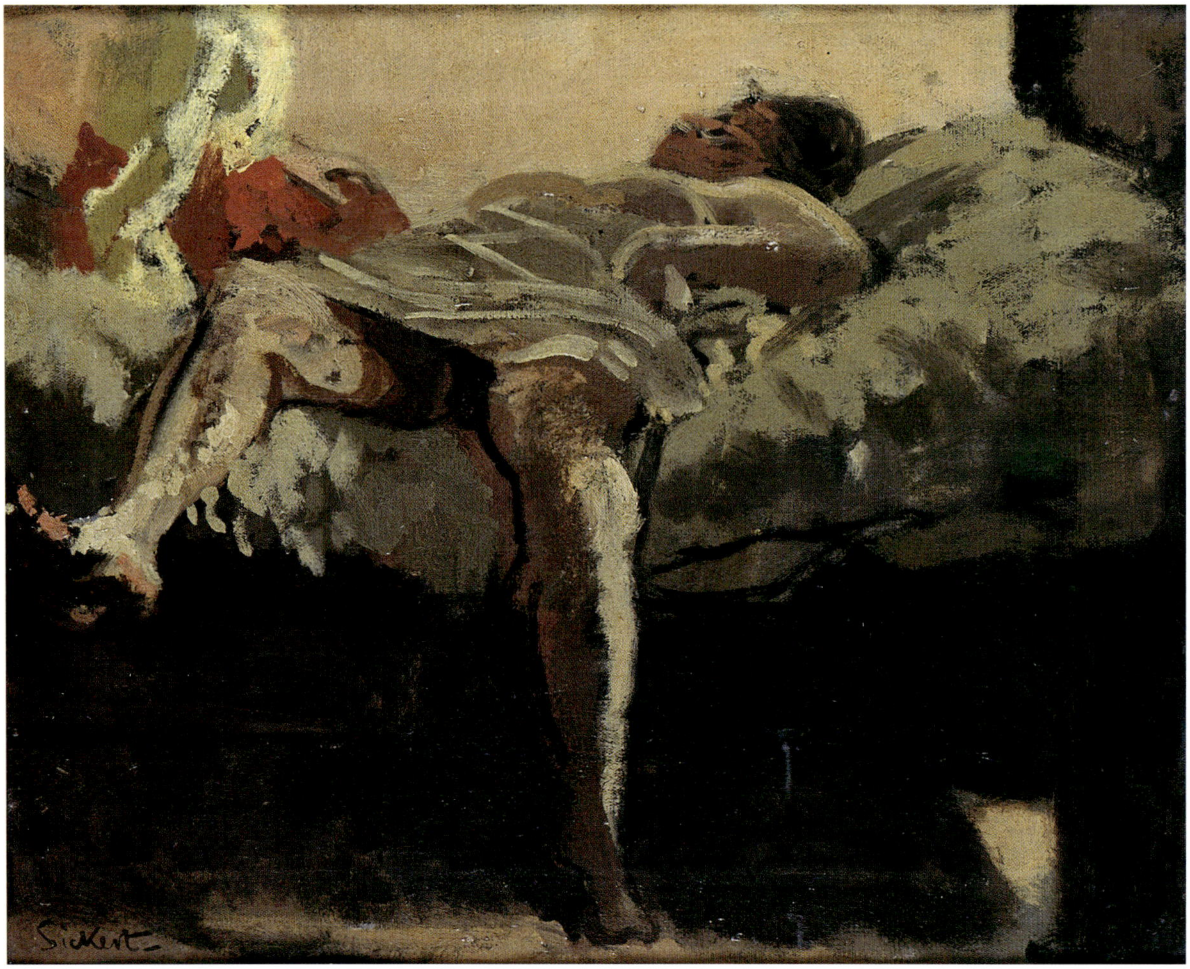

Fig. 21
Walter Sickert
Fille Vénitienne Allongée
1903–04
Oil on canvas, 37.5 x 46 cm
Rouen, Musée des Beaux-Arts

this to single-figure subjects. But now he elaborated the double-figure theme of *A Marengo* to also embrace the nude, by having one of the girls naked on the bed while her clothed friend chats to her, such as in *Fille Vénitienne Allongée* (fig. 21) or *Giuseppina and the Model* (1903–04).[77] It was a line of development that was to gestate and reach conclusion five years later in Sickert's 'Camden Town Murder' series. Canvases such as *The Camden Town Murder* (fig. 22) and the sinister *L'affaire de Camden Town* (1909),[78] each featured a clothed man and a naked woman on a bed. These apparently related to the notorious murder of local prostitute Emily Dimmock, according to their various titles, but Sickert's deliberate ambiguity, learnt in Venice, leaves the viewer pondering just what stage of the drama they are seeing, or even if it relates to a murder at all.

Fig. 22
Walter Sickert
The Camden Town Murder
*c.*1907–08
Oil on canvas, 64.5 x 61 cm
Daniel Katz Ltd

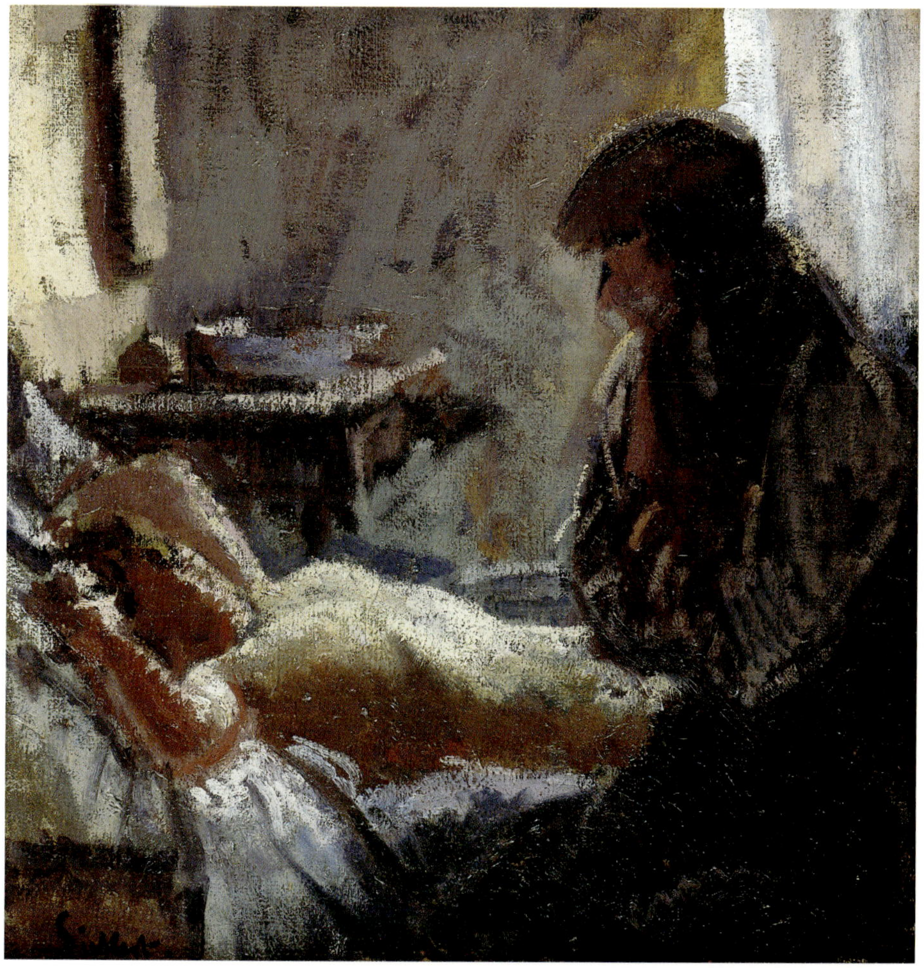

'To most contemporary viewers,' Sickert's biographer Matthew Sturgis has written, 'two women, whatever the state of their dress or undress, lounging together upon a bed, suggested only one setting: the brothel.'[79] In Sickert's pictures of such figure pairings there is certainly a subtext of sex, felt most strongly in those where one of them is naked. Sickert would have been familiar with Toulouse-Lautrec's pictures of brothel scenes, which are often characterised by a similar languid inaction of the figures. Sickert's biographer Denys Sutton, from his contact with those who knew the artist, believed that he certainly visited a brothel in Venice, so that in the manner of Lautrec and Degas he could make sketches.[80] Whether Sickert's relations with Giuseppina and Carolina extended to a physical dimension is unconfirmed, but it must seem likely. He admitted to his patron Sir William Eden that he had sex with prostitutes in Venice,[81] and he told Jacques-Émile Blanche that in the winter of 1903–04 he was for the first time infected with venereal disease, writing: 'Enfin me voilà tout à fait "grown up."'[82]

Looking back in 1920, Sickert wrote to Mrs Hulton:

> I live more in recollection of Venice than may seem likely... I regret too late that I painted buildings too much & 'from nature' ever. If I had my life over again I would have accumulated endless drawings of Venetian life & movement which would have served me to paint from till today.[83]

To Blanche, Sickert detailed his ideal method of painting on the figure paintings:

> Canvases size 8 prepared in grey (black and white) with oil. A good coat. The first session: everything is laid in from nature covering all the canvas and not permitting the model to move until it is all down. That takes about an hour more or less without moving. When the

canvas is covered I start another. Three days or more later (canvases kept round a stove that is always lit) I take up the series again. With a large brush I wash the canvas with linseed oil, which I remove afterwards with blotting paper, and then I finish off, being guided more by my own work from the first impression, than by the model, and keeping within the proportions first indicated, whether they seem right to me or not.[84]

The 'size 8' canvas Sickert mentions is a French canvas size, measuring 38.1 x 45.7 cm, which is the size of most of the Venice figure pictures. In another letter to Blanche, Sickert stated that he had adjusted his technique, although not his ambition to paint quickly:

> I have gained a great deal of experience working from 9 to 4... *Not* to paint in varnish. *Not* to embarrass the canvas with any preparations. And so to give the paint every chance of drying from the back of the canvas. To paint with 1/2 raw oil and 1/2 turps. To state general tones once and *once only*. And when the first coat is dry, to finish, bit by bit. I had the bad habit of re-stating the tones all over an indefinite number of times, and getting no further, not improving the colour, and making the canvas, especially in the darks, more and more disagreeable.[85]

Sickert's aim in his sequence of Venice figure pictures was to work rapidly and give a sense of spontaneous immediacy. It was this quality that he described to his friend Nan Hudson in offering her as a gift one of the pictures from the series: 'Do you remember one I had last Saturday of 2 Venetian girls in shawls, talking? It is one I like for the reason that it was immediately expressed during the pose, & is without thoughts or explanation.'[86]

In Neuville in 1902 Sickert had experimented with making a small number of drawings of a nude model in a bedroom,[87] but the setting of pairs of figures in distinct arrangements was a new advance. In such works, Sickert seems to deploy his models like actors on a stage, at once setting them in naturalistic poses but that are in fact highly contrived, to create a sense of dramatic tension. The surroundings in which they are positioned are also artificial; Sickert has furnished the everyday room in a naturalistic manner, but this is still in essence an artist's studio. Again, it is comparable with a piece of theatrical staging. Sickert had himself been an actor, in Henry Irving's company, and knew a great deal about the theory and practice of the dramatic arts. There is a strong resonance with the drama of Henrik Ibsen, which had been performed in London for the first time in the early 1890s. Ibsen enhanced traditional nineteenth-century theatrical conventions by interspersing dialogue and action with moments of motionlessness and silence in order to create mood, atmosphere and powerful psychological tension. There is some correlation with the method by which Sickert's subjectless figure studies exert their own intense effect on the viewer. His pictures' stillness and indefinite yet heightened atmosphere create a very similar tension that recalls naturalist drama. The frankness with which Ibsen confronted the baseness of human behaviour also makes interesting comparison. Sickert would have been familiar with the succession of Ibsen's plays performed in London, most notably *A Doll's House*, which caused a furore when it was performed in 1892. Other painters too responded to this new modern form of drama. In 1900 Sickert's friend William Rothenstein painted the moment in *A Doll's House* when Nora waits silently on the stairs for her infidelity to be uncovered, casting his new wife Alice in the female character and Augustus John as the model for her lover.

Sickert's setting of his models in the carefully constructed yet natural environment of Calle dei Frati might be compared to August Strindberg's call in the preface to *Miss Julie* for naturalist staging of his drama. It is unlikely the two ever met, although Strindberg stayed briefly with the Danish landscape painter Fritz Thaulow in Dieppe in 1896 after suffering his breakdown; Thaulow himself was on friendly terms with Blanche, but did not find Sickert's art sympathetic. Both Sickert and Strindberg are examples of how the impetus of naturalism in literature, drama and painting found expression, and connected them with a wider sphere of cultural forms.

Critical Reception

Sickert's Venetian canvases were much admired in Paris and they sold well. He wrote to Mrs Hulton: 'Paris happens to have taken to me as a Venetian painter de bon côté. They are very sentimental about Venice, & Dieu merci, rather ignorant, so I impress them.' He was, he told her, 'le Vénitien par excellence – à Paris'.[88] To Steer he wrote delightedly:

> Paris has taken kindly to the brush that struggled rather in Robert St[reet]. German papers quote new appearance in Paris of a painter 'of the first rank' etc. J'aime autant ça. As Jimmy [Whistler] said… 'mayn't all be true, but makes very pleasant reading'.[89]

When *Palace of the Doges* was exhibited at the Salon of the Société National des Beaux-Arts in 1902 it was widely praised. Léon Bénédite, director of the Luxembourg, considered acquiring it for the French national collection, much to Sickert's excitement, although this eventually fell through. London, however, was a far more conservative environment and the critics had in the past been hostile to Sickert's work. He sent a small number of his more prominent Venetian canvases, both architectural and figure subjects, for exhibition at the New English Art Club (NEAC) from 1896. His earliest offerings, of *St Mark's, Venice (Pax Tibi Marce Evangelista Meus* (cat. 4) and *The Lion of St Mark's* (fig. 8) in spring 1896, caused little stir at all and several commentators regretted how dull they claimed the NEAC had become. 'The admixture of cleverness, eccentricity, and audacity which is their chief stock-in-trade has ceased to be novel, therefore it has ceased to entertain,' wrote *The Scotsman*, and *Empire* especially regretted that, 'Those humourists, Messrs. Walter and Bernhardt Sickert, have apparently ceased from joking on canvas'.[90] But others found much to admire in Sickert's Venetian landscape *From the Hospital to the Grave* exhibited at the NEAC in November 1896.[91] *The Daily Telegraph* wrote of it that while he 'displays no adequate sense of form, he at any rate gladdens the eye with a brilliancy and sparkle of colour, a frank play of light, for which we had not given him credit' and the *Daily Chronicle* judged that Sickert 'at last begins to see colour in Venice, in the old buildings on its canal banks, in the rich shimmering blues of the distance framed by the long narrow perspective of houses'.[92]

Ten years later, Sickert's Venetian figure subjects were not to receive such easy passage. 'Mr Walter Sickert's sketches, for the naming of which he had to have recourse to a foreign tongue, are so slipshod, dirty, incomplete and meaningless that they are utterly unfit for exhibition,' thundered Paul Coddrington in *The World*.[93] The colouring and elusive narrative of Sickert's figure paintings was taken up by the *Daily Mail*, which complained the November 1906 NEAC exhibition consisted of 'partial and complete failures, and of would-be clever things that defy all rules of sound art and even of common sense. Mr Walter Sickert is one of the worst offenders, and the Italian names which are appended in the catalogue to his mud-coloured smears give but the vaguest clues to his meaning'; the headline was 'Art run amok'.[94] In that show were included *A Marengo* (cat. 53), a portrait of Maria Bonda, one of

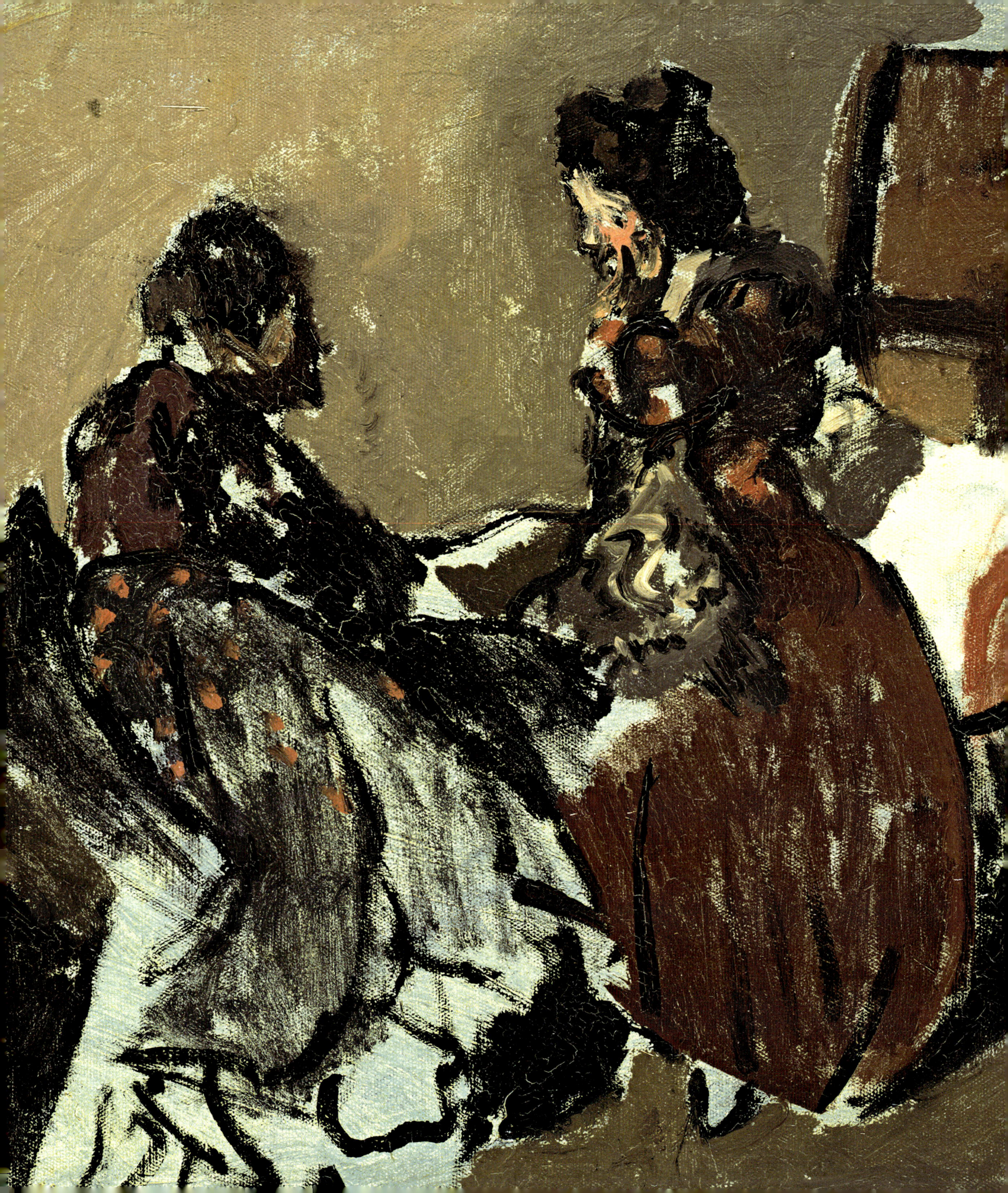

Sickert's Venetian sitters, a picture titled *Bonne Fille* and *Mamma Mia Poveretta* (cat. 43). 'The little pictures of strange people he has sent to this exhibition,' wrote *The Saturday Review*, 'must be seen by artificial light to appreciate properly their search for personal expression in colour and the witty anecdotes of their attitudes.'[95] The review interestingly compared him to the symbolist poet Mallarmé in giving only hints of his meaning rather than making it wholly explicit – 'he gives you a fragment here and a fragment there, enough to prove the reality of his vision, but not enough to render it visible to the world.'[96] This was a theme picked up by other critics of Sickert's figure pictures. 'In this exhibition,' complained *The Tribune*, 'there are several experiments of his, studies of pose and gesture, in which certain aspects of reality are very vividly presented. But they make no pretence to be pictures, and one cannot but feel that it is time that Mr Sickert should be painting pictures, after all the experiments he has made.'[97]

The *Daily Mail* grasped the subversive moral dimension of Sickert's figure subjects: 'with his touches of the grotesque… beauty becomes an uncanny insinuation and graciousness a kind of leer.'[98] The macabre or grotesque nature of Sickert's contribution was highlighted by other reviewers, most notably in relation to *Mamma Mia Poveretta*. To the *Manchester Guardian*, Sickert's return to the New English Art Club after a period in which he had focussed on exhibiting on the Continent heralded a new era:

> The return of Mr Walter Sickert to London and his re-election to the New English Art Club, and more particularly the nature of his contribution to its Winter Exhibition, must turn the thoughts of many visitors to the pioneer period of its history that, in a sense, closed some twelve years ago… Mr Walter Sickert having in four examples taken charge of the macabre side of the exhibition.[99]

Walter Sickert
A Marengo
1903–04
(cat. 53, detail)

Commerce

One of the principal attractions of Venice for Sickert was its affordability. Here an artist could live in reasonable style for a fraction of the cost in London. Rent was cheap; Sickert delightedly related to Blanche that Calle dei Frati was 'such a good studio 30 fr a month'.[100] This equated to just £1 4s, and must have been cheap even by Venetian standards as in the same letter he wrote of how his visits to see Carlo Goldoni's comedies cost 'Thirteen francs for a stalle d'orchestre for 12 representations.'[101] Other artists too were attracted to life in Venice for the same reason. The British painter William Logsdail was a permanent resident in the 1880s and 1890s and could not believe his luck in being able to rent a 20-room palazzo in Madonna dell'Orto with ceiling decorations by Tiepolo, a sixteenth-century chapel and a beautiful garden for just 'one thousand five hundred lire a year. That is £60'.[102] Published in 1906, Karl Baedeker's tourist guide to Northern Italy estimated that including hotel accommodation:

> The average expenditure of a single traveller, apart from railway-fares, may be estimated at 20-25 francs per day, or at 15–20 francs when a prolonged stay is made at one place; but persons acquainted with the language and habits of the country may easily restrict their expenses to still narrower limits.[103]

Sickert's poor finances kept him in Venice, where living was cheap. But he admitted to Sir William Eden in 1901 that if he could have an income of just £100 a year he would much rather live in London.[104] The same year he told a new Venice friend Edward Heron-Allen that he would have liked to spend even a month in London but could not afford it.[105] Sickert believed that it was possible for an artist to gain a living without having a popular following, like the stars of the Royal Academy, but only if one was prepared to produce work of real quality. In an insight into how he saw the production, sale and critical reception of his own work, he argued there would always be a small but lucrative and lasting market among those who could discern 'quality' as against fashion or popularity:

> What is it then that I would advise the painter to do? I would advise him to forget that he has been called a professional man, and to watch the markets, like any other skilled artisan that has his wits about him. He will then notice that quality always has a market value. Quality is a good investment. It is true that many of the larger money prizes have fallen to work which has no quality. But when it is found out, as it is at the next change of owners, the market value comes down with a run… But quality has always had its market value. Corot drove a roaring trade, and so did Turner. Keene left thirty thousand pounds, earned by his pen, Whistler has only to look at a piece of paper to turn it into a large cheque. Yet none of these artists have been in any sense popular. The topers know where the good wine is, and it is on the topers that your honest innkeeper grows fat.[106]

The sizes of the pictures Sickert made in Venice were deliberately aimed at a domestic market, based on the everyday realities of scale and space. 'Consider the conditions under which your true collector, your connoisseur with a palate, buys,' Sickert wrote in 1897. 'His space is limited… he will naturally ask the painter to put his thoughts into the smallest compass necessary to their complete expression. Here he may seem to be cramping the artist. On the contrary, he is his best friend.'[107] Sickert's last comment acknowledges the realities of artistic production, that the smaller the canvas, the faster it can be filled. Indeed, Sickert held that certain painters, such as Corot, were harmed when they tried to work on a larger scale, wonderfully likening it to taking 'green Chartreuse in a mug'.[108] Sickert even identified a recipe of three ingredients in the small paintings of the French realist painter Jean-Jacques Henner (1829–1905) that he believed ensured their success:

> The one is that if paint is skilfully and lightly brushed on, and not mauled, it looks nice, and, that when varnished, makes pretty furniture. The other is that a slip of human flesh, under trees, and near water, is a nice thing to think about. The third is that a certain pink, a certain mahogany, a certain blue, and a certain green go well together. So he brushes you in a little slip of pink nude, on grass of a certain green, by a little slip of blue lake, under mahogany boughs and a pearly blue sky.[109]

The abstract qualities of this recipe, of colours that sit harmoniously together and applied dexterously, might well describe Sickert's own practice at this time. His mention of the psychological attraction to buyers of 'a slip of human flesh' further binds his statements about Henner to his own way of working, and gives a highly interesting insight into his likely consideration of commercial motives when selecting subjects and the way in which he might paint them. It is entirely probable that Sickert consciously limited the scale of his own Venetian canvases, both for reasons of commercial viability and also because of their greater suitability to a smaller scale. He concluded in his article that if Henner's 'recipe' were 'expanded on to six feet of canvas for the Salon, the value of the picture is lessened.'[110] However, Sickert had reason to rue not heeding his own advice. In the early months of 1898 he painted a life-size image of the actress Hilda Spong as she appeared in Arthur Pinero's play *Trelawny of the Wells*.[111] At eight feet four inches square, this was the largest picture Sickert had painted to date, and an emphatic claim to elevate his theatrical subjects to the status and scale of high art. When it was exhibited at the New English Art Club the critic D. S. MacColl complained that the picture 'occupies a self-defeating quantity of wall space… Surely it would repay him to use the same material for a small colour engraving which would be more the size of his subject; for subjects have their sizes.'[112] Sickert could not sell the picture, and it remained on his hands until 1911 when it was bought anonymously by his friend Sylvia Gosse, knowing he was in need of funds.[113]

Poor critical reaction and the lack of return on an intensive amount of work must have formed a significant lesson for Sickert, emphasising to him the links between scale and marketability. Sickert was profoundly aware of the economic dynamics of painting, and that the amount of labour required had to be balanced strictly against a likely price. Most of his Venetian pictures are of a similar moderate and modest size, perfectly suited to a bourgeois drawing room or boudoir. The largest pictures he painted were the sequence of canvases of the façade of St Mark's (cats. 3–5). Made during and after his first visit to Venice in 1895–96, these were all painted on a larger and more impressive scale, the largest of the set measuring 152.4 cm wide.[114] In April 1901 Sickert was in correspondence with Durand-Ruel, writing with enthusiasm about his plan to paint a further series of five canvases of a corner of St Mark's which would all measure the same size of 100 x 85 cm.[115] In the event Sickert seems to have made only one canvas of these dimensions, and other treatments of the same composition were more domestic in scale.[116] Sickert suggested to Durand-Ruel an advance of 500 francs for his set of five large paintings, with the option to return the money if they did not like them. The French dealer took up the offer, suggesting they might be suitable for a special small exhibition.[117] At 100 francs each, these large pictures would work out at earning Sickert the equivalent of £4 each.[118] As he could charge them the same for smaller canvases, it hardly seems worth his while to have painted on a larger scale, with the added cost of materials as well as greater time. This may well explain his decision to reduce the scale of this sequence.

The prices Sickert obtained for his Venetian paintings were relatively modest, and the prices the Parisian dealers paid were less than he could achieve when he sold direct to local buyers. In 1904 he was particularly pleased with the sale of 'a nude on a bed and a girl in a shawl sitting on a sofa' to Henri Gonse and another picture to Johan Schlesinger that together netted him 900 Italian francs, the equivalent of £36.[119] He remarked somewhat wryly to Jacques-Émile Blanche that he would 'have had to do nine canvases for the Bernheims for the same money'.[120] This would work out to an equivalent of £4 per picture, which seems to have been the average price Sickert obtained from the dealers for his Venetian paintings. An important snapshot of his prices is contained in a postcard written by an anonymous author about negotiations with the artist to purchase *The Dogana and Santa Maria della Salute*[121] for a Miss Lillian Richardson. Postmarked August 1895, the postcard is attached to the reverse of the painting and reads:

> W. Sickert want[s] £5.5 for his Salute but will take £3.3.0, so I have closed the bargain. He will send it to you by post at once if you like; or will bring it to England early in September & post it in England – I advise the latter – I shd send him a cheque if you want to pay at once, as negociable [*sic*] here at his bank[122]

Although the panel, measuring 15.9 x 23.8 cm, was smaller than other works made at this time, three guineas was nevertheless a comparatively low price for Sickert to achieve.

The prices the dealers charged their clients for

Sickert's pictures, however, evidently also incorporated a hefty mark-up. When Sickert's friend Jean, Lady Hamilton previewed his solo exhibition at Bernheim-Jeune in Paris on 31 May 1904, she bought two of his Venetian pictures. Refusing to accept a discount, falsely hoping the full amount would be passed on to Sickert, she paid £28 for a view of the Salute and £32 for *St Mark's, Venice (Pax Tibi Marce Evangelista Meus* (cat. 4).[123] Evidently the Venice pictures sold well in Paris, Sickert writing to Mrs Hulton that he had heard from Durand-Ruel that 'apart from purely aesthetic considerations the firm considers them about the right article'.[124] Initially sending to Durand-Ruel, Sickert subsequently switched to Bernheim-Jeune. The two dealers applied different economic strategies with their artists. Durand-Ruel took works on commission, in the traditional manner, and Sickert only got paid when and if there was a sale. Bernheim's, however, followed a more speculative and commoditised policy, buying pictures outright, often in bulk, and then charging whatever they could get. It was initially more expensive and required greater capital speculation. But potentially it was an extremely canny way of working, for if an artist's reputation – and prices – rose, as a result of their exposure, then Bernheim-Jeune would have reserves of pictures they owned outright that would appreciate markedly in value. Under the traditional system, as at Durand-Ruel, the artist would receive a share of any rise in their market. Sickert however was clearly content with the Bernheim arrangement in that it delivered immediate payment. For such a deal, and for negotiating to purchase paintings in some numbers, Bernheim also expected a discounted rate. They bought one group of Sickert's pictures for just 60 French francs each. Two of these, both pictures of Venice, were sold immediately for 1,500 francs apiece, a differential that Jacques-Émile Blanche described as scandalous.[125] The rate of exchange was approximately 25 French francs to the pound, meaning that Sickert got only £2 10s per canvas.[126] Yet he was not necessarily downhearted by this return. Casting his mind back in 1935, he wrote to the Editor of *The Times*:

> The sons of my old friend Mr Tooth have got hold of the right end of the stick in their scheme for the hire purchase of pictures. Painters will be, for them, rich as soon as the *pauperise* (not *paupertas*) can buy pictures. I was rich when I lived in France, and when Bernheim jeune et fils bought my canvases in roped up (and unseen) batches of 10 at £40 the batch, with one batch thrown in as a make-weight, 'O! L'heureux temps que nous étions malheureux!'[127]

Sickert himself took a sophisticated economic view of the Paris art market. In a letter to Philip Wilson Steer he observed of Paris, 'Prices too low. But at low prices demand *unlimited*. *Very* able dealers.' Nevertheless, he was shocked that 'Some make, though, *hundreds* percent. Durand-Ruel, alone, very generous, almost quixotic. Takes 10 percent'.[128] But he realised that a high turnover was good for the market and good for building the reputation of the artist. On his way to Venice in September 1903, Sickert called at Bernheim's to discuss his postponed exhibition and also to discuss his prices. They agreed to accept all of Sickert's Venetian pictures as he made them.[129] The money he received began to edge up, obtaining a total of 600 French francs for four Venetian landscapes, a result with which he declared himself 'bien content', obtaining two hundred for two of them and a hundred each for the others.[130] This amount equated to a total of £24 sterling.[131] This was, however, still short of the mark Sickert had hoped for when he had first considered switching to Bernheim. Then he had written to Blanche: 'I hope soon to send the Bernheims some canvases. But I do well not to send till I have some stuff which is up to the mark. Also I want to screw them up to 200 francs

Walter Sickert
St Mark's, Venice
*c.*1895–96
(cat. 3, detail)

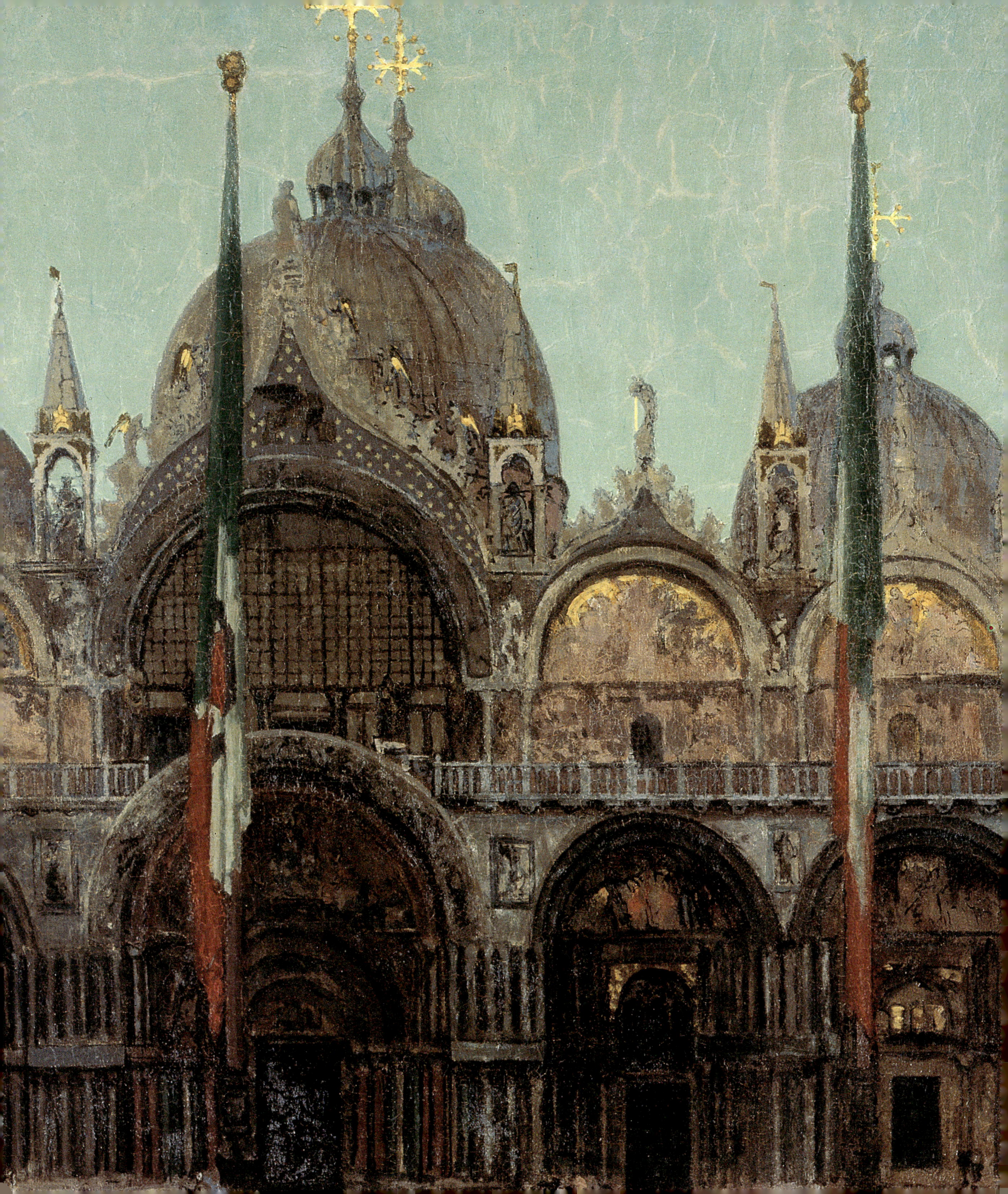

a canvas if I can.'[132] Unfortunately for Sickert his prices did not rise for quite some time.

Innovation and Experiment

Sickert followed a strict practice when drawing and presumably also painting directly from the figure. Artists, he believed, should place themselves at such a distance from their subject that the size of the figure as it was seen and the size on the paper would be the same. He wrote:

> Your drawing must be reduced in proportion until it and your sitter look the same size... The scale of your drawing, then, must vary with two factors – with your distance from the model, and with your distance from your paper or canvas ... If the rule is observed, the operation of drawing becomes a direct comparison. If it is defied, it becomes a proportion sum. Consider what an added wear on brain and eye must be the change of scale, every time the draughtsman looks up at the model, and down at his work!... One of the surest instincts of genius is to avoid useless difficulties.[133]

This gives some indication of Sickert's proximity to his models Giuseppina and Carolina. For the canvases painted 'alla prima' before the subject in which they are close up, he must have sited himself just a short way from his model. Sickert saw drawing and painting as quite independent activities, and that it was a 'fatal confusion' to see one simply as a link to the other: 'Drawing and painting are two separate things,' he wrote, 'and should be studied separately, each for its own sake; and, again, each in relation to each other. Lord Leighton failed as painter, because he painted only like a draughtsman.'[134]

Sickert was notoriously adamant in his views, but frequently changed them, often contradicting his previously held conviction with equal vigour. Painting directly from nature was a particularly thorny topic. Sickert was clear that a painter should work only from drawings made of his subject, rather than painting directly before it. For him this was a conviction which held certain personal dimensions. His first master Whistler followed a highly personal practice when painting of working from a carefully memorised set of details. Turning his back on a subject, Whistler would call out his observations of the scene and ask his assistant Sickert to verify them, a sequence repeated until perfected. Once sufficiently committed to memory it would then be painted in the studio. This was a kind of intense inventiveness, a mental abstraction from the raw material of life viewed through the lens of the mind's imagination. But Degas, to whom Sickert transferred his respect, followed a pragmatic and workmanlike practice of making drawings and studies on which he then based his oils. It was a process, Sickert liked to point out, that rewarded industry. Sickert allowed his acidity towards Whistler to spill over into print in small ways calculated to needle his former friend and master. 'Whistler's genius has been purely personal,' he wrote in April 1897,

> he has had no following, and left no pupils. His sublimated realism is inimitable, and, like a fine organ, of no use to anyone but the possessor. And so with Manet. Degas, on the other hand, has always practiced the synthetic method, a path on which, at whatever distance, it is possible for a student to follow, by the exercise of mere intelligence.[135]

Suggesting Whistler had no lasting inheritance in imitators was designed to be wounding, and chiefly asserted Sickert's own independence. He compounded the slight by highlighting the transfer of his allegiance to Degas, whose technical principles were held to be more practical.

But evidently Venice inspired Sickert to experiment. This was behind his decision to break his own rules and paint *en plein air* or directly from his models. A number of small oil on panel *pochades* survive from his first Venetian painting trip that indicate he took up established impressionist practice and worked directly before the subject. The flickering brushwork and modest size of *Piazza San Marco* (cat. 7) indicates Sickert made it while sitting in St Mark's Square, capturing passing figures against the backdrop of the Basilica. Similarly, his oil study of the Jewish ghetto (cat. 12), in which the wooden ground of the panel is cleverly allowed to show through and define the space, was evidently also painted out of doors. Such works would be used as reference material for fully developed paintings, in the same manner as drawings. But later Sickert was quick to draw a veil over his working from nature in Venice. Lecturing to a group of students at the Euston Road School of Painting and Drawing in 1938, he advised them emphatically, 'Never work from nature':

> 'Have you never worked from nature?' asked [Victor] Pasmore. 'Not since I was grown up', said Sickert. Which, as Clive [Bell] pointed out, was not true and that he certainly painted from nature in his Venetian period. 'Oh Venice,' said Sickert 'What do you know of Venice?' and then went on at great length to describe an old print of the Piazza dei Frati with beggars and a corpse on a shutter etc. etc. and added 'that was a subject if you like'.[136]

The realist *plein air* painter William Logsdail encountered Sickert painting in the open air when he arrived at the Ponte della Paglia to set up his own easel. His technique rather bemused Logsdail, who watched Sickert with glee as he started

> to caper like a master of fence, backing and lunging with sudden stabs at the canvas… the American [painter William Gedney] Bunce… caught sight of a button on the pavement which he pickt up and offered to Sickert and looking at his trousers said 'Excuse me Sir, but I think this has worked loose'.[137]

This description of Sickert has a certain resemblance to accounts of Whistler's vigour of movement while painting. Logsdail recalled this incident as being while he was at work on a picture he exhibited at the Royal Academy in 1893, but it is presumably an error of memory as this was before Sickert had visited the city.

Photography

It seems extremely likely that in Venice Sickert experimented with the use of photography in making certain of his architectural paintings. This is surprising, because in the 1890s he was an outspoken challenger of those who used photographs, and photography is only commonly associated as a feature of Sickert's late work.

As a vociferous opponent of the use of photographs, Sickert wrote a letter of complaint to the *National Observer* in 1891 that Mortimer Menpes's exhibited views of India were copied from photographs, and that in not pointing it out critics failed in their duty to 'those whose drawing is the result of special gifts of brain and eye and hand, arduously and painfully cultivated.' Ultimately, 'an artist who spends the best years of his life in colouring or copying tracings of instantaneous photographs does not progress'.[138] This was a theme Sickert developed in *The Studio* in answer to the question asked of a selection of artists, 'Is the camera the friend or foe of art?' Sickert wrote: 'In proportion as a painter or a draughtsman works from photographs, so he is sapping his powers of observation and expression. It is much as if a swimmer practiced in a cork jacket, or a pianist by turning a barrel-organ.' In the words of John Gilbert, he said, 'an artist must do it all by himself'.[139]

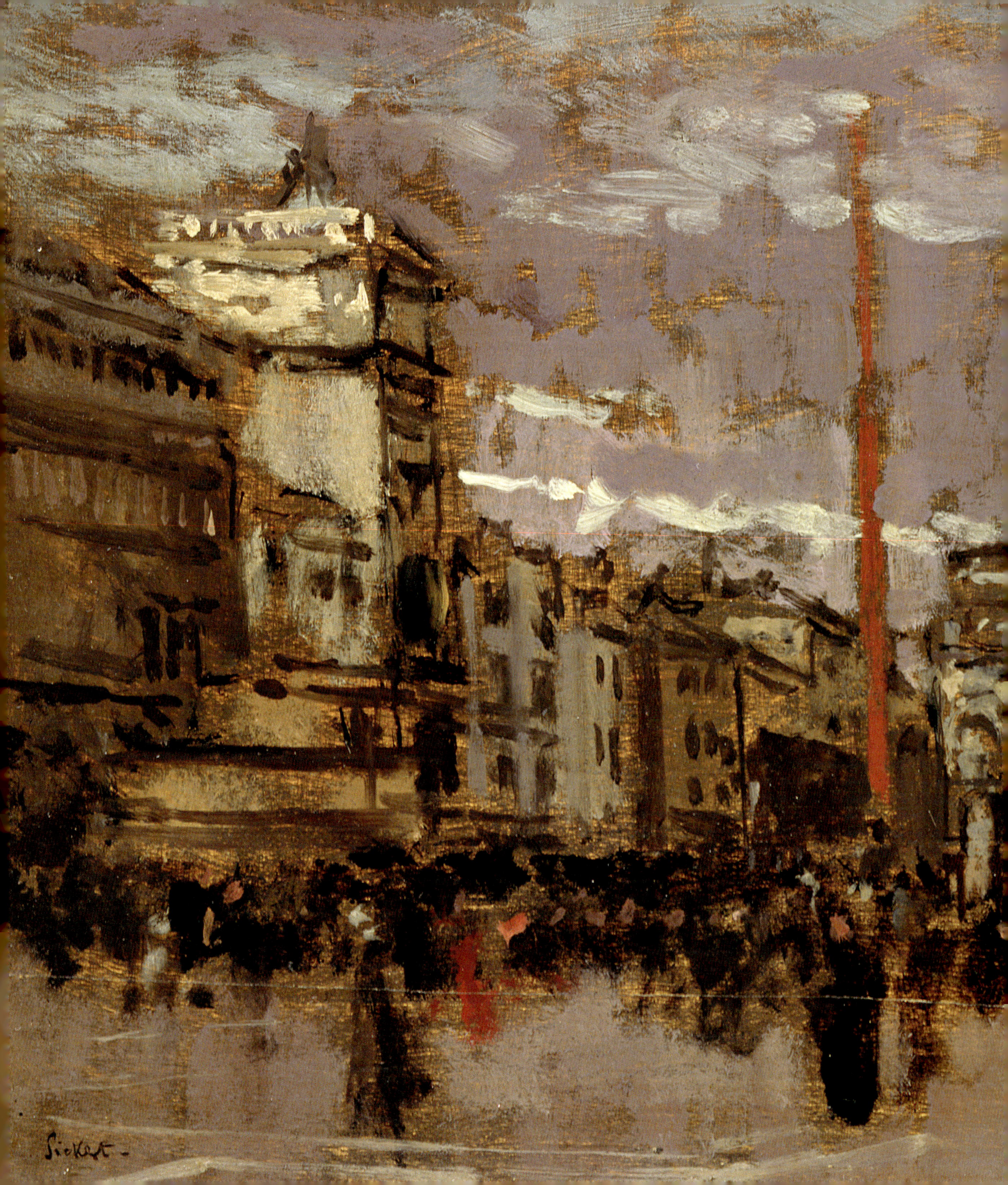
Sickert

However, in the last phase of his career Sickert joyfully utilised photographs, often taken from newspapers, which he squared up and translated into paintings. They captured fleeting moments and effects that were impossible to rehearse in the studio with a live model, and they animated his art into a wholly new idiom. By 1929 Sickert was openly championing the usefulness of the camera for the artist, writing to *The Times*:

> A couplet in one of the most treasured music-hall songs of the last century runs:
>
> Some do it *h*openly,
> Some on the sly… &c.
>
> A photograph is the most precious document obtainable by a sculptor, a painter, or a draughtsman. Canaletto based his work on tracings made with the camera lucida. Turner's studio was crammed with negatives… Millet found photographs of use. Degas took photographs. Lenbach photographed his sitters. To forbid the artist the use of available documents, of which the photograph is the most valuable, is to deny to a historian the study of contemporary shorthand reports. The facts remain at the disposition of the artist.[140]

However, there is a strong hint in a letter to Gwen Ffrancon-Davies that he may have resorted to photography far earlier than is usually assumed. Sickert wrote: 'The *Gatti's Hungerford* of 1887 is so admired that I shall do, I hope, many play and opera scenes. Photography has progressed enormously since then.'[141] Sickert's first, freely admitted use of photographs was for the commission of a portrait of the politician Charles Bradlaugh in 1891.[142] Bradlaugh was already dead and, while Sickert borrowed a suit of his clothes, of necessity he also used a photograph. Sickert was careful to announce the fact in print before the picture's exhibition, and also in the catalogue to the New English Art Club, crediting the photographer Van Der Weyde in both.[143] Other portraits of the 1890s were also made using photographs. To the wife of his patron Sir William Eden he wrote in early 1898: 'Keep in… mind the possibility of making an appointment here for me to get my photographer to photograph you in the light I want.'[144] It is significant that Sickert wished to control the lighting and effects, to use a professional photographer and direct the creation of the photograph. It signified a highly sophisticated approach to photography that essentially replicated his creative control in the studio environment.

The issue was a serious one, as the Royal Academy, along with almost all the other exhibiting societies, prohibited the showing of works that had been created using photographs.[145] Sickert detailed his technique, essentially making an abstraction from the photograph rather than simply copying it. 'I have myself had occasion to paint portraits from photographs,' Sickert admitted in *The Speaker*,

> and the method pursued is this. The photograph is carefully traced on to the panel, and then pinned up beside the easel, and painted from, with the same freedom which an artist would use in painting from a drawing… The question is what can be got by these methods in the ablest hands. Saving of time; the possibility of painting portraits of people who are dead, or who cannot give sittings; and nearly as much accuracy of form as the given photograph may contain. But colour, in the real sense of the word, there is none.[146]

The evidence for Sickert's use of photographs for some of his Venetian pictures is suggestive rather than definitive. But in a letter from around 1899 concerning clearing out his studio in Robert Street in London, Sickert wrote to Florence Humphrey men-

Walter Sickert
Piazza San Marco
*c.*1900–01
(cat. 7, detail)

tioning a parcel of 'small scale drawings, of panels of Venice, that is to say St Mark's façade and the Rialto, pen drawings and photographs of sitters and photographs of Venice'.[147] His possession of Venetian photographs suggests the possibility that he utilised them in the manufacture of paintings. And photographs of Venice were readily available: 'Everyone,' wrote Henry James, 'has brought back a collection of photographs,' and there were numerous sellers throughout the city.[148] By the 1890s the Venetian bookseller Ferdinando Ongania was publishing books of photographs of both the main sights and lesser-known districts and studies of the inhabitants which sold briskly to foreign tourists (fig. 23). His collection *Calle e Canali in Venice and in the Islands and Lagoons* was published in an English edition in 1899.

There are tantalising clues in certain of Sickert's pictures, which hint at the use of photography. The figures in front of Sickert's *St Mark's, Venice (Pax Tibi Marce Evangelista Meus)* (cat. 4) are blurred, for instance, contrasting with the crispness of the architectural details, and suggesting exactly that quality found in contemporary photographs.[149] In 1903, Sickert wrote to Blanche – it is ambiguous whether he was being ironic or literal – 'I would not say I have not taken a single photograph'.[150] Interestingly, when Blanche quoted the letter in his memoirs, he changed the opening from 'I would not' to 'I need not', subtly altering its meaning.[151]

The description of making tracings from photographs that Sickert published in 1897 could well be connected in some way with his use of draughtsman's copy paper. In *The Piazzetta and Old Campanile, Venice* (cat. 1) he has transferred a carbon paper tracing onto the new sheet and then heightened it with coloured pastel. The work has a grainy quality, particularly in the sky and lagoon area, which is characteristic of a transfer technique. While it covers almost the full extent of the paper sheet, the edges of the carbon paper, used to transfer the composition, are just visible along the edges and form a black rectangle. Sickert applied peach, blue, green, red and purple pastel after the carbon tracing to colour and emphasise certain elements of the image, and sections of the architecture, sky and lagoon have been embellished with various coloured pastels. Cross-hatching was next applied on top of the pastel in a black graphic medium, either using the carbon paper or working directly onto the paper in pencil, to give depth to the sky and certain architectural features. Although this work has a sketch-like quality, the image lines are not loose but highly controlled, and the architectural features are carefully proportioned, reflecting Sickert's carefully planned process.[152]

No original drawing is known of this composition, begging the question of how Sickert obtained the design. If it was based on first-hand sketches, then these would have had to be made from the vantage point of a boat. However, this is such a classic Venetian view, it must be possible that Sickert simply drew it from postcards or from pictures in guide-

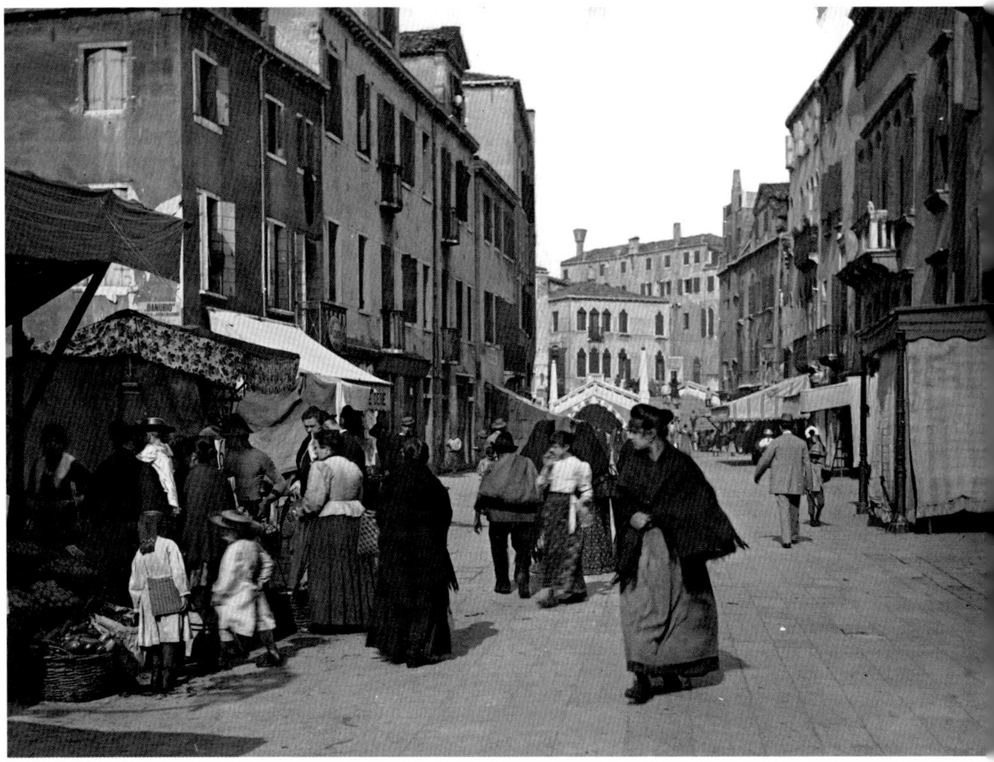

Fig. 23
Tomaso Filippi
Street Scene (Venezia – Rio Terra la Maddalena)
*c.*1894–1903
Photograph

Photographs of Venice and her inhabitants sold well to visiting tourists.

books. If this were so then the relatively large size of *The Piazzetta and the Old Campanile, Venice* raises the possibility that the original carbon copy drawing from which it was transferred was scaled up using a pantograph, a drawing instrument that can also be used to trace from photographs. In his 1897 description of how to transfer a design from a photograph it is important – and perhaps revealing – that Sickert drew comparison with how 'Canaletto based his work on tracings made with the camera lucida'.[153] Evidently he had been considering and investigating the working methods of the Venetian master. In the same article he asserts that one of photography's advantages for the artist was 'as much accuracy of form as the given photograph may contain'. This would have been invaluable when drawing detailed architectural forms and relationships. Sickert's interest in drawing instruments is further confirmed by his possession of his own camera lucida.[154] Purchased from a shop in Jermyn Street, London, it is made from silver and has a set of a dozen lenses to change the scale of the projected image. Enid Bagnold borrowed it sometime around 1913, and never returned it to Sickert.[155] It is not possible to know how long Sickert had owned it.

Whether in using carbon paper Sickert was investigating some form of producing multiples is unknown, but it remains an intriguing possibility. Being able to manufacture several drawings simultaneously would save considerable time, and hand finishing would make certain their status as original works. It was a way of working that artists had used in the past, albeit not with the new modern material of carbon paper. In the eighteenth century, for instance, Thomas Rowlandson (1756–1827) had combined printing with a form of graphite medium to imitate original drawing, and then hand coloured the results. Also related, and undoubtedly known to Sickert, was Degas's practice of making multiple traced images, applying pastel over the top and nuancing each image, so that each was wholly individual.[156]

Sickert produced a number of oil versions of the Piazzetta composition.[157] Each is finished in a slightly different way, and one titled *Le Palais des Doges au Crépuscule* is a nocturne. But in each the architectural drawing is essentially the same and, crucially, it is the same size. Such close correlations indicate some association between the carbon drawing and these oils. It must be a possibility that Sickert used carbon paper in some way to transfer his design onto the canvas itself, and do away with the necessity of squaring up. When writing in 1897 of any advantages of photography to the artist, the first Sickert suggested was 'saving of time'.[158] This was a fundamental aspect of Sickert's life in Venice. Producing as many oils as possible for Durand-Ruel and Bernheim, any speeding of the drawing process he could achieve would offer a tempting advantage. Painting before the subject was a verified part of Sickert's practice in Venice. But occasional judicious use of copy paper for certain subjects would explain the immense speed with which he was able to complete works. If the drawing was transferred, it would save a great deal of time. Similarly, it would also explain why some works are noticeably more calligraphic and others, presumably painted before the subject, more painterly.

There is a tantalising possible further link to a specialist form of photography. Stereoscopic photographs of Venice were commonplace (fig. 24), and enjoyed great currency throughout late-Victorian parlours. When viewed through a stereoscope, these double photographic images took on a pronounced three-dimensional quality, forming an interesting way in which to experience the architecture of the city. Stereoscopic photographers would deliberately choose scenes that 'layered' elements of the photographic composition, aligning them so they overlapped each other between foreground, middle ground and distance. In Venice a common and natural approach was to introduce gondolas into the foreground or ships' masts rising before the Ducal Palace. Indeed, the Piazzetta was a particularly pop-

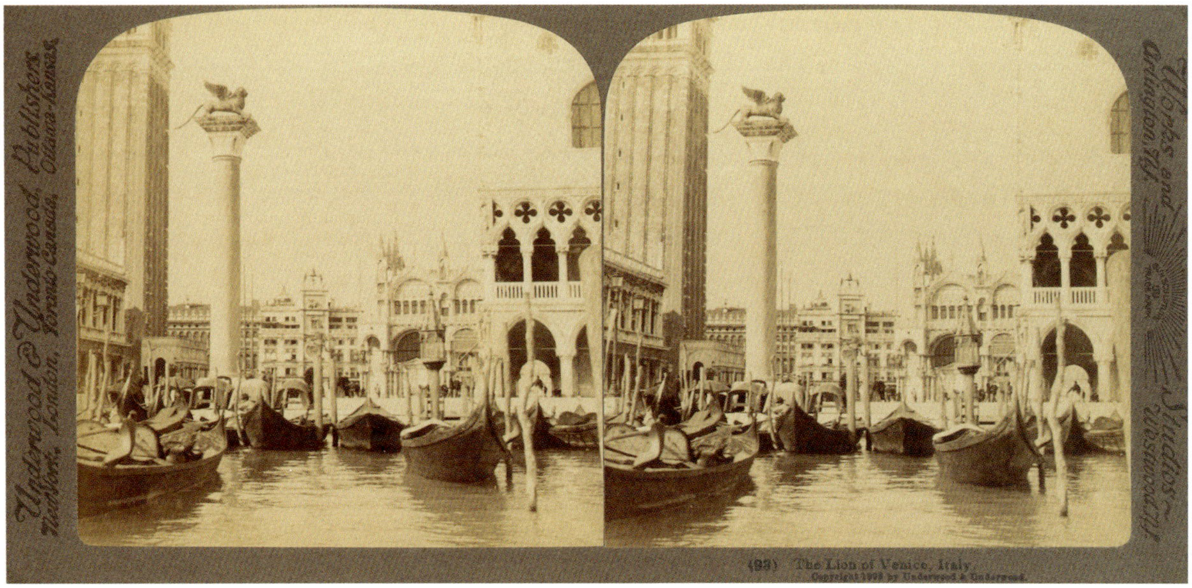

Fig. 24
The Lion of Venice – Stereoscopic
Stereoscopic photograph
Courtesy of Adelson Galleries, New York

ular stereoscopic view, not just because it was the most famous, but because the Campanile and columns bearing the Venetian Lion and St Theodore, and the corner of the Ducal Palace and projecting Basilica, all provided natural visual 'interruptions' that would heighten the three-dimensional effects. A further characteristic of stereoscope photographs was that they were usually square, so that when looking through the stereoscope the eye could take in the whole picture. There was also a deliberate tendency to crop certain architectural or city images to emphasise their three-dimensional layers.

When we look at *The Lion of St Mark's* (fig. 8) we are struck by how inventive a composition it is, unlike anything in Sickert's art before his first visit to Venice. But its similarity to stereoscopic images is quite arresting. It has a square format, and the column is carefully positioned so that it occupies the middle distance, interrupting and energising our view of the Ducal Palace. The cut-off, compacted foreground emphasises the three-dimensionality of the column's position, just as in a stereoscopic image. Exposure to the stereoscope might perhaps have been one inspiration for Sickert to think of architectural composition in new ways. Cropping and 'layering' are found in a number of his Venetian views, but their function in the composition of paintings was closely allied to their function in stereoscopic photography. Both painters and photographers dealt in the fundamental business of composition. Cropping was one of Sickert's favourite practices in these pictures, and there were strong artistic prototypes with which he was familiar. Monet's series paintings of Rouen Cathedral showed only a portion of the building. But more importantly, Degas had taught Sickert how cropping figure compositions would invigorate them, and make them visually more interesting and unusual. Sickert's extension of this to architectural views was a natural progression. In *Venice: La Salute* (cat. 16), for instance, Sickert shows only a close-up of part of Santa Maria della Salute. It enabled him to give a sense not simply of the detail of the architecture, but its bulk and mass, and there is also an impression of approaching or retreating from the church steps. He also adopted this principle in *The Horses of St Mark's* (cat. 6). These ancient gilded bronze horses were one of the most famous sights in Venice, and in prior times had been believed to have once adorned the triumphal arch of Nero. But Sickert gives them new energy and visual tension by presenting them as part of a tightly cropped composition, viewed from a steeply oblique angle. In all these and other such works Sickert is likely to have taken a fuller drawing of the whole building and transferred only a portion of it onto canvas. This is clear when comparing two canvases he made in *c.*1895–96 of *The Rialto Bridge and Palazzo dei Camerlenghi* (cats. 21–22). In one Sickert records the full panoramic arc of the Grand Canal round the Palace towards the Rialto Bridge. But in the other he has reduced the composition to focus on just the Palace, and changed the lighting effects. Manifestly it has been based on the same drawing, but Sickert has distilled an abbreviated picture from the same source. And Sickert would also come back to such source material at a later date. In *The Rialto Bridge* (cat. 20), painted around 1901, Sickert has concentrated on a different part of the same scene, this time treating only the bridge. Such practices demonstrated the skilful economy with which he would treat studies and source material, an archive on which to base multiple compositions.

The Venetian Old Masters

With his studio just around the corner from the Accademia and everywhere evidence of the artistic achievements of previous generations, Sickert must have been highly conscious in Venice of both previous depictions of the city and the triumphs of the Venetian Renaissance painters. Before he ever visited Venice, Sickert had studied Canaletto in the National Gallery in London.[159] Here he was able to see a significant number of Venetian views, including major works such as *A Regatta on the Grand Canal*, *The Stonemason's Yard*, *The Feast Day of St Roch*, *The Doge's Palace*, *The Grand Canal with S. Simeone Piccolo* and *The Entrance to the Cannaregio*. His appreciation of Canaletto's painterly qualities was registered as early as 1890, in an article he contributed to *The Whirlwind* in which he took astounded exception to a claim by Ruskin that Canaletto 'is a little and poor painter'.[160] The other principal view painter, Guardi, was not a feature of the National Gallery's collection until the major Salting bequest in 1910, but Sickert would have seen here *Venice: Piazza San Marco*, a large painting acquired in 1846 that showed the view straight down St Mark's Square, finishing with a frontal rendering of the Basilica.

By the 1890s the National Gallery had built, through purchase, gift and bequest, a wide-ranging and stunning collection of Venetian Old Master paintings, and it was possible to study these artists in some considerable depth. There were half a dozen Titians, including *Bacchus and Ariadne*, *The Holy Family* and *The Tribute Money*. Sickert appears to have been particularly interested by Veronese, and he is known to have had photographs of pictures by Veronese pinned up on his studio wall in Dieppe, incongruously alongside some of Pompeii.[161] In 1929 Sickert wrote to his friend Mrs Hulton about the Leicester Gallery's retrospective of his work, 'so much of it done in the Calle dei Frati within sight of Veronese's grave (none the better for that)'.[162] In London the National Gallery had an unrivalled representation of Veronese's art, including the *Allegory of Love* series which was acquired in 1890–91 and joined a further six major paintings already in the collection. Sickert evidently examined them all closely, and wrote about his observations in 1890:

> When Veronese expresses, in terms of an inspired convention, the breadth of illumination on a brocaded gown, a nearer examination of his canvas does not reveal the texture of the stuff nor the single strands of gold. It is something quite else that we perceive and delight in, in proportion to our capacity for appreciation. It is the strange and incredible decorative beauty of the touches of paint, which is inseparable from, and is, indeed, the mark and seal of mastery, of means well fitted to end. Painters call it quality.[163]

The Old Masters were utilised by Sickert to argue against what he considered the pernicious modern practice of painting without lines – 'No one ever saw a painting by Tintoretto, or Titian, without a thick outline' – again demonstrating a careful study of their techniques and methods.[164] In Venice, Sickert decided that modern painting was however the match of any of the Old Masters, and simply different in its mode of expression. This, however, was a view he would confide only to his closest allies. He wrote to Philip Wilson Steer in 1895:

> Of course one gets as familiar with Tintoretto and Titian and Veronese as one was with Reginald Cleaver and F. C. Gould.[165] The more one sees them (the former I mean) the more preposterous is the pessimistic contention that we who live now should not paint. We aim at and achieve totally different results, results that they neither dreamt of nor could compass. A fine Whistler or Degas or Monet could hang with any of them. It would be intrinsically every bit as good, and for us have the added sparkle and charm of novelty. Don't tell MacColl or anyone about these sentiments. He would deduce therefrom that I considered the sisters Lloyd superior to the presentation of the Virgin![166] You, thank God, are too damned clever to understand anything.[167]

In *La Nera* (cat. 48) Sickert seated Carolina del'Acqua in front of a large Old Master painting. It effectively combines old and new, the art of the past with that of the present, inviting comparison and connection. Sickert wrote to the first owner Hugh Hammersley that he had effectively bought two pictures for the price of one – 'a Jacopo Bassano thrown in!' Bassano was highly visible in Venice, a trademark being pictures of the Holy Family in a pastoral setting, portraying his models in a naturalistic rather than elevated manner. There is the possibility Sickert's title *La Nera* may have been wrongly applied,[168] yet it is curiously fitting for both the sitter and the painting that is in the background. The glittering darkness of Bassano, his rich colouring and low tone might be compared with Sickert's own, and the tangible pleasure in paint is shared between the two.

Other Renaissance artists also engaged Sickert's imagination. Sickert may have seen in Verrocchio's epic depiction of Bartolomeo Colleoni, the conquering general, an echo of his own ambition. Made in 1897, probably as a design for publication, one of Sickert's few self-portraits from this time is a pen-and-ink drawing showing him in profile against the backdrop of the Colleoni Monument.[169] His bowler hat is raffishly tilted, and Verocchio's masterpiece looms above him as if emerging out of his head. It is more than a simple record of his presence in Venice, or linking his name with the city and its sights. It is an assertion of artistic stature, inviting comparison between the eminence of one of the greatest Renaissance sculptors and the modern artist. And Sickert was evidently enduringly fond of the Colleoni statue. Painted around 1927, his 'in character' self-portrait *Lazarus Breaks his Fast* showed the ageing painter frailly spooning up food after an illness of several months.[170] It was based on a photograph[171] taken by Thérèse Lessore in which, on the wall behind Sickert, can be seen a framed print of the Colleoni Monument and Scuola Grande di San Marco. As in the drawing of thirty years before, Sickert is again in profile, again with Colleoni behind him. It is almost certainly simple coincidence, but the photograph invites comparisons between the Sickert of these different stages of his life, and between his decrepitude and the martial arrogance of the Venetian general. 'It is odd,' Sickert observed to Mrs Hulton in 1928, 'our dining room is filled with engravings (17th cent) of Venice.'[172] Evidently Sickert also considered making a painting in oils of the Colleoni Monument and Scuola, as another squared pen and ink drawing testifies (cat. 11). Made around 1900, Sickert considered the drawing again after 1924, when as with many others, he signed it a second time, now with the proud initials 'ARA' to signify becoming an Associate member of the Royal Academy.

Sickert's ruminations on the Venetian Old Masters appear to have lasted throughout his long career, but his interest appears to have renewed itself in the last years of his life. Around 1932–33 he painted a copy of *The Rape of Lucretia* by Jacopo Palma (fig. 25). When it was exhibited at the Beaux Arts Gallery in London in 1934 Sickert explained in the catalogue that it was 'based on an old engraving after a picture ascribed to Palma'; the print was by Picart of a painting then in his own collection. The disturbing subject of Lucretia's rape by Tarquin was treated several times by Jacopo, and his most famous version is now in the Hermitage. Sickert's treatment synthesised Jacopo's design with his own thoroughly modern style, in which he painted with dry colours and added exaggerated highlights. It was part of a long sequence of pictures Sickert dubbed 'Echoes' in which he took compositions from old, frequently Victorian illustrations, and recreated them in a more contemporary idiom, which breathed fresh vigour and interest into historical material.

Departure

In June 1904 Sickert's solo exhibition at Bernheim-Jeune opened in Paris. It was a major survey of Sickert's achievement in which he exhibited nearly a hundred pictures, and the critical reception was full of praise. In August he travelled to Dieppe. He had every expectation of returning to Venice, but instead

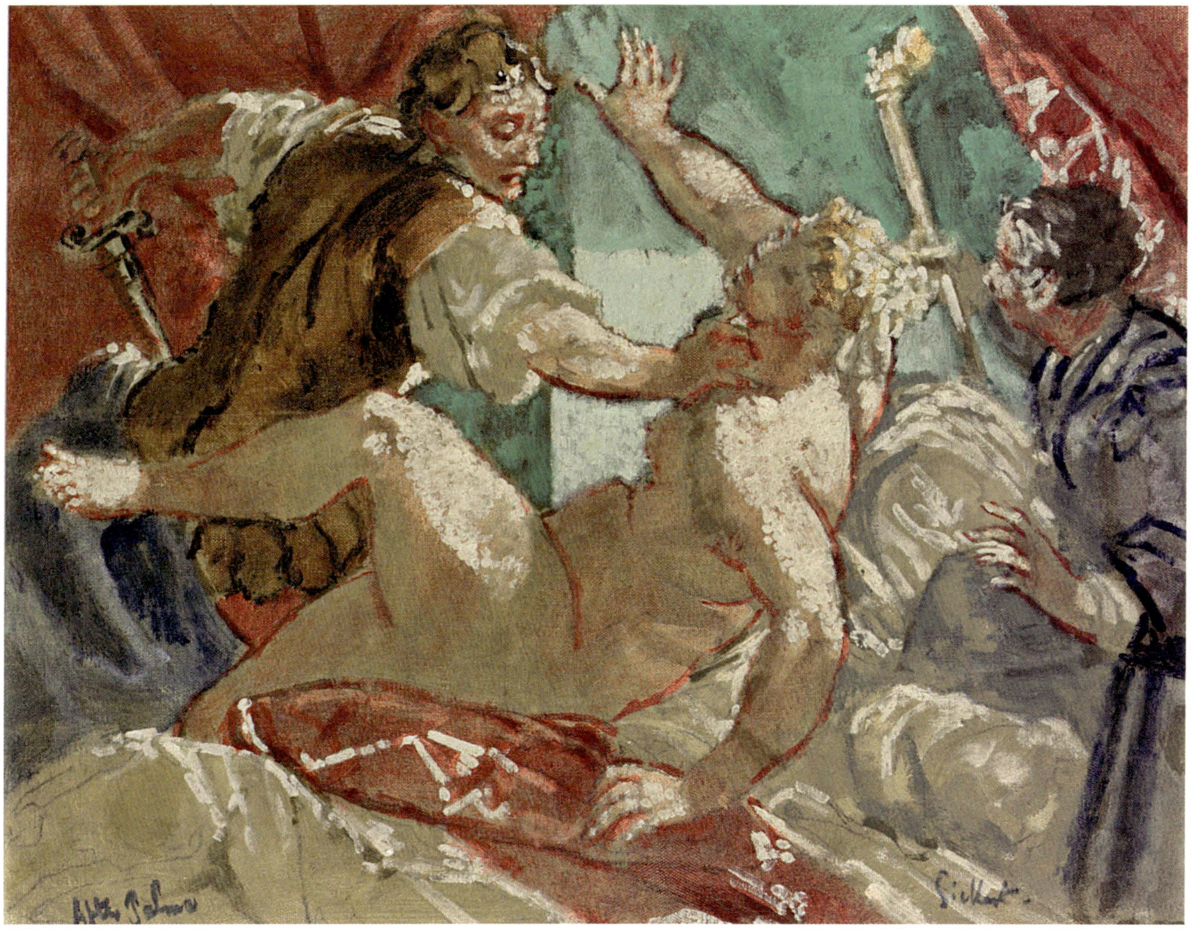

Fig. 25
Walter Sickert
Rape of Lucretia (after Palma)
*c.*1932–33
Oil on canvas, 50.8 x 61 cm
Sotheby's

he lingered in France working on new pictures and developing his experiments with painting the nude. At Dieppe he was visited by Albert Rutherston, who introduced him to a young painter accompanying him, Spencer Gore. At 26, Gore was eighteen years younger than Sickert, but the pair appear to have struck up an immediate rapport. Gore's account of the London art world and the evidence of his own personal and artistic capability seem to have played a significant part in persuading Sickert to end his exile in Europe and return again to live in London. In 1905 Sickert took up lodgings at 6 Mornington Crescent in London's Camden Town. Here he continued his experiments with the figure, using local models taken from the streets. Gore lived a short distance away. Together, Sickert and Gore grouped around them some of the most talented younger painters in London, with the older artist able to pass on his accumulated knowledge of modern French painting. These gatherings in Fitzroy Street formed the nucleus of an avant garde, and began the hesitant beginnings of modern art in Britain that would eventually flourish under the banner of the Camden Town Group. London street scenes and studies of figures in interiors were the hallmark of these painters, and Sickert saw his Venice experiments reach full maturity in London, the city that would now come to define him.

Sickert did not to return to Venice until the winter of 1929–30, a gap of 25 years. In the summer of 1930 he was given the honour of a special display of his works at the Venice Biennale. This time they were shown in the British Pavilion. Sickert was 70 and in the flush of a last, late re-flowering of his career. He appeared in the newspapers regularly, and there was revived critical and popular appreciation of his painting. In 1934 he was elected a full Royal Academician, an accolade of which he was intensely proud. Considering which work to offer to the Academy as his Diploma piece, one which would stand to represent him to posterity, Sickert did not select a picture of the music hall, or Camden Town, or one of his recent adventurous paintings based on newspaper photographs. Instead he chose a sparkling canvas from around 1901 of Santa Maria della Salute.[173] It was doubtless a recognition of what the city had meant to him, and to the role it had played in the forming of his art.

This event seems to have sparked Sickert's interest in reviving his painterly engagement with Venice and a consideration of all his feelings about it. In 1934 he began work on a portrait of the actress Peggy Ashcroft (fig. 26), whom he adored. Sickert was 74 and she was 28, but the two enjoyed a mutually nourishing friendship, and they were probably lovers too. The picture was based on a photograph of Peggy on holiday in Venice, standing on the new wooden bridge over the Grand Canal with Santa Maria della Salute beyond. The photograph appeared in the *Radio Times*, and Sickert took the monochrome illustration and turned it into an extraordinarily livid, anti-realistic colour harmony of pulsating greens and pinks. It was a strikingly modern methodology that completely transformed the subject. His ability to produce innovative, startling work still held, and Sickert's picture was lauded by the *News Chronicle* under the headline 'An Old Man's Brilliance'.[174] As well as being new and innovative, the picture also looked backwards, linking past and present. The device of a portrait in which the subject occupied the foreground, hard up against the edge of the picture space, and was silhouetted against a Venetian backdrop was not new. It was the identical approach Sickert had used for his portrait of Israel Zangwill (cat. 30) in 1896–98, some 38 years earlier, and which he repeated again in 1905 for a picture of Mrs Swinton.[175]

Other Venetian pictures now followed, and in the mid-1930s he made a pair of paintings of *Il Cannaregio*.[176] With billowing clouds and industrious figures, they appear Old Masterly in their conception but dis-

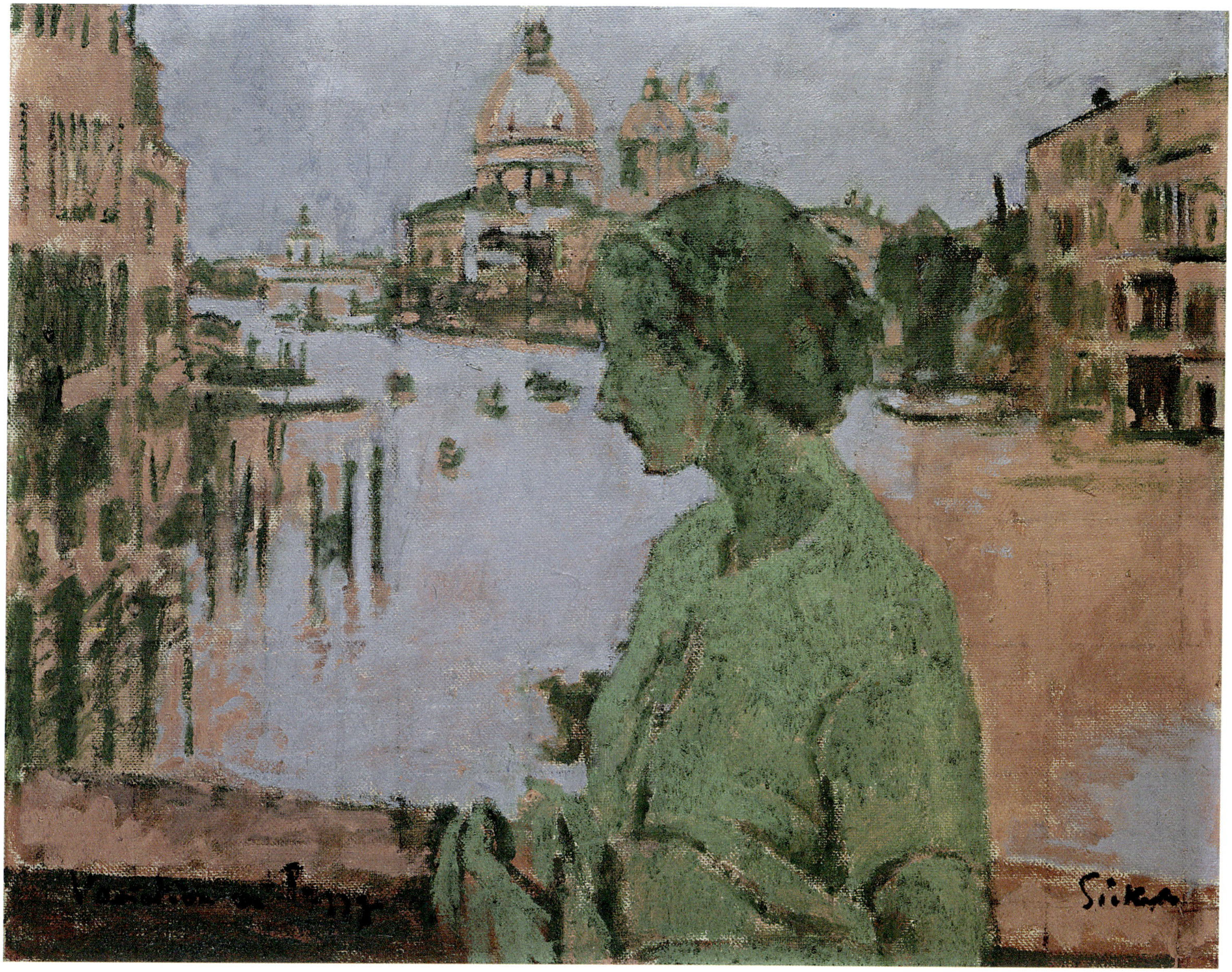

Fig. 26
Walter Sickert
Variation on Peggy
1934–35
Oil on canvas, 73.5 x 66 cm
Tate, London. Bequeathed by Dame Peggy Ashcroft 1992

tinctively contemporary in execution. This motif of busy figures was repeated more intensively in *Outside the Frari, Venice*.[177] Seemingly painted at the very end of the 1930s, this was Sickert's last Venetian canvas. With its visible squaring, smudgy touches of dry paint and strong, flickering lighting, it was wholly characteristic of Sickert's late style. But it is transformed by the extensive cast of lively street characters, and even a pair of scampering dogs, suggesting it was most likely partly copied from an antique print, perhaps one of the many engravings of Venice that once decorated Sickert's dining room.

His creative facilities were waning, but as Sickert's final painted consideration of the city to which he had formed such a strong emotional attachment it was a fitting last tribute. Nearing the end of his long artistic journey, Sickert painted a homage to the people whose lives were acted out against the backdrop of what he had called 'the loveliest city in the world'. Whatever Venice's architectural beauties, it was her people who held Sickert's imagination and affection, for with La Giuseppina and Carolina del'Acqua he had discovered an approach to his art that framed the rest of his career.

NOTES

1. Walter Sickert to Nan Hudson, 1907; Tate Archive TGA 9125.
2. Walter Sickert, 'The New Life of Whistler', *Fortnightly Review*, December 1908; Anna Gruetzner Robins (ed.), *Walter Sickert: The Complete Writings on Art* (Oxford: 2000), p.182.
3. *ibid.*
4. Walter Sickert to Rudolf Dircks, September 1894; see Matthew Sturgis, *Walter Sickert: A Life* (London: 2005), p.693 n.13, 15.
5. Karl Baedeker, *Northern Italy* (London: 1906), p.281.
6. D. S. MacColl, *The Spectator*, 2 March 1895, p.295.
7. Baron no. 94.
8. Baron no. 48.
9. Roger Fry to Helen Coombe, 20 January 1895; quoted in Frances Spalding, *Roger Fry: Art and Life* (London: 1980), p.46.
10. Walter Sickert to Brandon Thomas, 1898; Sturgis, *Walter Sickert: A Life*, p.226.
11. William Rothenstein, *Men and Memories* (London: 1931), I, p.169.
12. Sturgis, *Walter Sickert: A Life*, p.227.
13. *ibid.*, p.228.
14. *ibid.*, p.694 n.1.
15. Walter Sickert to Philip Wilson Steer, autumn 1895; quoted in Robert Emmons, *The Life and Opinions of Walter Richard Sickert* (London: 1941), p.107.
16. *ibid.*
17. 'Sickert v. Sickert', *The Times*, 19 July 1899, p.4.
18. 'Miles Amber' [Ellen Cobden Sickert], *Wistons* (London: 1902), p.136.
19. Julian Halsby, *Venice: The Artist's Vision* (London: 1990), p.127.
20. Walter Sickert to Constanzia Hulton, 1 January 1904; Hulton Papers, Bodleian Library, University of Oxford.
21. Baron no. 100.1.
22. See Wendy Baron in *Sickert Paintings*, Royal Academy exhibition catalogue (London: 1992) (22).
23. See for instance J. M. W. Turner's *The Interior of San Marco: the Atrium, looking North*, 1840, Tate (TB CCCXVIII-22; D32241), or *The Interior of San Marco, looking into the North Transept*, 1840, Tate (TB CCCXVIII-7; D32226).
24. Sickert's copy is now in the Courtauld Institute Library.
25. Technical analysis by Stephen Hackney, Tate Conservation; Peter Booth, 'The Interior of St Mark's Venice, 1896' in *Completing the Picture: Materials and Techniques of Twenty-Six Paintings in The Tate Gallery* (London: Tate Gallery, 1982), pp.69–72.
26. Walter Sickert to Philip Wilson Steer, autumn 1895; quoted in Emmons, *The Life and Opinions*, p.107.
27. *ibid.*
28. Andrew McLaren Young et al, *The Paintings of James McNeill Whistler* (New Haven and London: 1980), no. 213.
29. E. R. & J. O. Pennell, *The Life of James McNeill Whistler* (London: 1911), p.192.
30. Wendy Baron, *Sickert: Paintings and Drawings* (New Haven and London: 2006), p.33.
31. Walter Sickert, 'French Pictures at Knoedler's Gallery', *Burlington Magazine*, July 1923; Robins (ed.), *Walter Sickert*, p.464. Sickert is referring to Monet's *The Ducal Palace, View from San Giorgio*, 1908 (Wildenstein no. 1754).
32. Frank Richards, 'Letters from Artists to Artists. No. X. Venice as a Sketching-Ground', *The Studio*, Vol. III, 1894, p.171.
33. Technical analysis by Stephen Hackney, Tate Conservation.
34. Malcolm Easton, *Sickert In the North*, University of Hull exhibition catalogue (Hull: 1968), p. vii.
35. Walter Sickert to Durand-Ruel, April 1901; quoted in Sturgis, *Walter Sickert: A Life*, p.289.
36. Baron no. 174.1.
37. Quoted in Sturgis, *Walter Sickert: A Life*, p.233.
38. See forthcoming article by Robert Upstone, 'Between Innovation and Tradition: Waterhouse and Modern French Painting', *John William Waterhouse*, Royal Academy exhibition catalogue (London: 2009).
39. Sturgis, *Walter Sickert: A Life*, p.295.
40. Walter Sickert to Constanzia Hulton, undated; Hulton Papers, Bodleian Library, University of Oxford.
41. Walter Sickert to Jacques-Émile Blanche, undated; Institut de France, Paris.
42. Walter Sickert to Philip Wilson Steer; quoted in Emmons, *The Life and Opinions*, p.89.
43. Sturgis, *Walter Sickert: A Life*, p.318.
44. Walter Sickert to Philip Wilson Steer; quoted in Emmons, *The Life and Opinions*, p.89.
45. Walter Sickert, 'Literature', *The Whirlwind*, 28 June 1890; Robins (ed.), *Walter Sickert*, p.69.
46. Walter Sickert ('St. P.'), 'The New Gallery', *The Speaker*, 1 May 1897; Robins (ed.), *Walter Sickert*, p.165.
47. Walter Sickert ('St. P.'), 'Schools of Art', *The Speaker*, 23 January 1897; Robins (ed.), *Walter Sickert*, p.132.
48. See David Peters Corbett, *Walter Sickert* (London: 2001), pp.21–25.
49. Henry James, 'The Grand Canal', *Scribner's Magazine*, Vol. XII, no. 5, November 1892, p.532.
50. Baron no. 271.
51. Henry James, 'Venice', *The Century Magazine*, Vol. XXV, no. 1, November 1882, p.3.
52. *Art Journal*, 1886, p.97.
53. Letter from Walter Sickert to Nan Hudson and Ethel Sands; Tate Archive TGA 9215, *c.*1907.
54. Walter Sickert, 'Impressionism', preface to *A Collection of Paintings by the London Impressionists*, Goupil Gallery exhibition catalogue (London: December 1889); Robins (ed.), *Walter Sickert*, p.60.
55. Sturgis, *Walter Sickert: A Life*, pp.221, 223.
56. Letter from Walter Sickert to Jacques-Émile Blanche, Institut de France, Paris, 7055XI/175–178; translation quoted in Sturgis, *Walter Sickert: A Life*, p.329.
57. Henry Perl, *Venezia* (London: 1895), p.92.
58. Horatio Brown, *Life on the Lagoons* (London: 1884), p.249.
59. Baedeker, *Northern Italy*, p.xiii; James, 'Venice', p.15.
60. James, 'Venice', p.23.
61. *ibid.*
62. Henry James, 'The Grand Canal', p.532.
63. *ibid.*, pp.534, 538, 539.
64. See *Sickert Drawings*, Art Gallery of Western Australia exhibition catalogue (Perth: 1979), p.12.
65. The watercolour of Mrs Hulton is Baron no. 186.
66. Walter Sickert to Jacques-Émile Blanche; quoted in Baron, *Sickert: Paintings and Drawings*, p.54 n.5.
67. Walter Sickert to Jacques-Émile Blanche; Institut de France, Paris 7055XI/173.
68. Richards, 'Letters from Artists to Artists', pp.175–76.
69. Walter Sickert to Constanzia Hulton, 1 January 1904; Hulton Papers, Bodleian Library, University of Oxford.
70. 'To the sympathetic and genial Signor de Rossi from his friend Sickert'.
71. Alastair Grieve, *Whistler's Venice* (New Haven and London: 2000), p.186.
72. Henry Perl, *Venezia* (London: 1895), p.77.
73. *ibid.*, p.78.
74. Brown, *Life on the Lagoons*, p.234.
75. Grieve, *Whistler's Venice*, pp.185–86.
76. See Peters Corbett, *Walter Sickert*, p.20.
77. Baron no. 217.1.
78. Baron no. 354.
79. Sturgis, *Walter Sickert: A Life*, pp.329–30.
80. Letter from Denys Sutton to Wendy Baron, 21 November 1974, Sutton Papers, University of Glasgow Library; see Sturgis, *Walter Sickert: A Life*, p.330.
81. Letter from Walter Sickert to Sir William Eden, University of Birmingham Library, AP22/23/3; see Sturgis, *Walter Sickert: A Life*, p.330.
82. Letter from Walter Sickert to Jacques-Émile Blanche, copy in Sutton Papers, University of Glasgow Library; see Sturgis, *Walter Sickert: A Life*, p.330.
83. Walter Sickert to Constanzia Hulton, received 2 January 1929; Hulton Papers, Bodleian Library, University of Oxford.
84. Letter from Walter Sickert to Jacques-Émile Blanche, Institut de France, Paris; quoted in Sturgis, *Walter Sickert: A Life*, p.710 n.62.
85. Letter from Walter Sickert to Jacques-Émile Blanche, Institut de France, Paris; quoted in *ibid.* and in *Sickert Paintings*, Royal Academy exhibition catalogue (34).
86. Undated letter from Walter Sickert to Nan Hudson, ?1907; Tate Archive TGA 9215.
87. Baron no. 190.
88. Walter Sickert to Constanzia Hulton, undated [1903]; Hulton Papers, Bodleian Library, University of Oxford.
89. Walter Sickert to Philip Wilson Steer, quoted in Emmons, *The Life and Opinions*, p.89.
90. *The Scotsman*, 14 November 1896. *Empire*, 29 November 1896.
91. See Baron no. 103.
92. *The Daily Telegraph*, 19 November 2008. *Daily Chronicle*, 14 November 1896.
93. Paul Codrington, 'In the Picture

Galleries: The New English Art Club', *The World*, 27 November 1906.
94. 'Art Run Amok: The New English Art Club', *Daily Mail*, 27 November 1906.
95. 'The New English Art Club', *The Saturday Review*, 1 December 1906.
96. *ibid.*
97. 'New English Art Club', *The Tribune*, 22 November 1906.
98. 'Round About', *Evening Standard*, 21 November 1906.
99. *Manchester Guardian*, 20 November 1906.
100. Walter Sickert to Jacques-Émile Blanche, undated; Institut de France, Paris, 7055XI/171.
101. Price converted using 'Money-Table', Baedeker, *Northern Italy*, opposite title page.
102. William Logsdail, manuscript memoirs; private collection *c.*1925–27.
103. Baedeker, *Northern Italy*, p.xi.
104. Walter Sickert to Sir William Eden, 15 November 1901, University of Birmingham Library; Sturgis, *Walter Sickert: A Life*, p.295.
105. Walter Sickert to Edward Heron-Allen, 9 October 1901, Getty Research Institute, Los Angeles; Sturgis, *Walter Sickert: A Life*, pp.295–96.
106. Walter Sickert ('St. P.'), 'Small Pictures', *The Speaker*, 2 January 1897; Robins (ed.), *Walter Sickert*, pp.124–25.
107. Walter Sickert ('St. P.'), 'Small Pictures'; *ibid.*, p.125.
108. *ibid.*, p.125
109. *ibid.*
110. *ibid.*
111. *The Pork Pie Hat. Hilda Spong in 'Trelawny of the Wells'*, 1898, Johannesburg Art Gallery; Baron no. 98.
112. D. S. MacColl, *The Saturday Review*, 23 April 1898.
113. Sturgis, *Walter Sickert: A Life*, p.430. Gosse offered the picture as a gift to the Tate Gallery, but it was declined.
114. Walter Sickert, *The Façade of St Mark's*, *c.*1895–96; Baron no. 102.4.
115. Walter Sickert to Durand-Ruel, received 2 April 1901; Fondation Custodia.
116. See Baron no. 166.
117. Sturgis, *Walter Sickert: A Life*, p.290.
118. Price converted using 'Money-Table', Baedeker, *Northern Italy*, opposite title page.
119. See Jacques-Émile Blanche, *Portraits of a Lifetime* (London: 1937), pp.46–47; prices converted using 'Money-Table', Baedeker, *Northern Italy*, opposite title page.
120. Walter Sickert to Jacques-Émile Blanche; Denys Sutton Papers, Glasgow University Library; Sturgis, *Walter Sickert: A Life*, p.330.
121. Baron no. 111.2.
122. See Christie's, London. 6 June 1991, lot 78; quoted in Sturgis, *Walter Sickert: A Life*, pp.695–96, no. 49.
123. Diary of Jean, Lady Hamilton; Liddell Hart Centre for Military Archives, King's College, London (20/1/1); Sturgis, *Walter Sickert: A Life*, p.336.
124. Walter Sickert to Mrs Hulton, Bodleian, Oxford; Sturgis, *Walter Sickert: A Life*, p.294.
125. Jacques-Émile Blanche to André Gide in Georges-Paul Collet (ed.), *Cahiers André Gide 8 – Correspondence André Gide–Jacques-Émile Blanche* (Paris: 1979), pp.135–36; Sturgis, *Walter Sickert: A Life*, p.306.
126. Price converted using 'Money-Table', Baedeker, *Northern France*, opposite title page.
127. [Walter] Richard Sickert, 'Hire Purchase for Pictures', *The Times*, 21 January 1935, p.13.
128. Walter Sickert to Philip Wilson Steer, quoted in Emmons, *The Life and Opinions*, p.89.
129. Jacques-Émile Blanche to André Gide, 26 September 1903, in Collet (ed.), *Cahiers André Gide 8*, p.67; Sturgis, *Walter Sickert: A Life*, p.320.
130. Walter Sickert to Jacques-Émile Blanche, undated; Institut de France, 7055XI/179.
131. Price converted using 'Money-Table', Baedeker, *Northern France*, opposite title page.
132. Walter Sickert to Jacques-Émile Blanche undated; Institut de France, Paris.
133. Walter Sickert ('St. P.'), 'Schools of Art'; Robins (ed.), *Walter Sickert*, p.132.
134. *ibid.*
135. Walter Sickert ('St. P.'), 'Charles Hazelwood Shannon', *The Speaker*, 24 April 1897; Robins (ed.), *Walter Sickert*, p.161.
136. Lecture description by Duncan Grant, 7 July 1938; see Richard Shone, 'Duncan Grant on a Lecture by Sickert', *The Burlington Magazine*, vol. 123, no. 944, November 1981, p.672.
137. Quoted in *William Logsdail 1859–1944*, Usher Gallery exhibition catalogue (Lincoln: 1994), p.13.
138. Walter Sickert, 'Drawing and Photography', *National Observer*, 2 May 1891; Robins (ed.), *Walter Sickert*, p.85.
139. Walter Sickert, 'Is the camera the friend or foe of art?', *The Studio*, July 1893; Robins (ed.), *Walter Sickert*, p.97.
140. [Walter] Richard Sickert, 'The Haig Statue: Artists and the Camera', *The Times*, 15 August 1929, p.6.
141. *Gatti's Hungerford Palace of Varieties. 2nd Turn of Katie Lawrence*, see Baron no. 44. Walter Sickert to Gwen Ffrancon-Davies, undated, *c.*1930–32; quoted in Rebecca Daniels, 'Richard Sickert: The Art of Photography', *Walter Sickert: 'Drawing is the Thing'*, Whitworth Art Gallery exhibition catalogue (Manchester: 2004), p.26.
142. *Mr Bradlaugh at the Bar of the House of Commons*, Baron no. 60.
143. *The Artist*, 6 November 1891.
144. Walter Sickert to Lady Eden; University of Birmingham Library, AP22/14/43.
145. Sturgis, *Walter Sickert: A Life*, p.186.
146. Walter Sickert ('St. P.), 'Van Beers and Menpes', *The Speaker*, 22 May 1897; Robins (ed.), *Walter Sickert*, p.171.
147. Walter Sickert to Florence Humphrey; quoted in Baron, *Sickert: Paintings and Drawings*, p.31.
148. James, 'Venice', p.3.
149. See Baron, *Sickert: Paintings and Drawings*, p.32.
150. Walter Sickert to Jacques-Émile Blanche, undated; Institut de France, 7055XI/173.
151. Blanche, *Portraits of a Lifetime*, p.47.
152. Technical analysis by Kate Jennings, Tate Paper Conservation.
153. Walter Sickert ('St. P.'), 'Van Beers and Menpes'; Robins (ed.), *Walter Sickert*, p.171.
154. Tate Archive TGA 971/18.
155. Note accompanying the gift of the camera lucida. Bagnold wrote that she borrowed it when she was aged around 24. She was born in 1889.
156. See Richard Kendall, 'Drawing, Tracing and the Sequence' in *Degas: Beyond Impressionism*, National Gallery exhibition catalogue (London: 1996), pp.186–88.
157. See Baron no. 157.
158. Walter Sickert ('St. P.'), 'Van Beers and Menpes'; Robins (ed.), *Walter Sickert*, p.171.
159. Sturgis, *Walter Sickert: A Life*, p.223.
160. Walter Sickert, 'Literature'; Robins (ed.), *Walter Sickert*, p.69.
161. Sturgis, *Walter Sickert: A Life*, p.296.
162. Walter Sickert to Constanzia Hulton, 2 June 1929; Hulton Papers, Bodleian Library, University of Oxford.
163. Walter Sickert, Preface to the exhibition catalogue *Water-Colour Drawings by Francis E. James*, Dudley Gallery, December 1890; Robins (ed.), *Walter Sickert*, p.82.
164. Walter Sickert, 'On Line', *The Speaker*, 1896; Robins (ed.), *Walter Sickert*, p.112.
165. Reginald Thomas Cleaver (1864–1954), illustrator for *The Daily Graphic*, the first illustrated daily newspaper, from its beginning in 1890. Cleaver specialised in parliamentary scenes, but also contributed to *Punch*. Francis Carruthers Gould (1844–1925), illustrator who contributed to the *Pall Mall Gazette* from 1887.
166. The sisters Lloyd were music hall performers whom Sickert painted *c.*1889, Baron no. 51.
167. Walter Sickert to Philip Wilson Steer; quoted in Emmons, *The Life and Opinions*, p.108.
168. See Baron no. 209.
169. *Self-Portrait*, 1897, Baron no. 78.1, untraced.
170. Baron no. 681.
171. Sickert Collection, Islington Council, reproduced in *Walter Sickert: 'Drawing is the Thing'*, p.150.
172. Walter Sickert to Constanza Hulton, received 3 November 1928; Hulton Papers, Bodleian Library, University of Oxford.
173. Baron no. 168.1. Sickert's position as an RA was short-lived. He resigned in 1935 in protest at the President's refusal to sign a petition against the removal of Epstein's sculptures from the British Medical Association building in the Strand.
174. 'An Old Man's Brilliance', *News Chronicle*, 15 July 1935.
175. Baron no. 241.
176. Baron nos. 773, 773.1.
177. Baron no. 774.

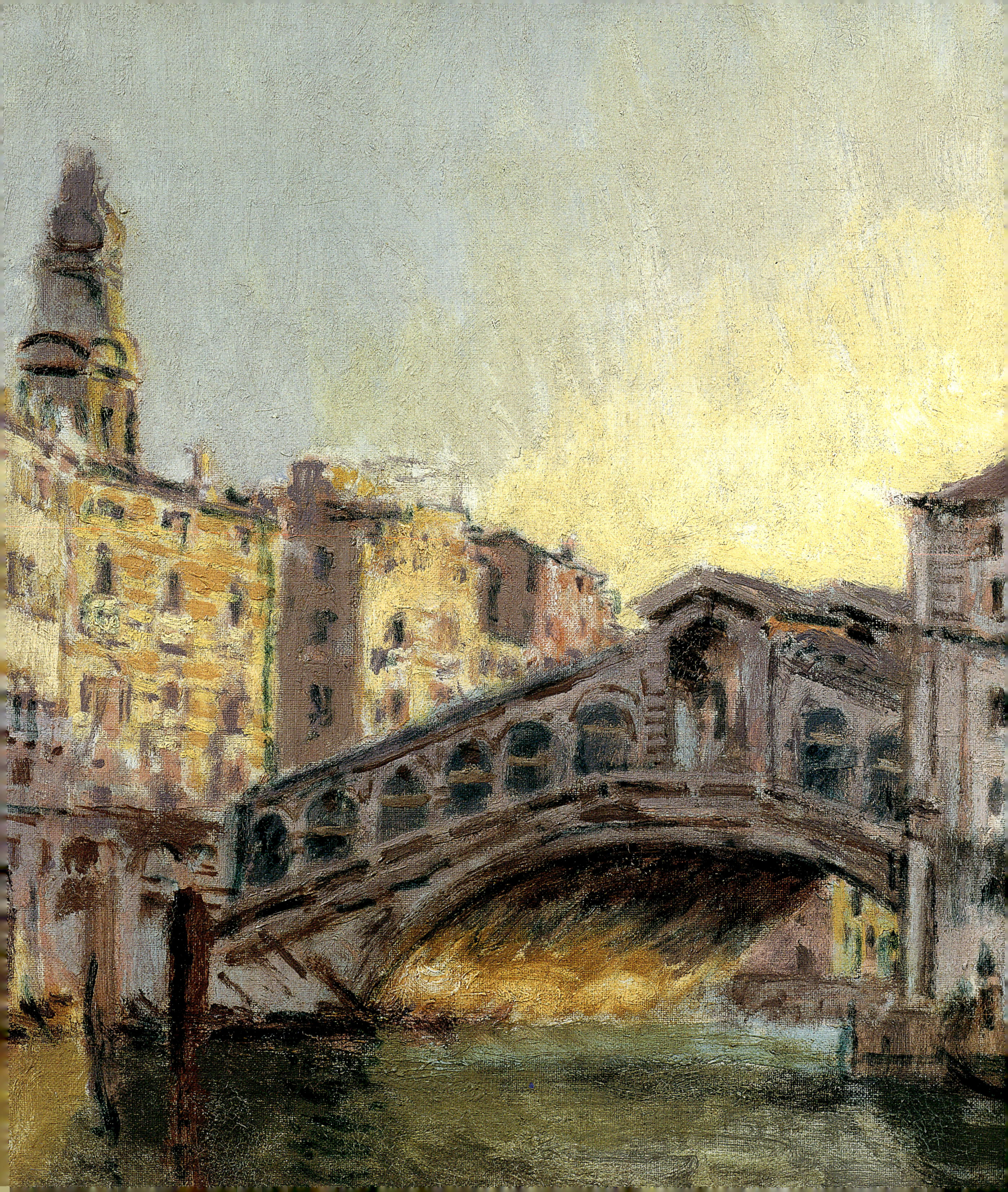

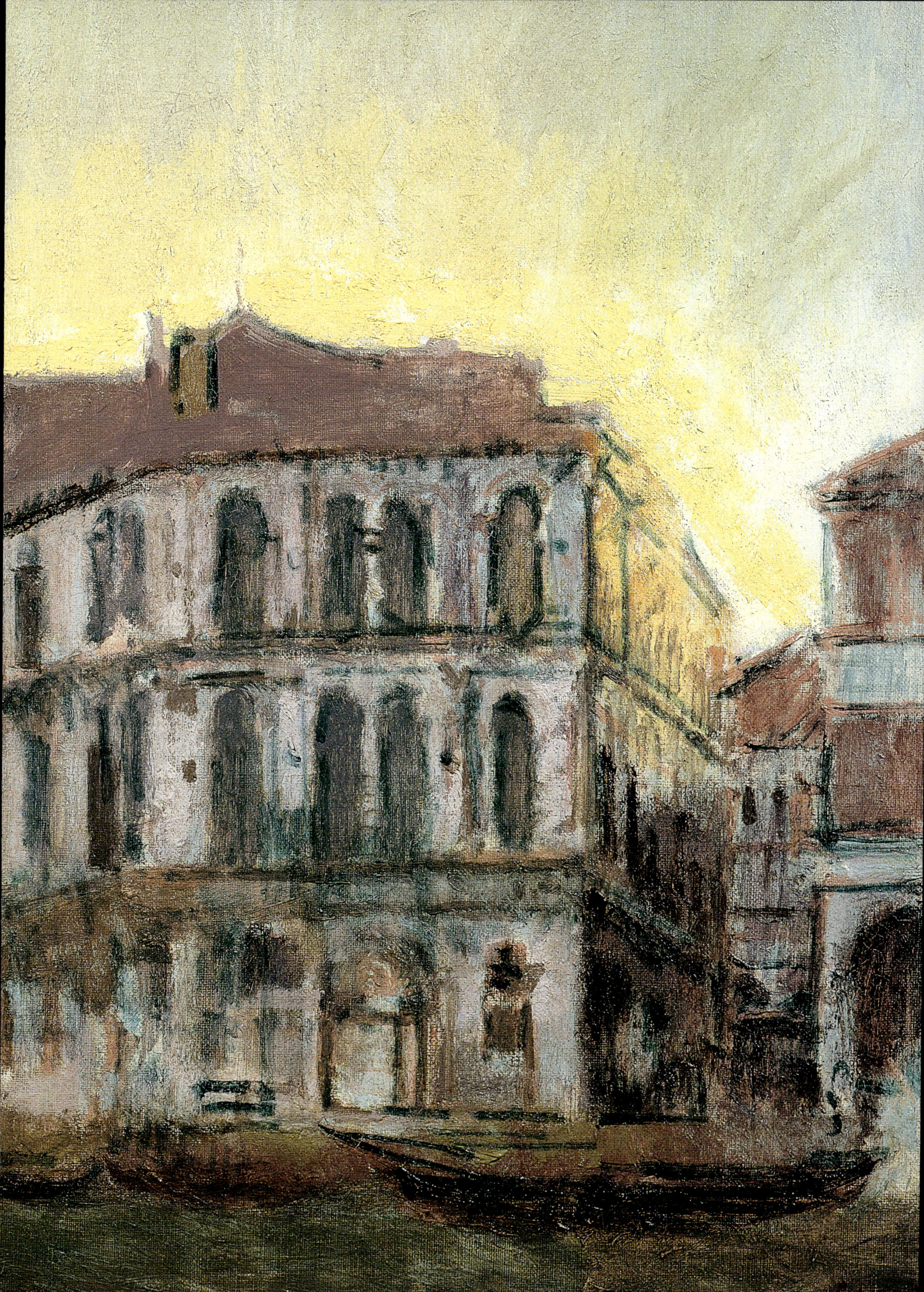

1

VIEWS AND VISTAS

The Rialto Bridge and Palazzo dei Camerlenghi
c.1895–96
(cat. 21, detail)

By the time Sickert visited Venice in the 1890s, Venice was a popular destination for European and American travellers. A city like no other, it was revered as a collection of architectural jewels, uniquely set against the sparkling watery setting of the lagoon and network of canals. East met West in its architectural influences, and the distinctive Venetian Gothic style was a source of considerable interest. British enthusiasm was stimulated by the enormous and lasting success of John Ruskin's *The Stones of Venice*. In three volumes appearing between 1851 and 1853, Ruskin set out in mesmeric and lyrical prose his passionate enthusiasm for the great city. He argued that in the simplicity of the Venetian Byzantine and Gothic styles was found a spiritual honesty and integrity lacking in the riper sophistication of Renaissance architecture. At the time his book first appeared Venice was a city of former greatness and shadows that had almost been forgotten about. Ruskin stimulated enormous interest and also concern for Venice's crumbling vulnerability.

When he first started painting in Venice, Sickert stuck exclusively to architectural subjects. He focussed on well-known sites, partly because he found them interesting but also because he was undoubtedly aware they would sell well. He wrote to his friend Philip Wilson Steer in 1895, 'St. Mark's is engrossing and the Ducal Palace and 2 or 3 Renaissance gems, the Miracoli and S. Zaccharia and the Scuola di San Marco.' Sickert made an ambitious sequence of large canvases of the façade of St Mark's in 1895–96, and also continued to work on them when he returned to London. Although almost identical, each showed the Basilica under different lighting conditions, something that he may have been prompted to do by seeing Monet's series paintings of Rouen Cathedral. Sickert's practice was to repeat compositions and subjects several times, sometimes exactly, until his investigations of the potential of paint were exhausted. But even if the composition was the same, each picture would have its own very distinct character and handling. An example of this is the series of paintings of the church of Santa Maria della Salute that offer quite distinct and individual treatments of the subject, almost like a series of fugal musical variations.

On his visits to Venice in 1895–96, 1900 and 1901, Sickert avoided figure subjects and devoted himself to painting architecture. He experimented with the method he employed in approaching his pictures. Usually convinced of the formula that a painter should make paintings based solely on drawings, Venice inspired Sickert to explore again painting before the subject in the open air and to make small oil sketches on which to base larger pictures. There is also evidence that Sickert utilised photographs of Venice to copy architectural detail and the possibility that he experimented with drawing instruments and even carbon paper to help him transfer multiple images.

1
The Piazzetta and Old Campanile, Venice
*c.*1901
Monotype print with ink wash on paper,
49.5 x 33 cm
Tate

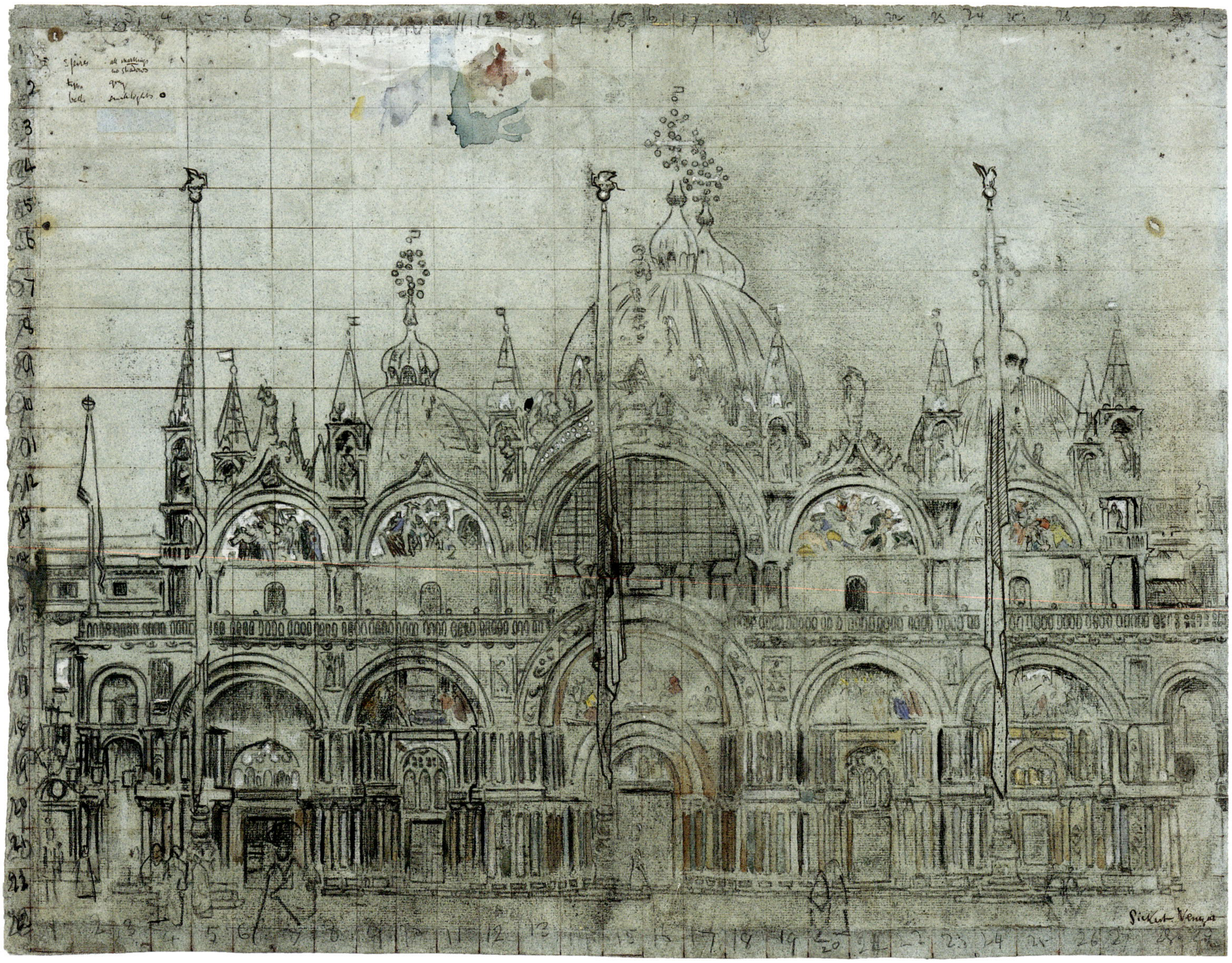

2
Façade of St Mark's
*c.*1896
Black chalk, watercolour and gouache on blue paper squared in red, 45.1 x 58.4 cm
Manchester City Galleries

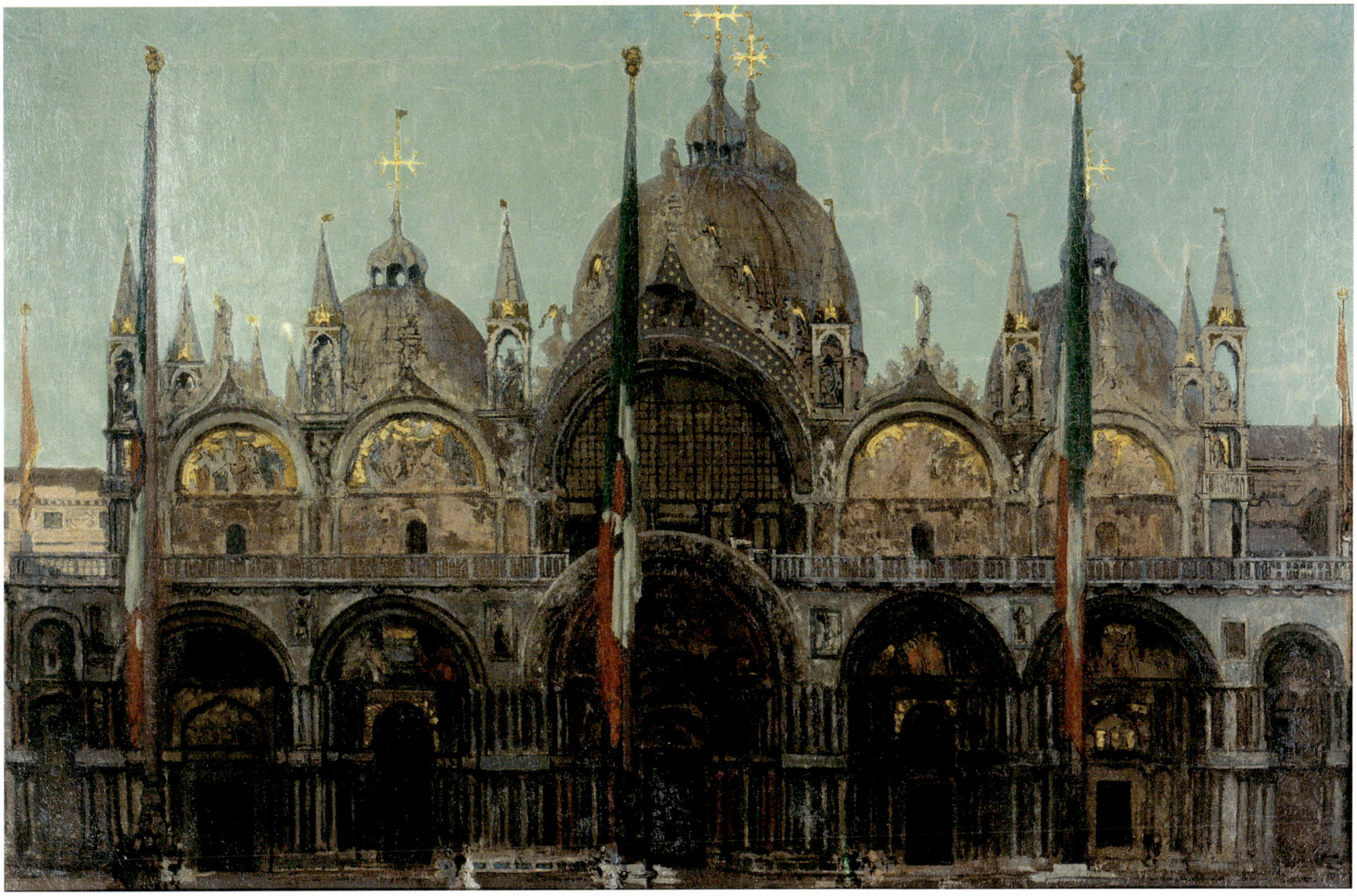

3
St Mark's, Venice
1895
Oil on canvas, 100.5 x 151 cm
British Council

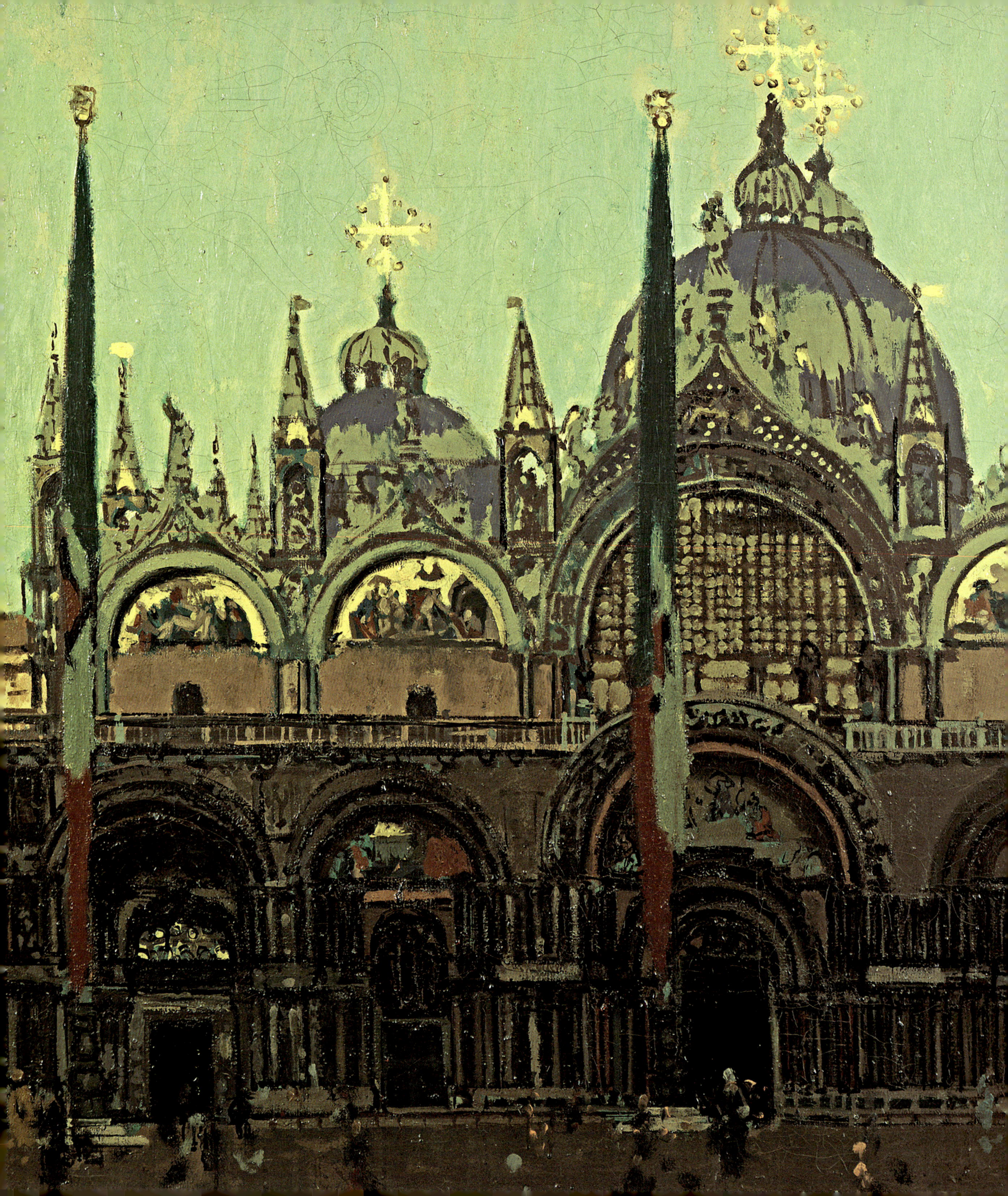

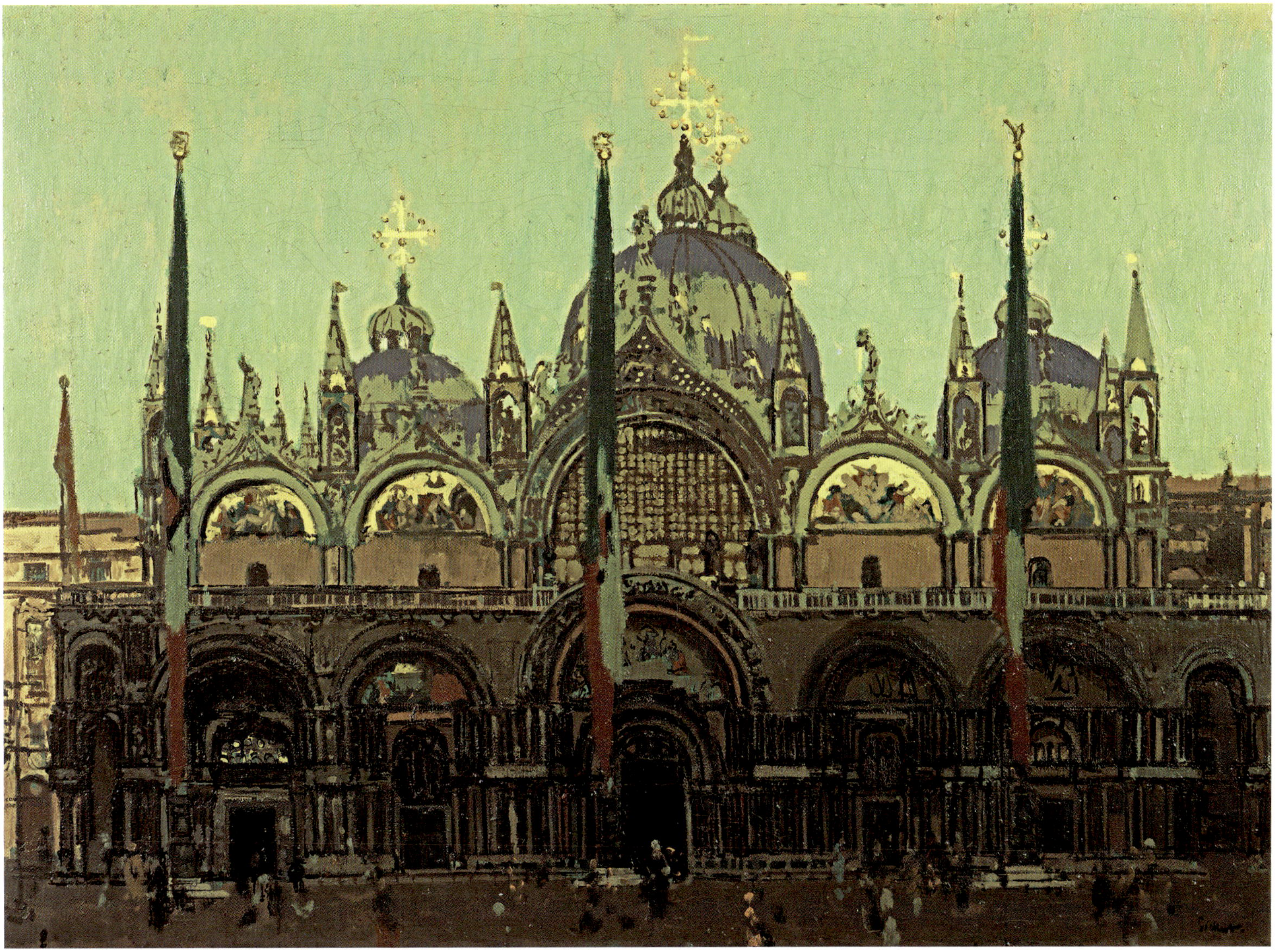

4
St Mark's, Venice (Pax Tibi Marce Evangelista Meus)
*c.*1895–96
Oil on canvas, 90.8 x 120 cm
Tate, London

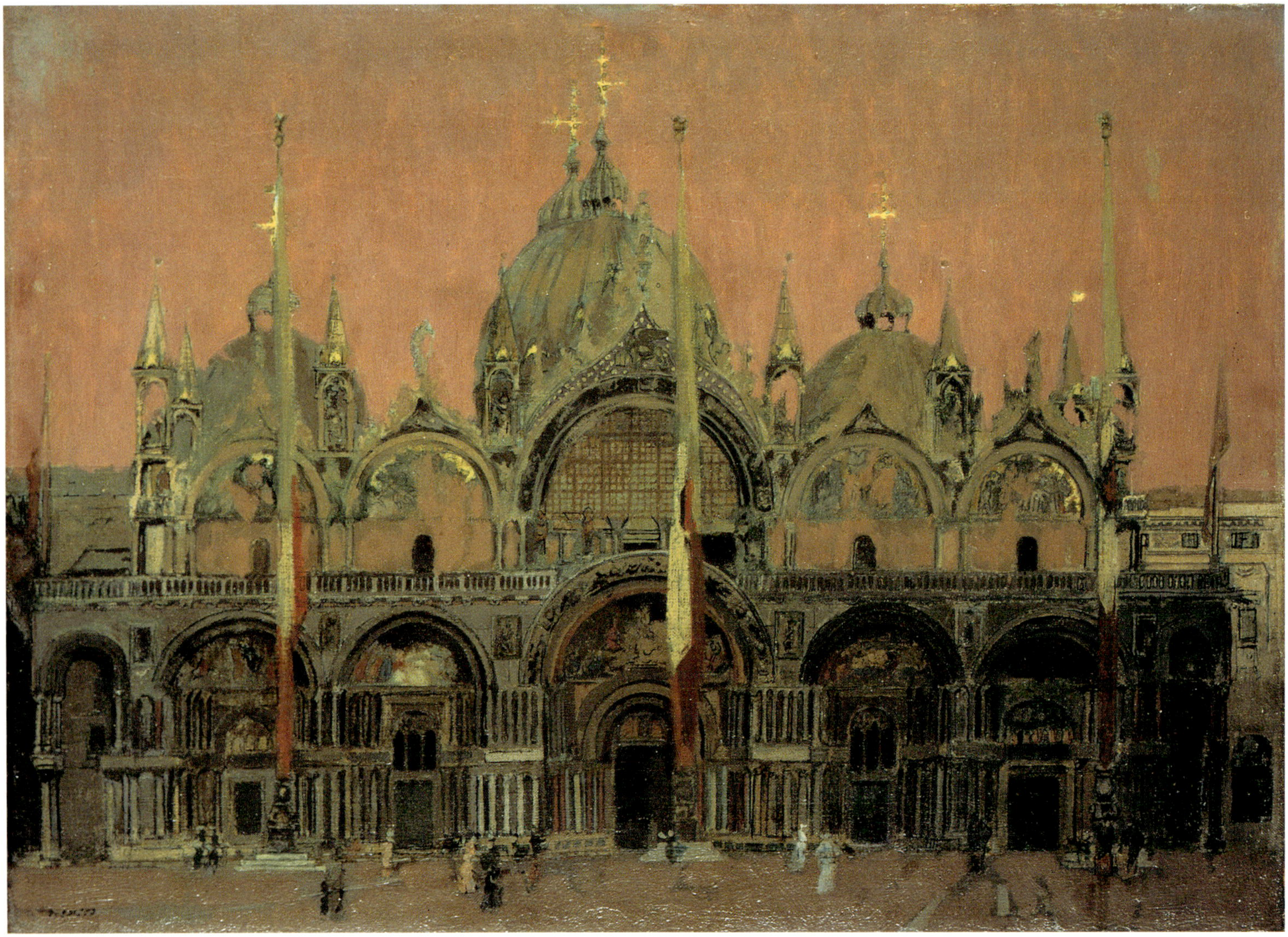

5
The Façade of St Mark's: Red Sky at Night
*c.*1895–96
Oil on canvas, 45.4 x 61 cm
Southampton City Art Gallery

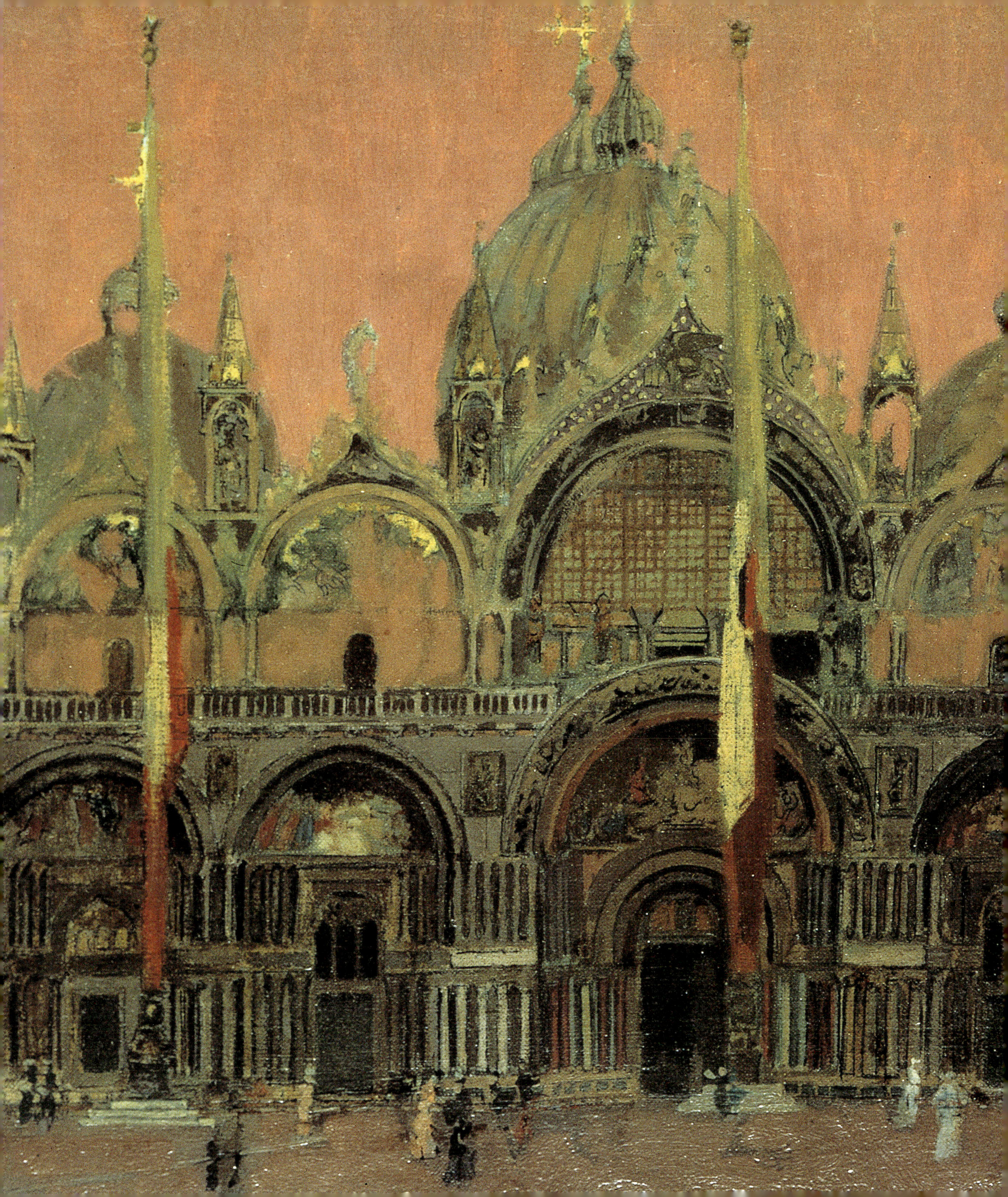

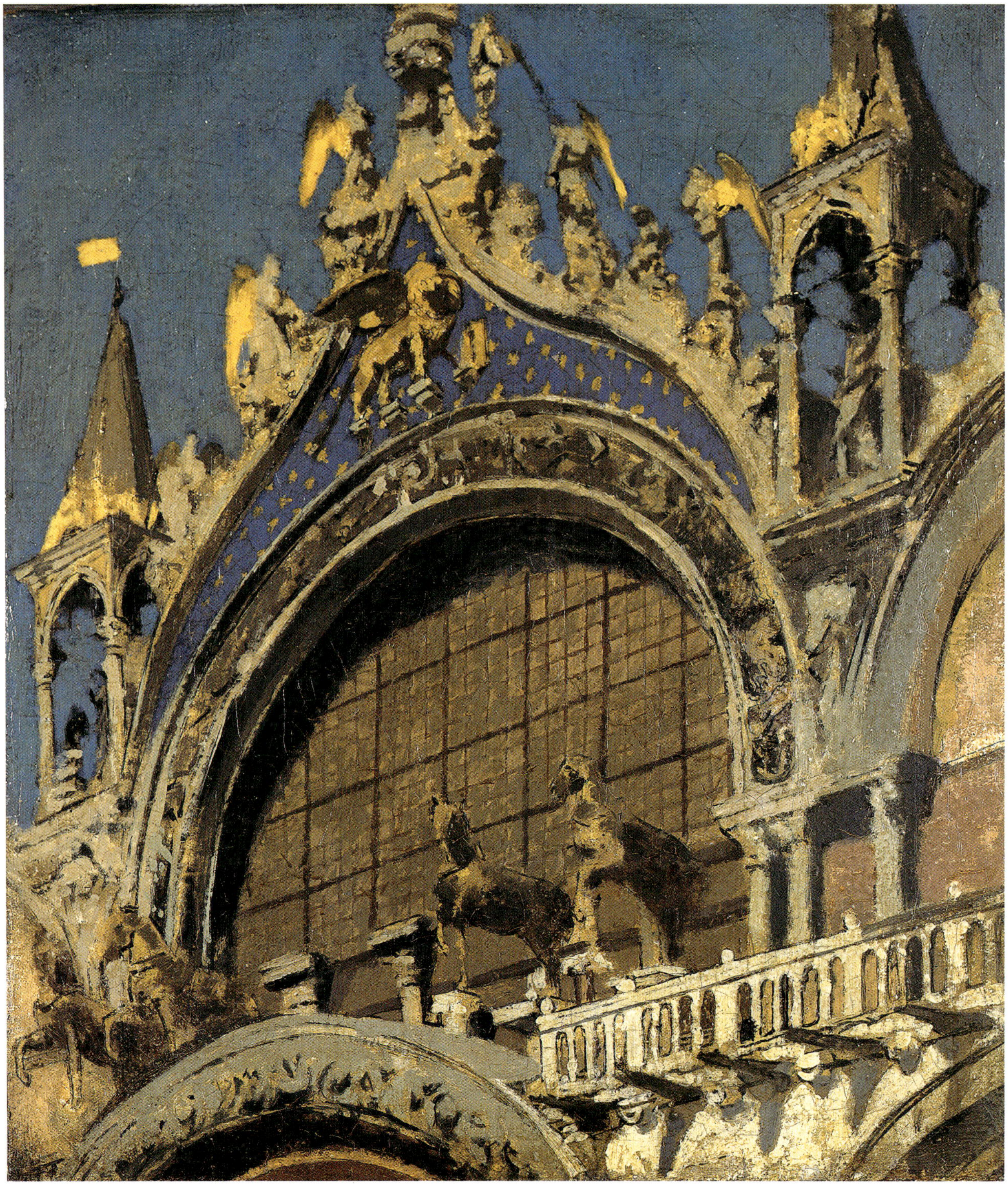

6
The Horses of St Mark's
1905–06
Oil on canvas, 50.2 x 42.2 cm
Birmingham Museums &
Art Gallery

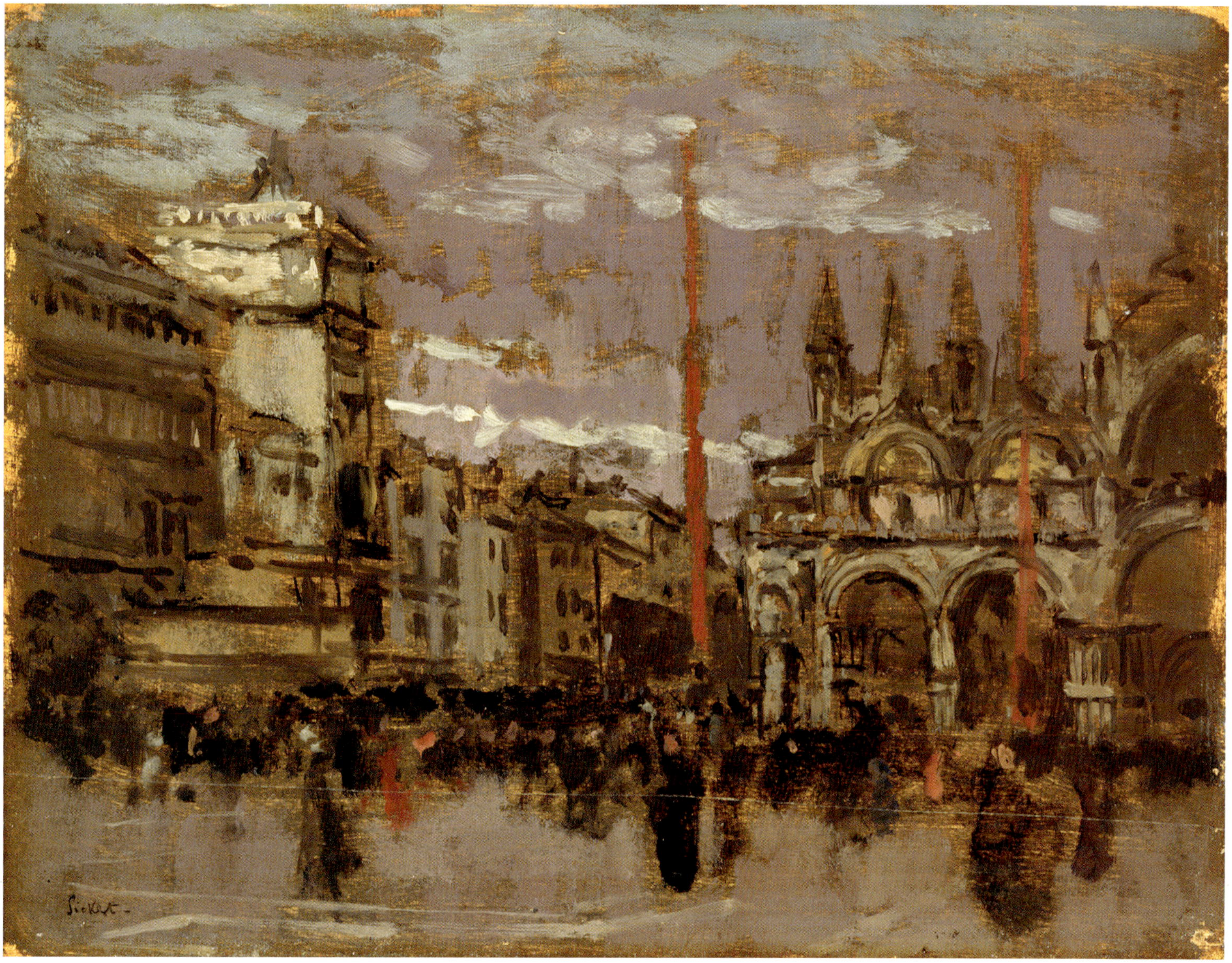

7
Piazza San Marco
*c.*1900–01
Oil on panel, 20 x 24.6 cm
Fitzwilliam Museum,
Cambridge

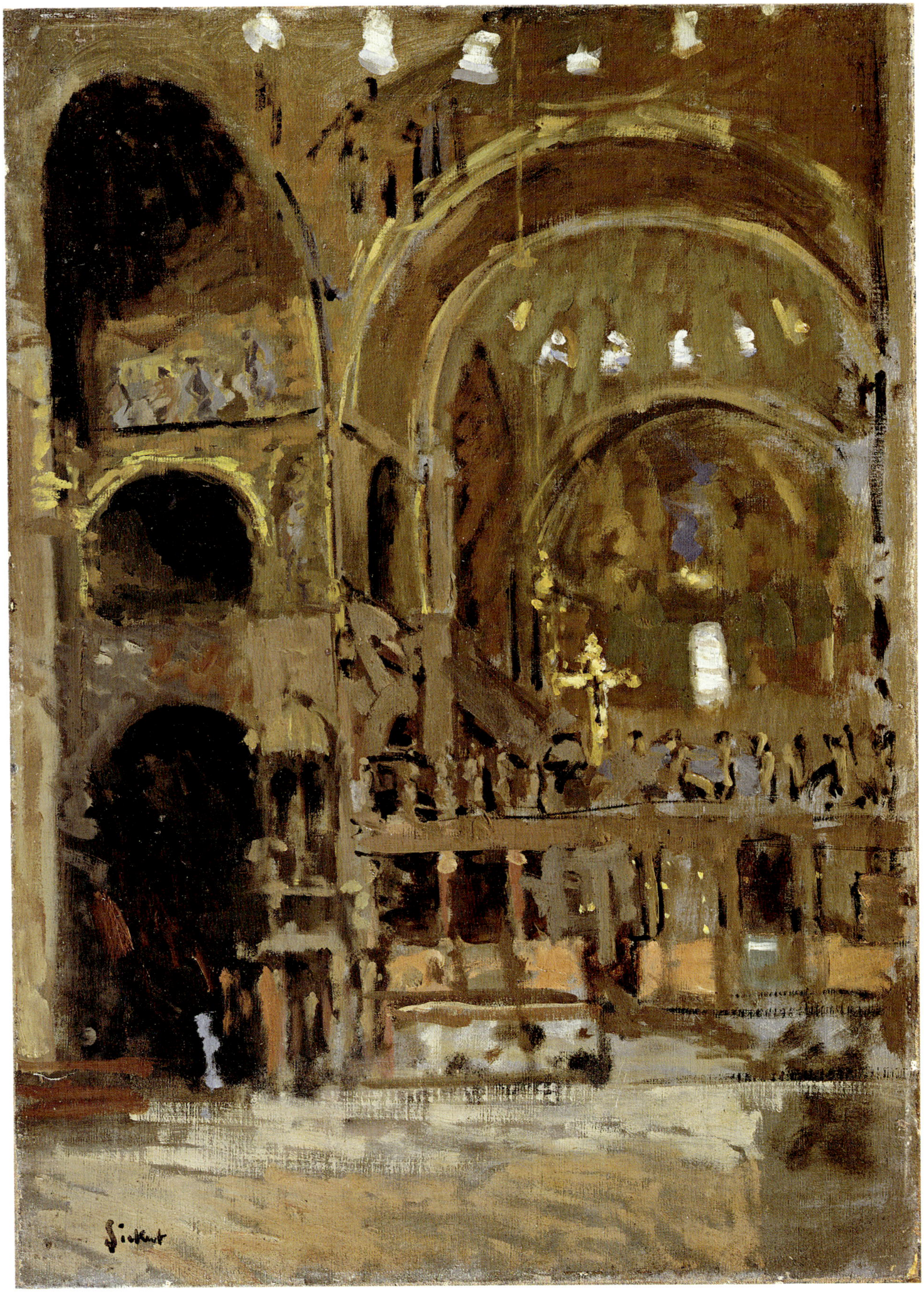

8
Interior of St Mark's, Venice
1896
Oil on canvas,
69.8 x 49.2 cm
Tate

9
Gli Scalzi: The Church of the Barefoot Friars
*c.*1895–96
Oil on canvas,
67.3 x 55.9 cm
Private Collection

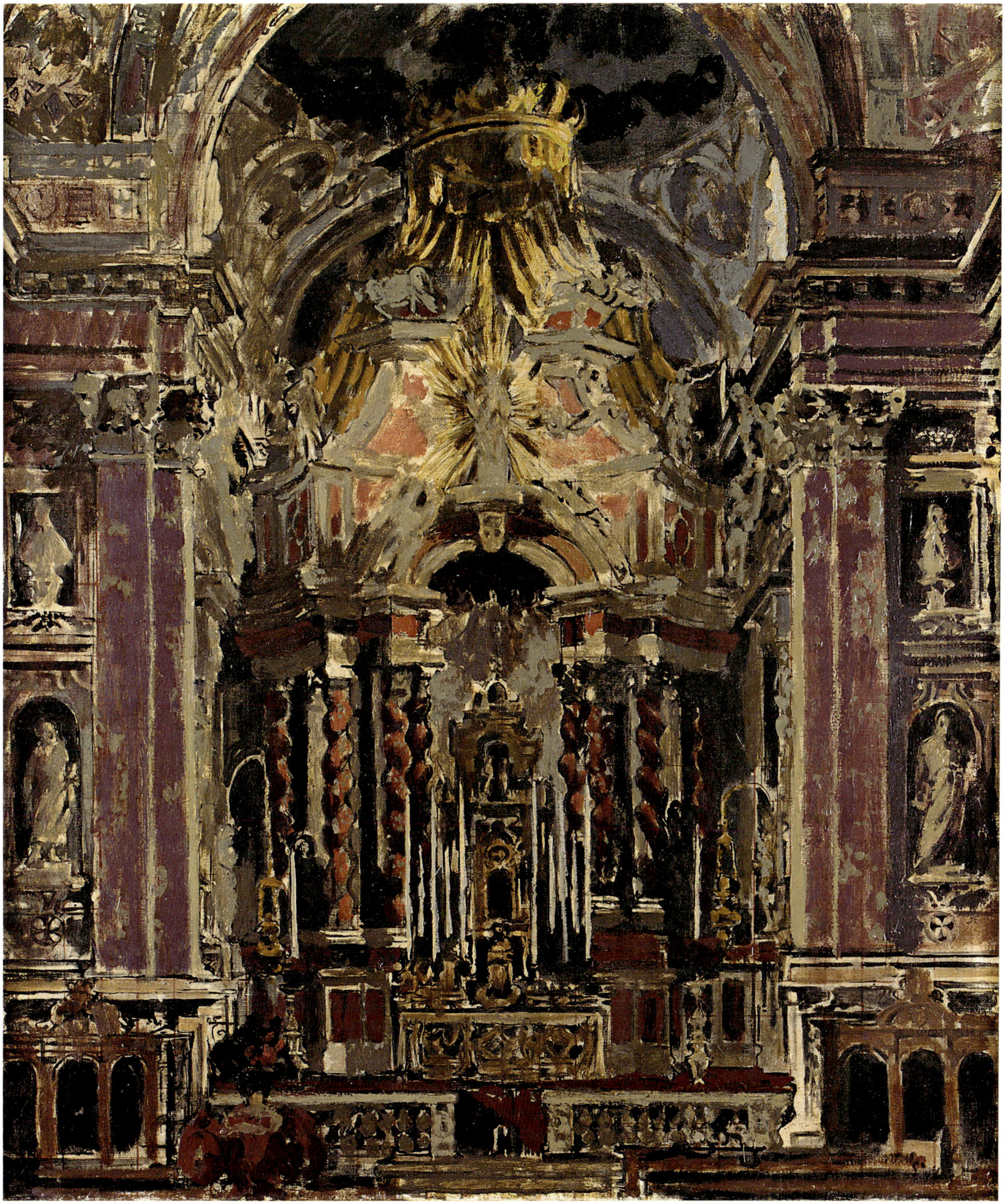

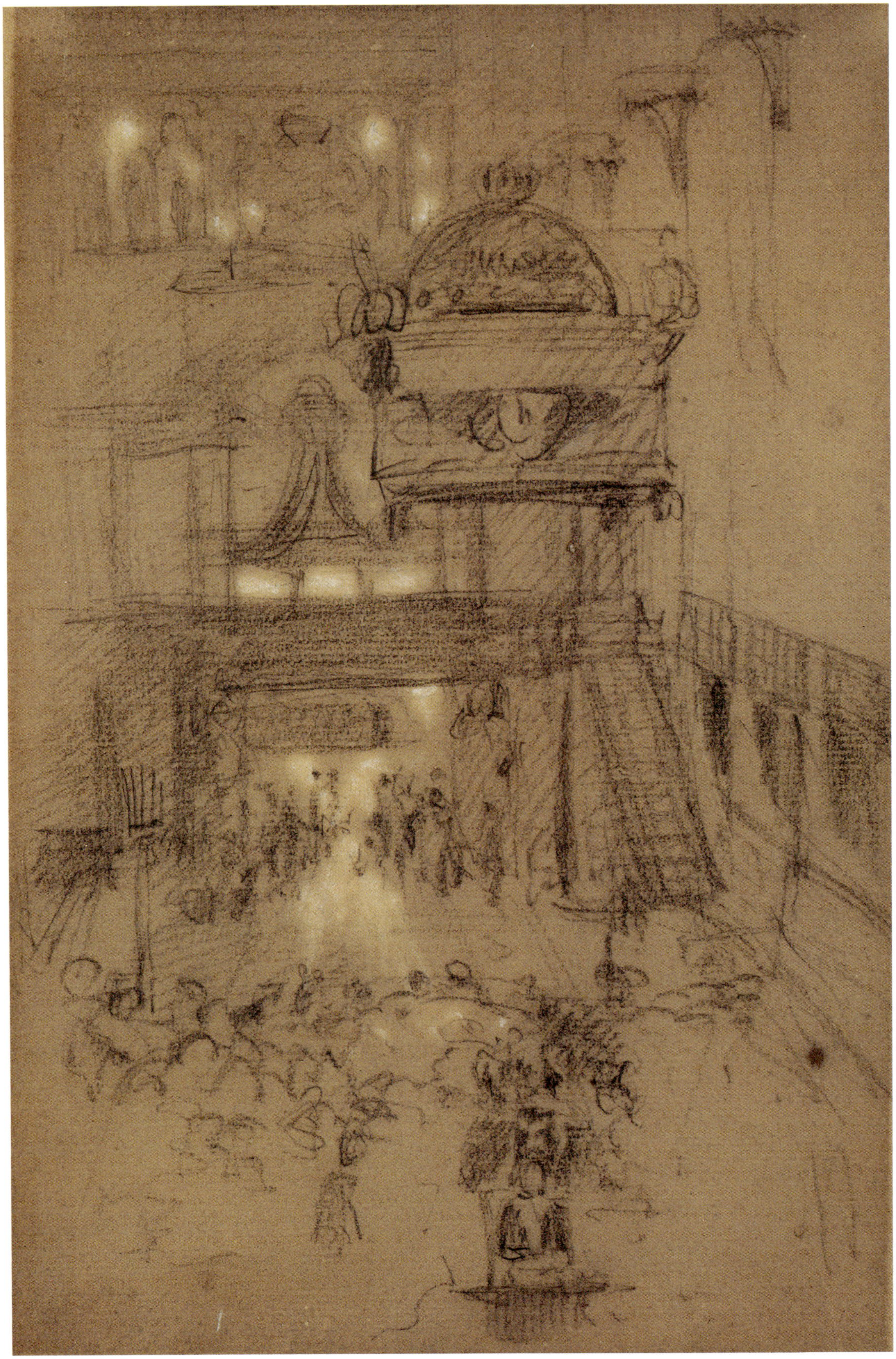

10
Interior of St Mark's, Venice
1898
Pencil and white chalk on toned paper, 21.5 x 14 cm
Private Collection

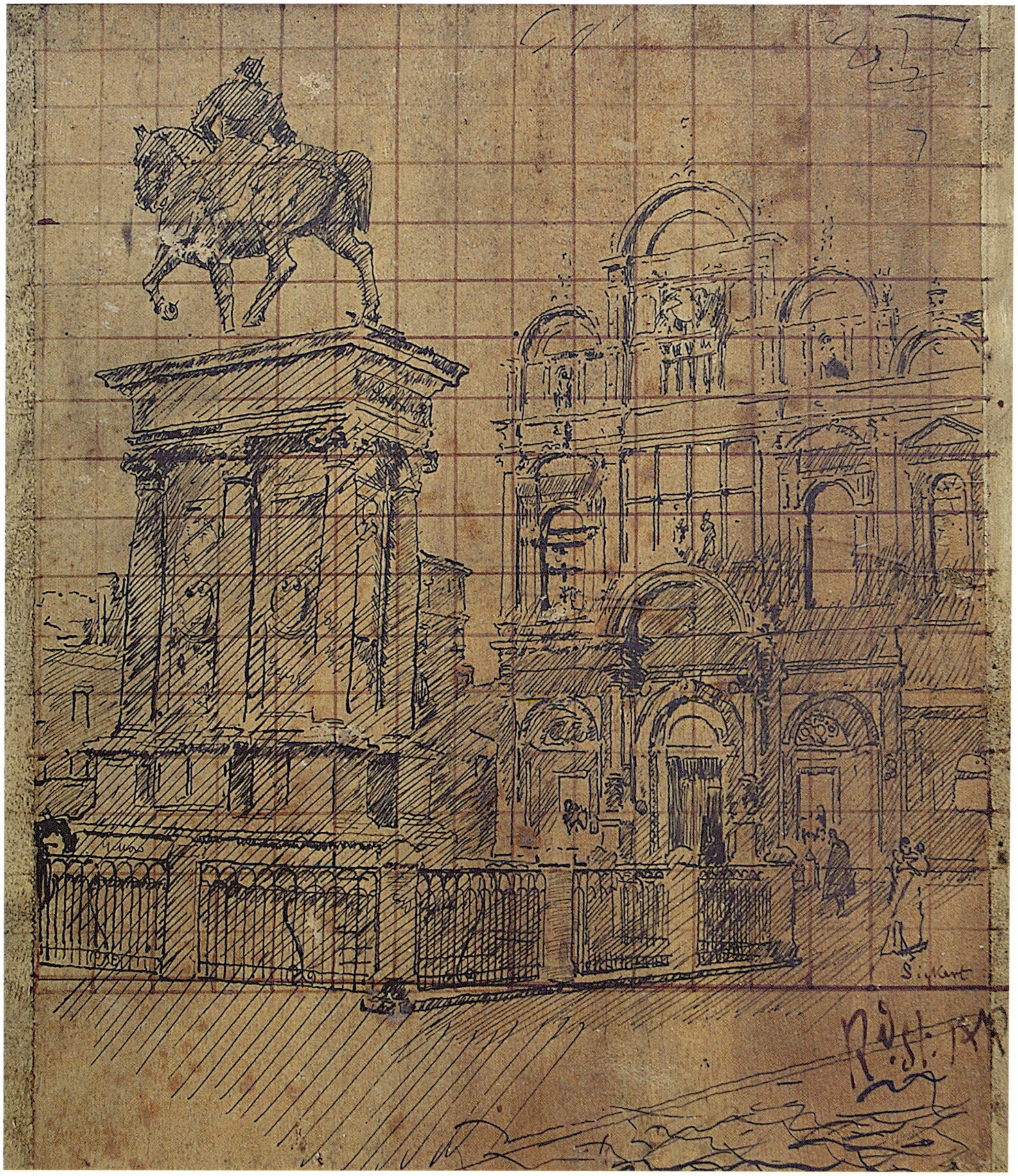

11
The Colleoni Monument
c.1900
Pen and black ink squared in red on brown paper laid down on board, 21.6 x 16.5 cm
Private Collection

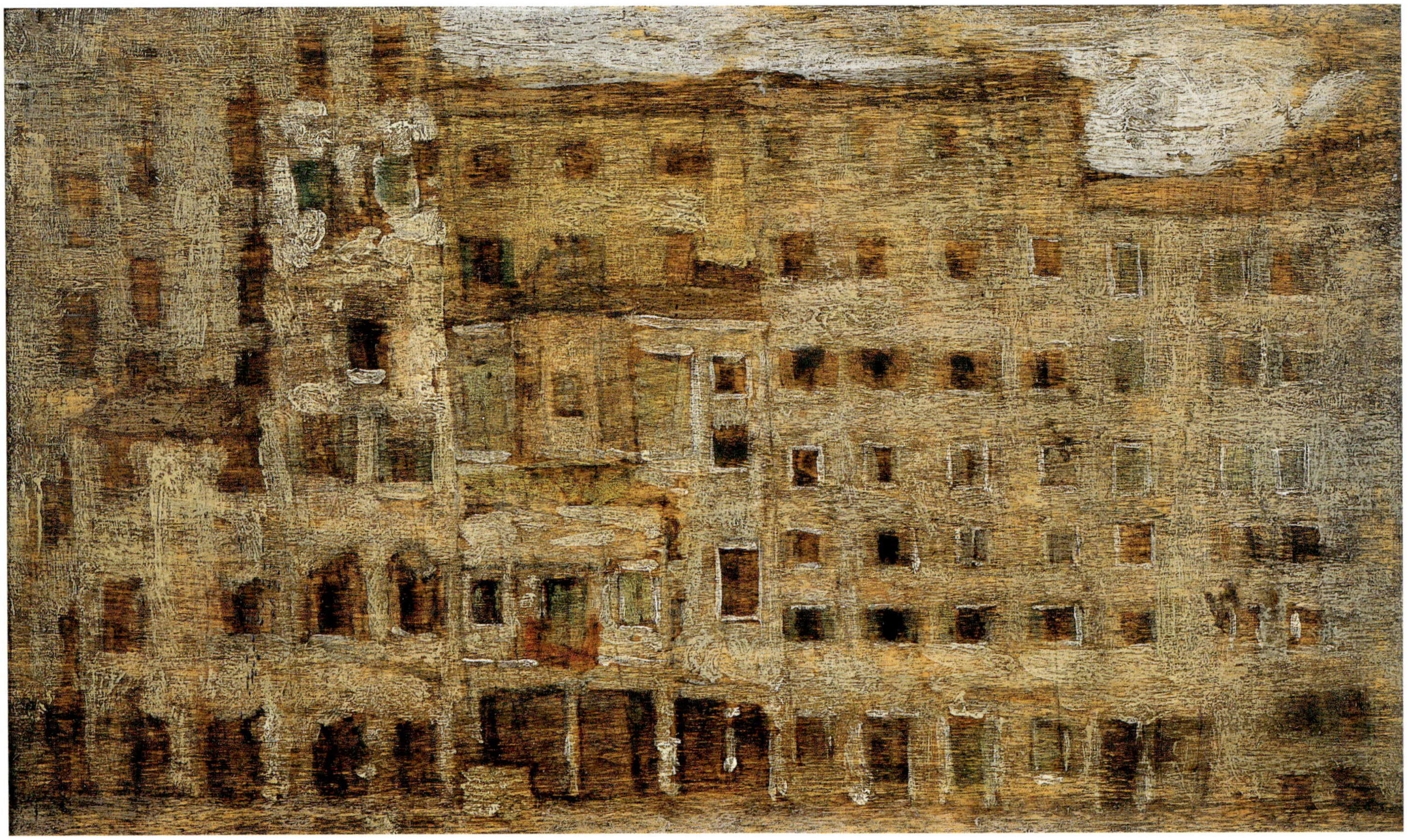

12
The Ghetto, Venice
1897–98
Oil on panel, 14 x 22.9 cm
Private Collection

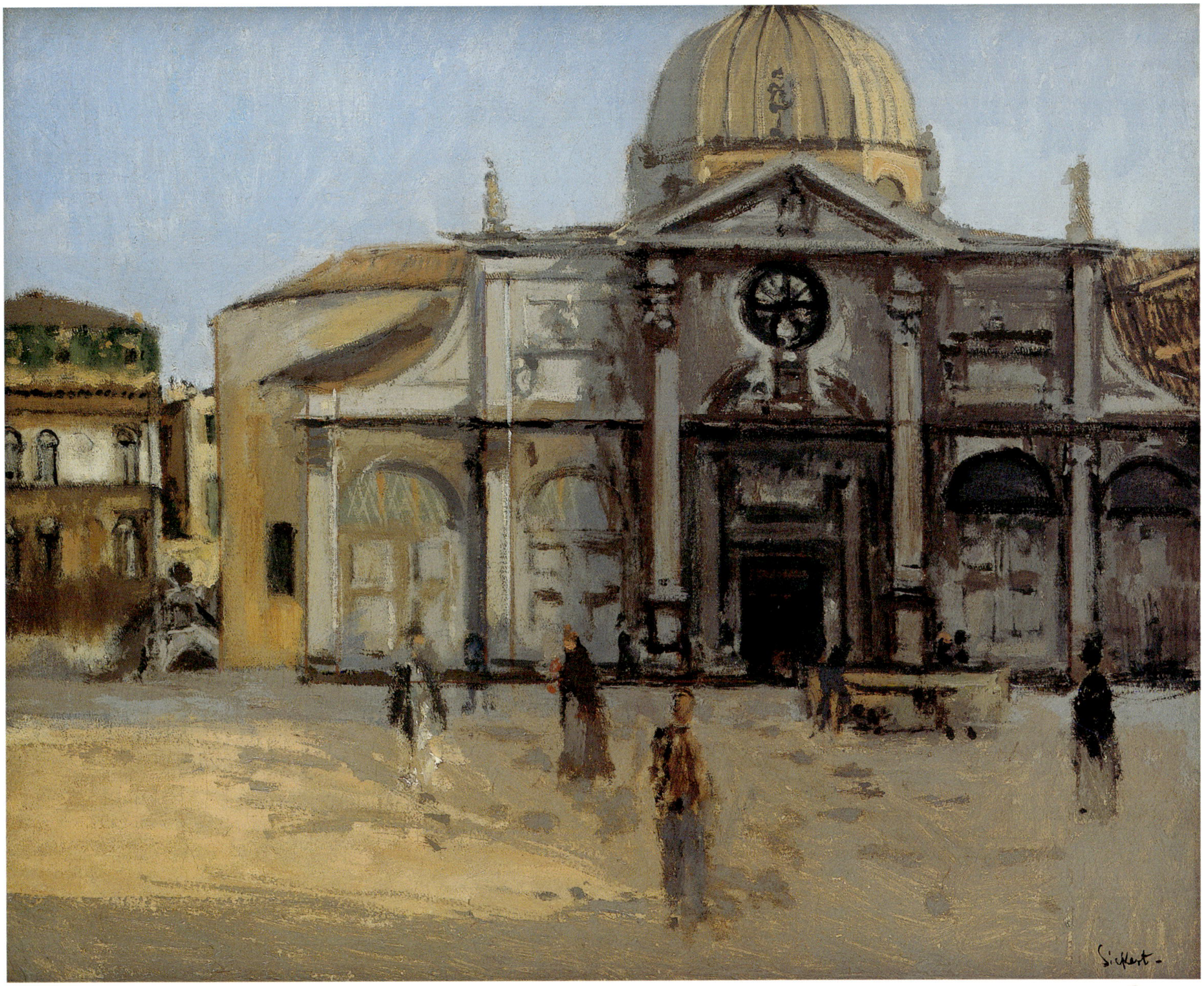

13
Santa Maria Formosa
c.1900–01
Oil on canvas, 48.2 x 55.9 cm
Private Collection, courtesy of
Offer Waterman & Co., London

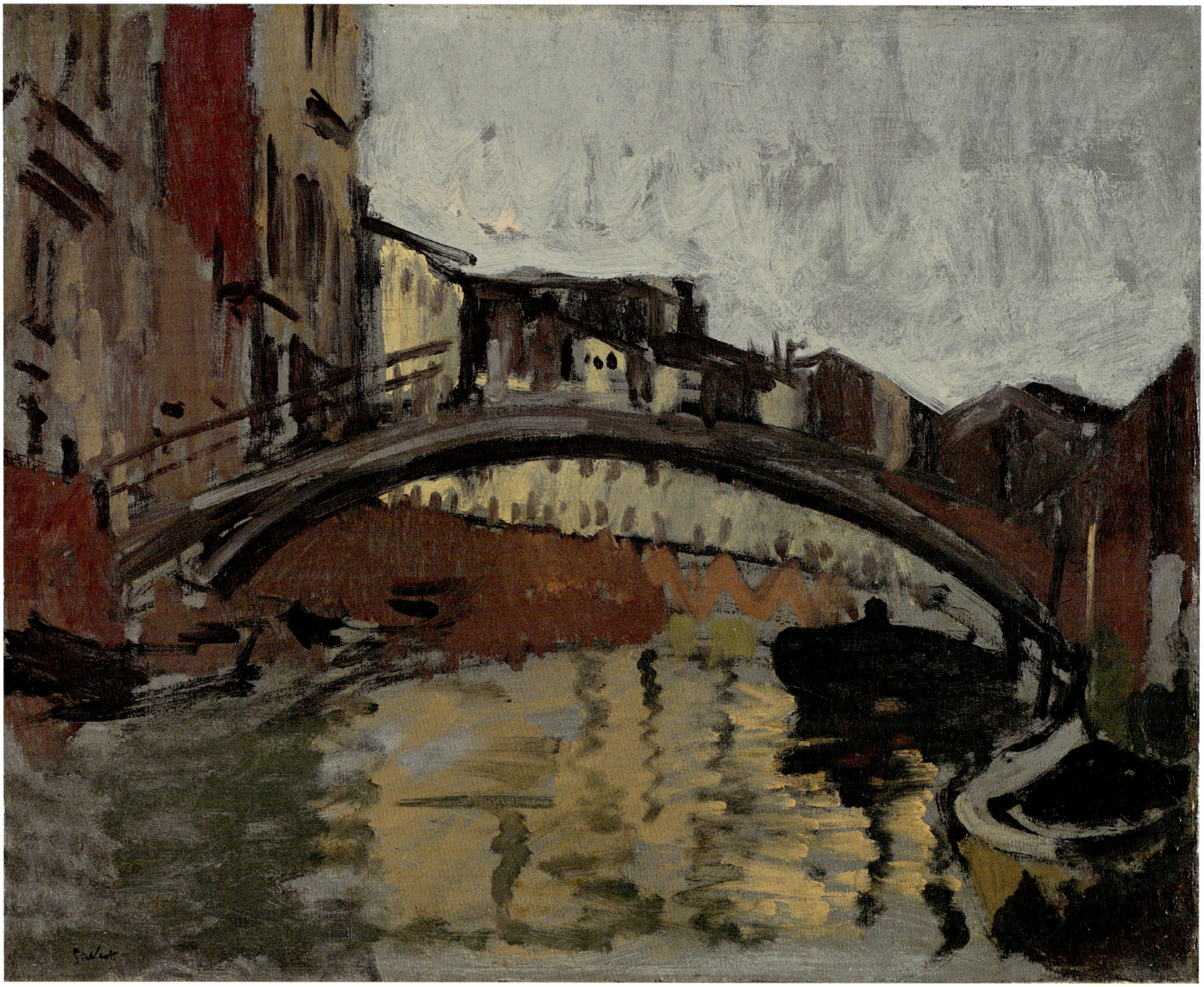

14
San Trovaso, Venice
c.1904
Oil on canvas, 39 x 45.4 cm
The Samuel Courtauld Trust,
The Courtauld Gallery,
London

15
A Canal, Venice: Palazzo Montecuccioli
1901–04
Oil on canvas, 46 x 38.5 cm
Courtesy of Austin/Desmond
Fine Art, London

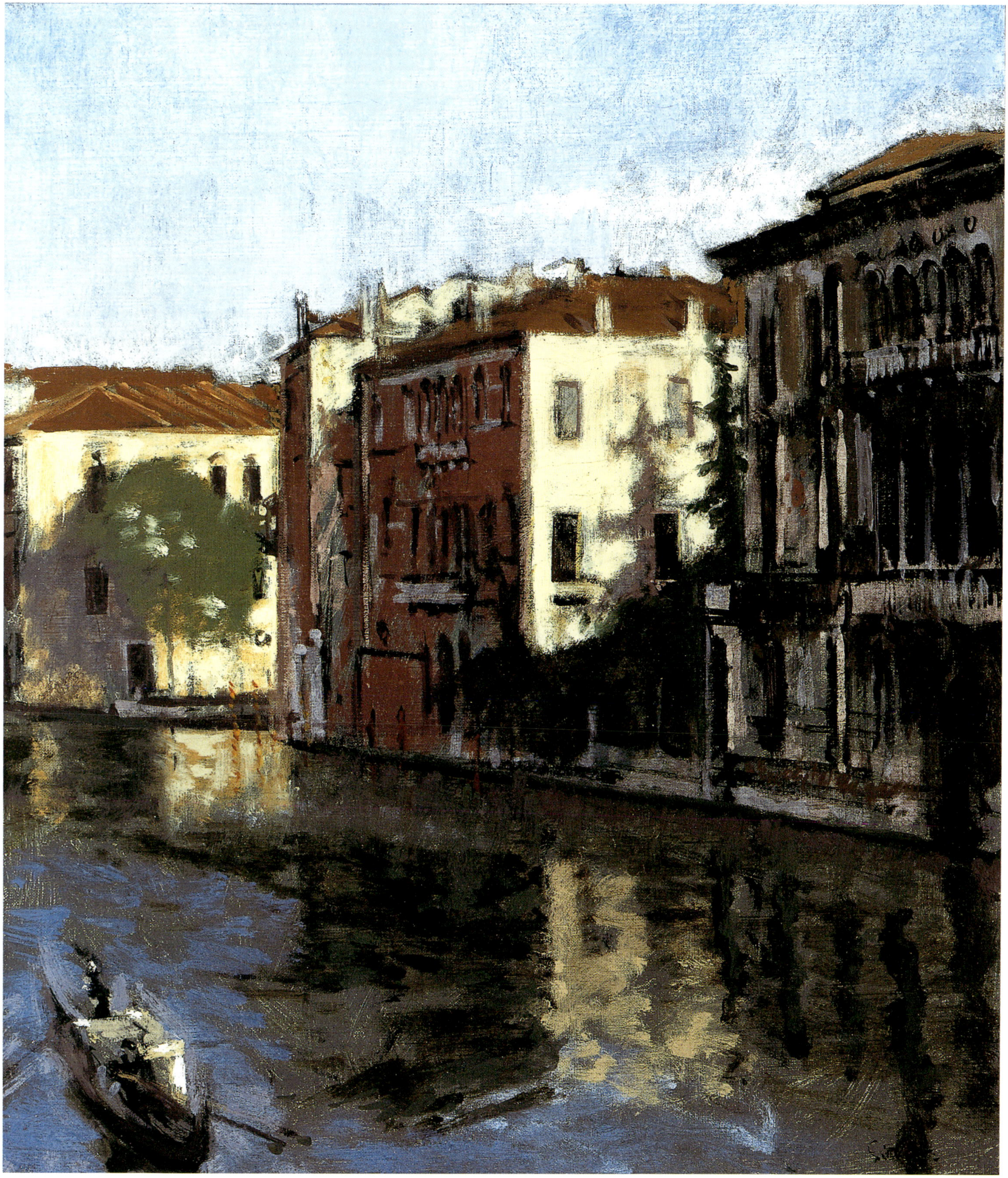

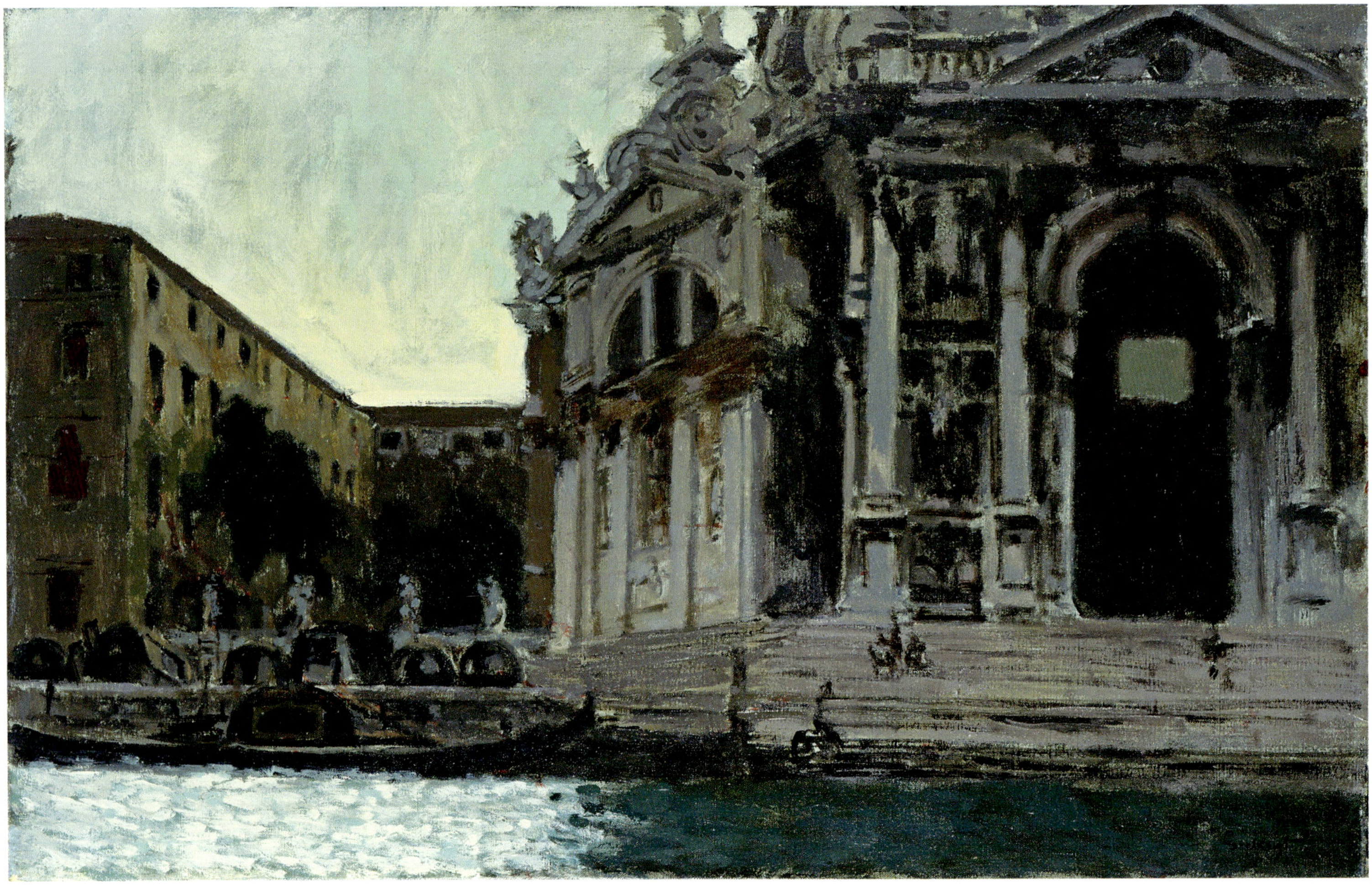

16
Venice: La Salute
*c.*1901–03
Oil on canvas, 45.1 x 69.2 cm
Tate

17
Santa Maria della Salute
*c.*1901
Oil on canvas, 73 x 55.9 cm
Private Collection

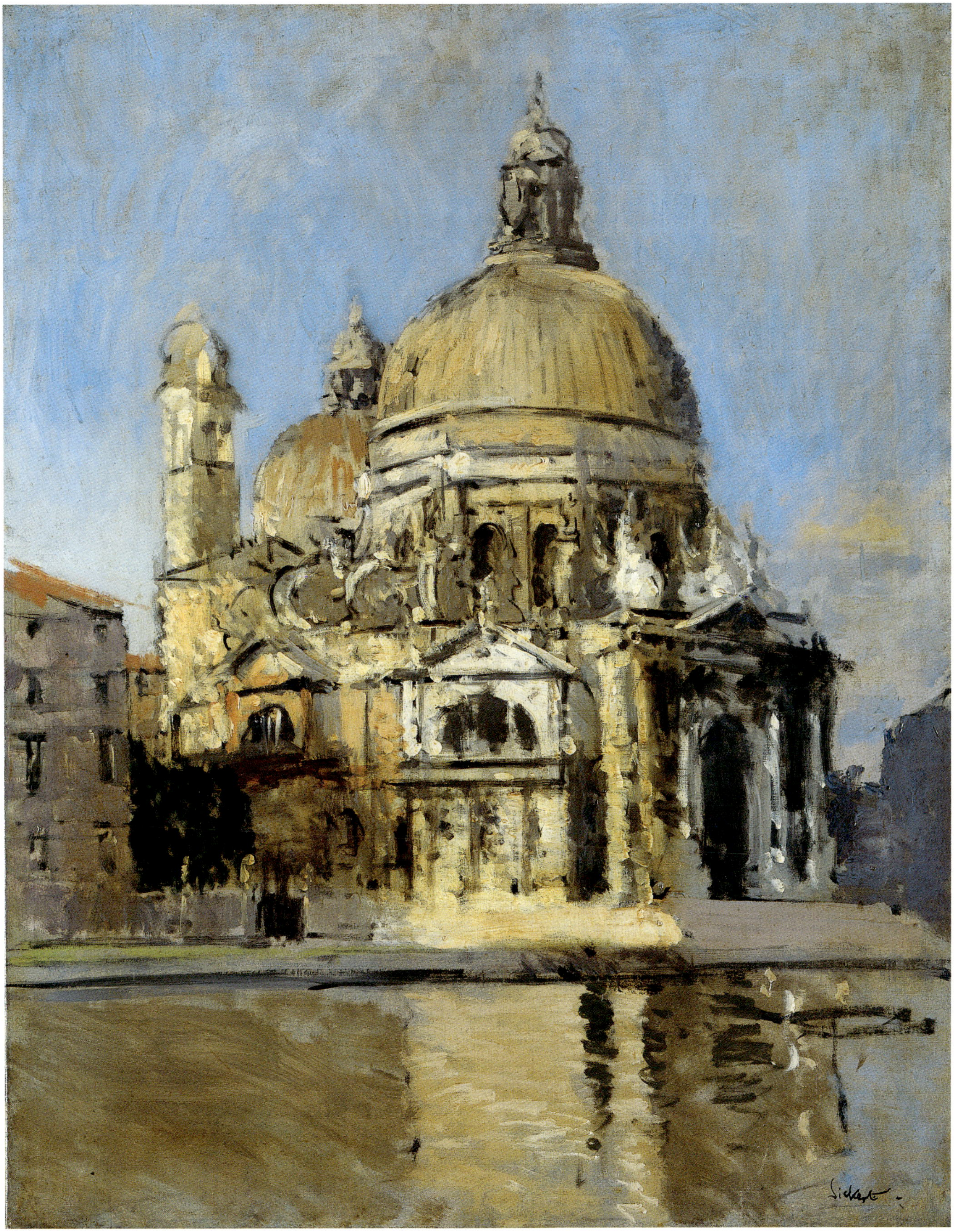

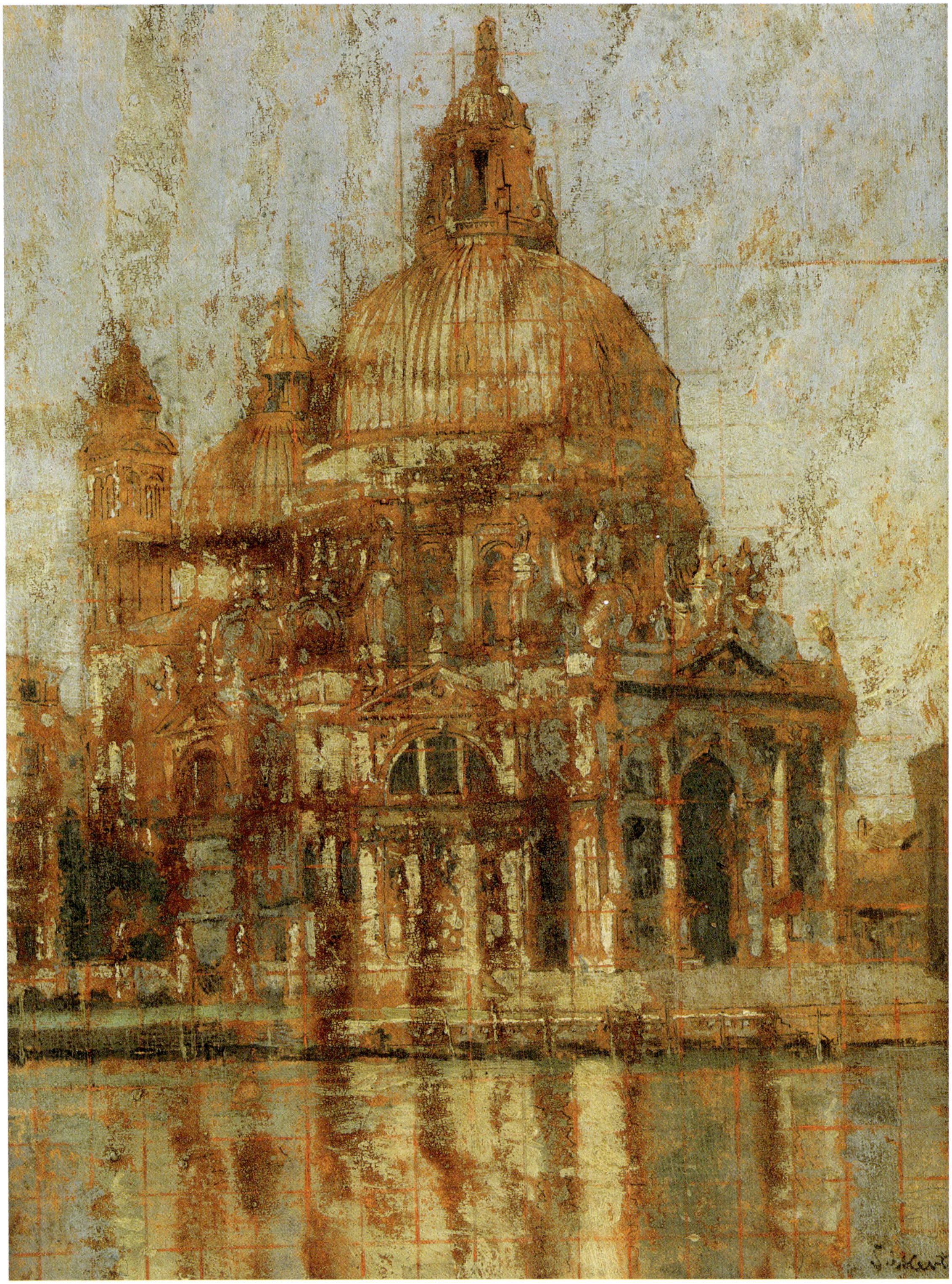

18
Santa Maria della Salute
*c.*1901
Oil on panel, 23.5 x 19 cm
Private Collection, courtesy of
Offer Waterman & Co., London

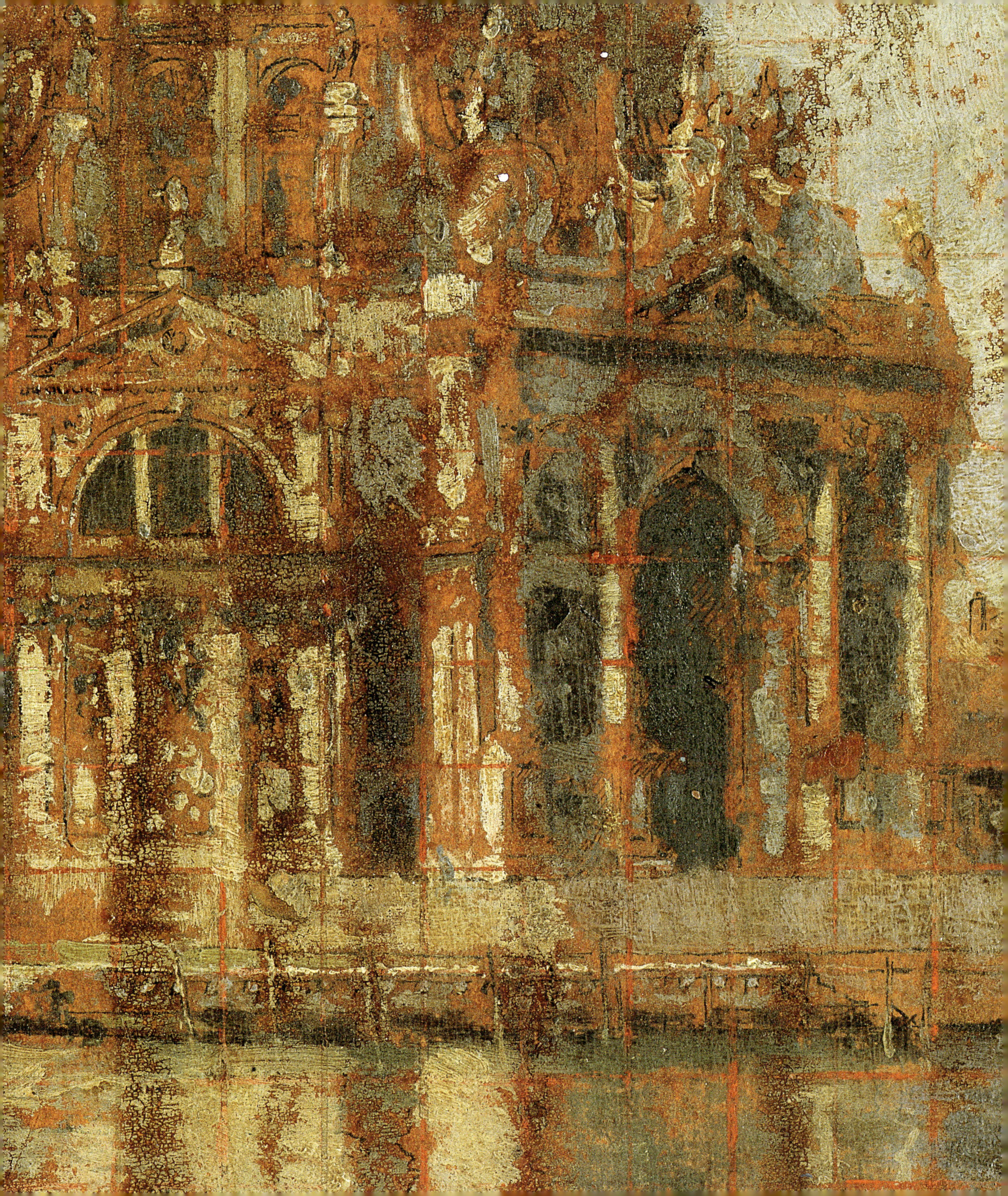

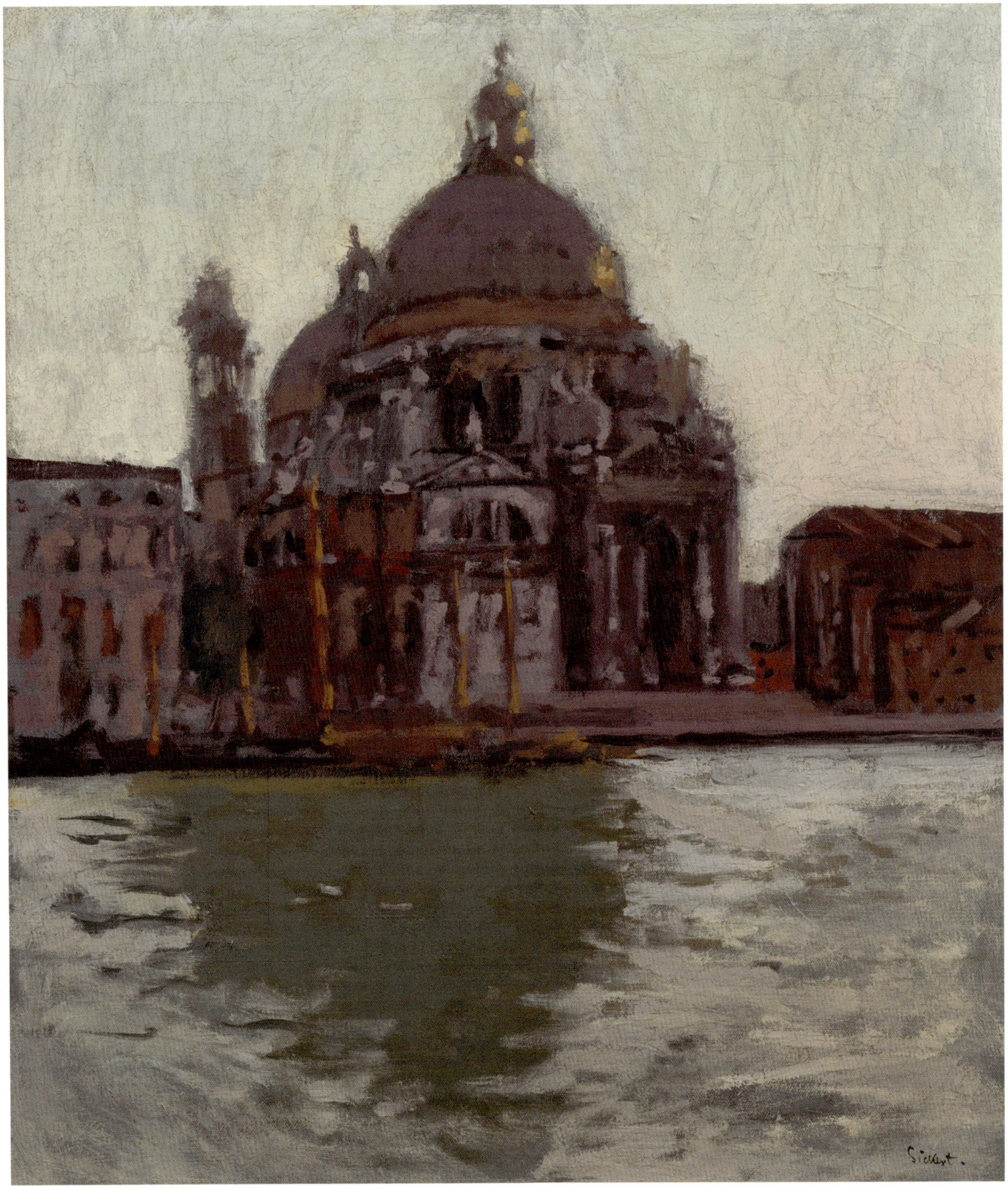

19
Venice: La Salute
c.1901
Oil on canvas, 54.6 x 45.7 cm
Richard Green, London

20
The Rialto Bridge
c.1901
Oil on canvas, 61 x 50.8 cm
Courtesy of Hazlitt
Holland-Hibbert

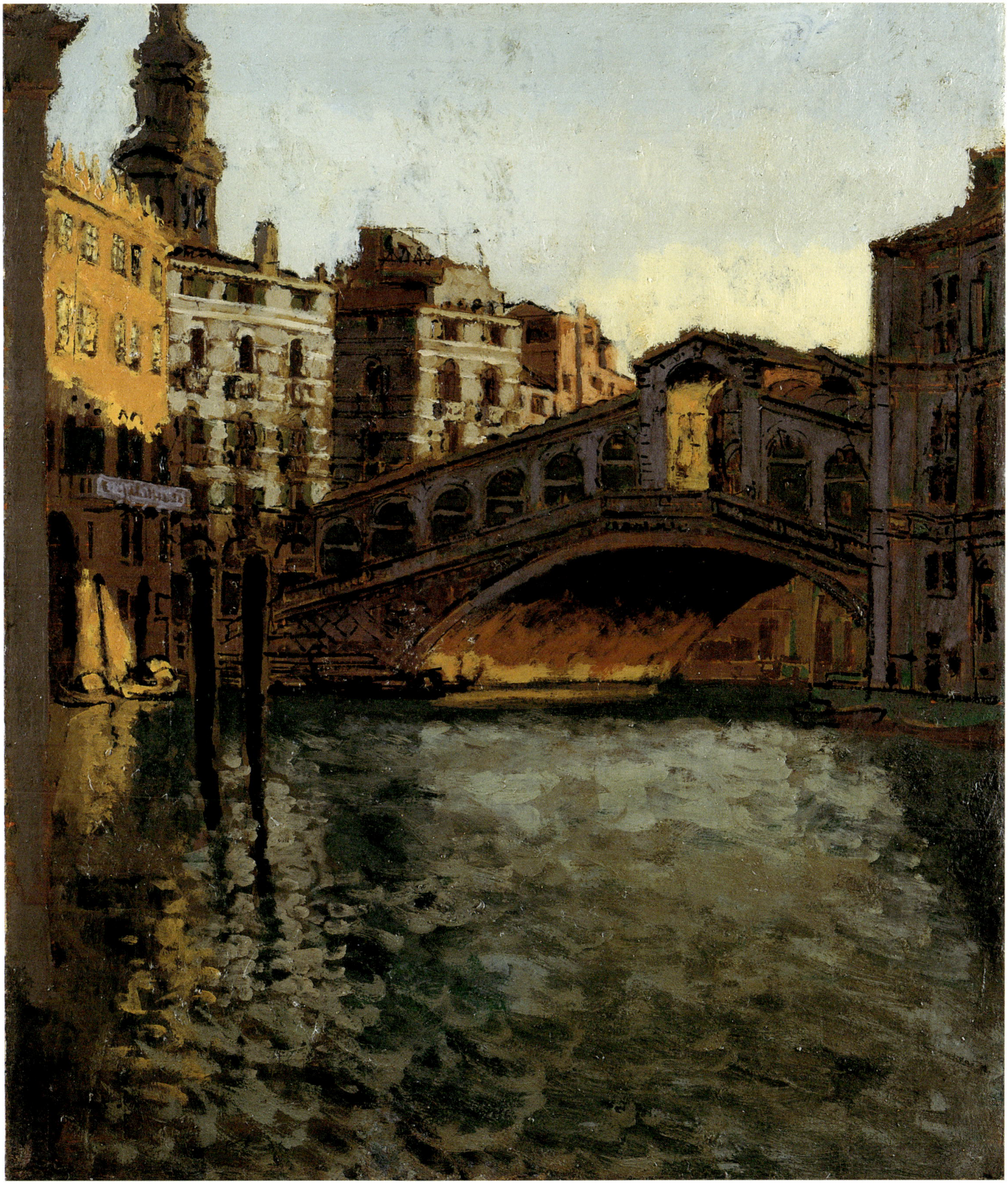

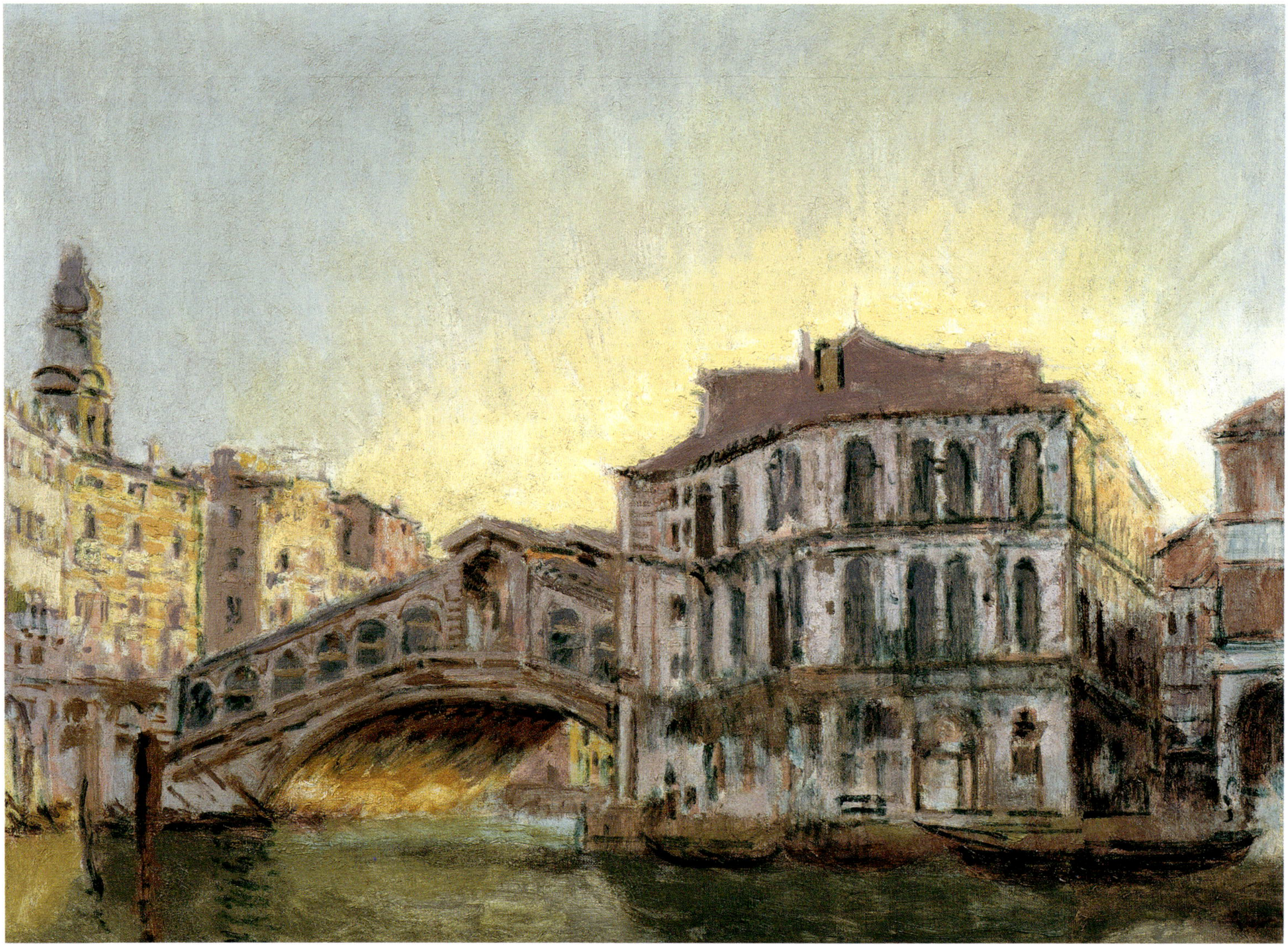

21
The Rialto Bridge and Palazzo dei Camerlenghi
*c.*1895–96
Oil on canvas, 55.9 x 74.3 cm
Private Collection

22
The Rialto Bridge and Palazzo dei Camerlenghi
*c.*1895–96
Oil on canvas, 61 x 50.8 cm
Private Collection

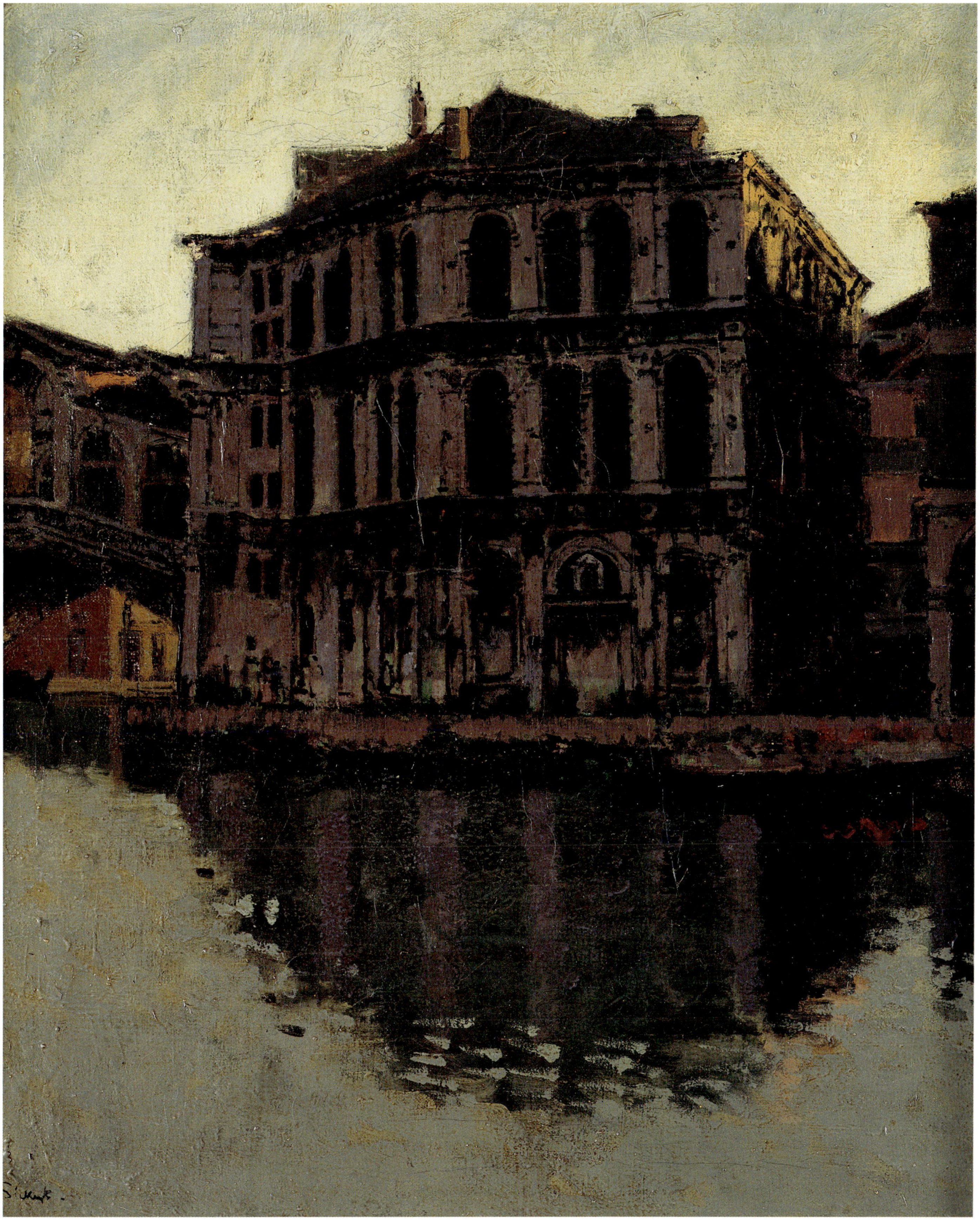

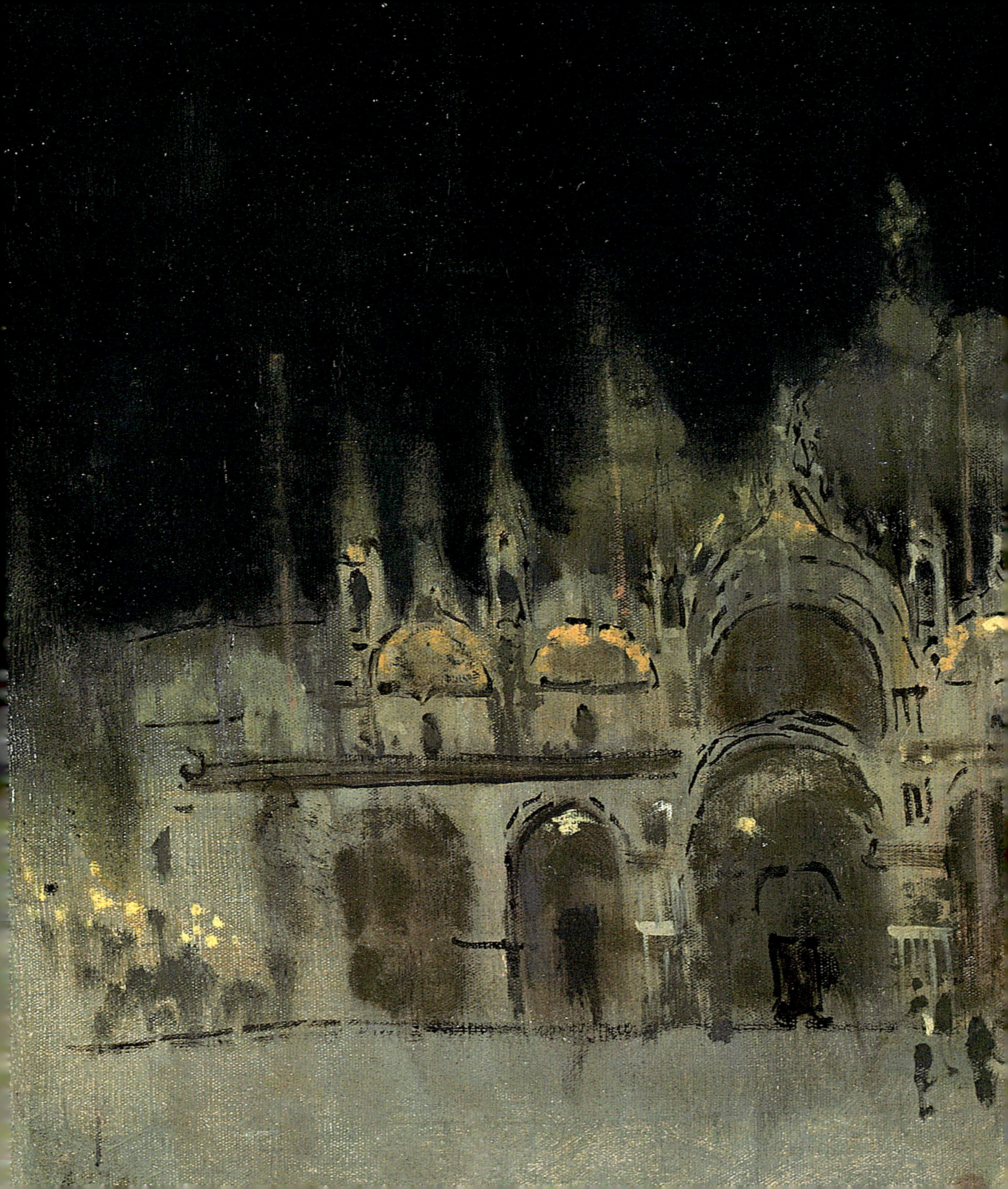

2 NOCTURNES

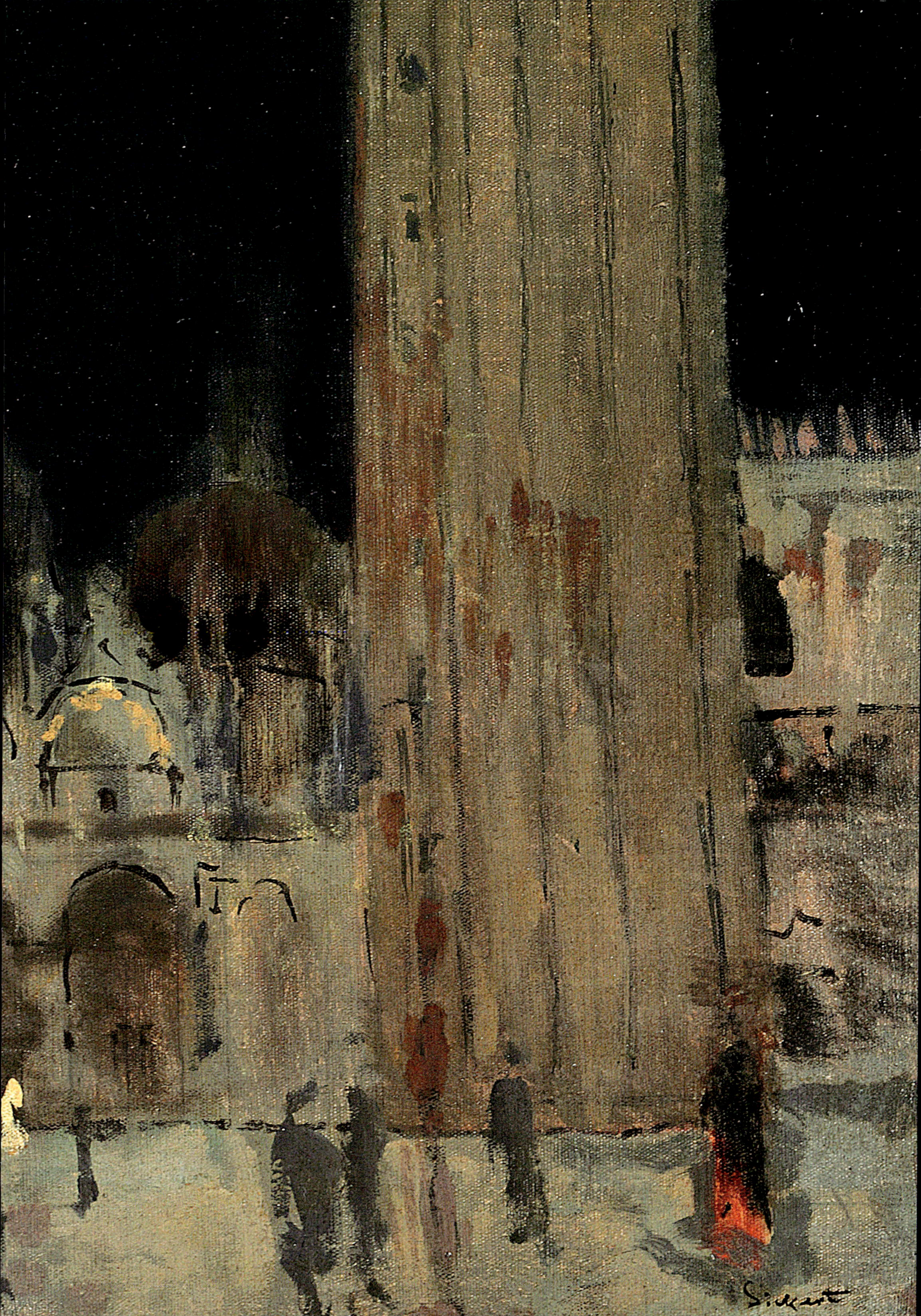

The Campanile, Venice
c.1901
(cat. 28, detail)

It had been Sickert's former master James McNeill Whistler who had first introduced the musical term 'nocturne' into the title of his paintings. It implied that, like music, the picture should act on the viewer's emotions directly, without the intervention of any narrative or explicit meaning. Sickert took up the practice in Venice and painted a number of night or dusk scenes of the city and lagoon. They are among the most beautiful and lyrical pictures he made there. In one sense they are a logical extension of the sequence of studies Sickert had made showing St Mark's under different effects of light. But the darkness and deep shadow create a whole new genre of cityscape that emphasises an aura of mystery and expressive beauty in night-time Venice. One source of inspiration for these nocturnes could have been the watercolours J. M. W. Turner made of Venice by night, which Sickert may have seen in the National Gallery in London. But principally it was the influence of Whistler, who had pioneered this form and made it his own, that prompted Sickert to realise the potential of the nocturne. There may even have been an element of competition in choosing a subject type that had been pioneered by Whistler and making it his own.

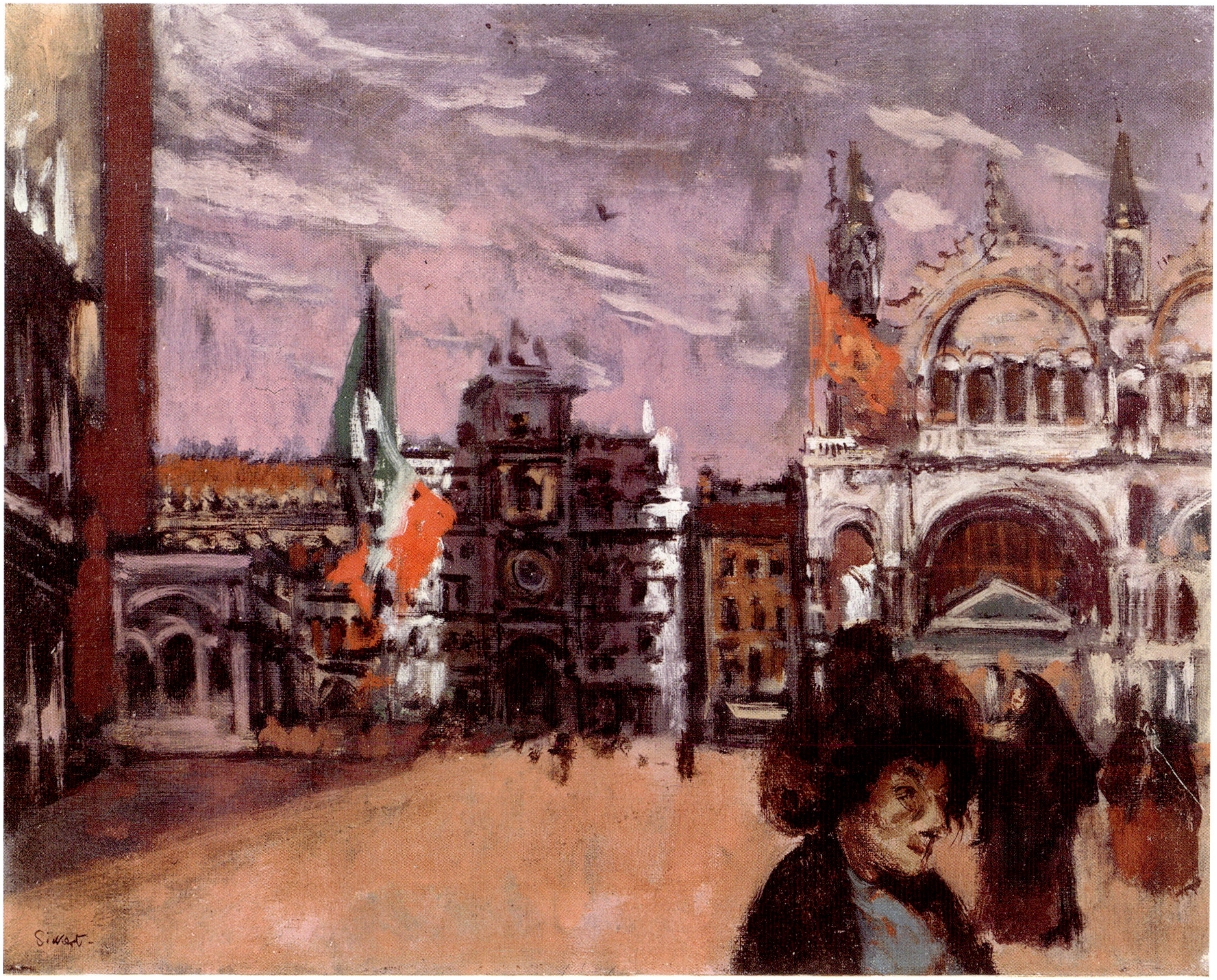

23
Piazzetta di San Marco
1900
Oil on canvas, 40.7 x 50.8 cm
Laing Art Gallery, Tyne &
Wear Museums

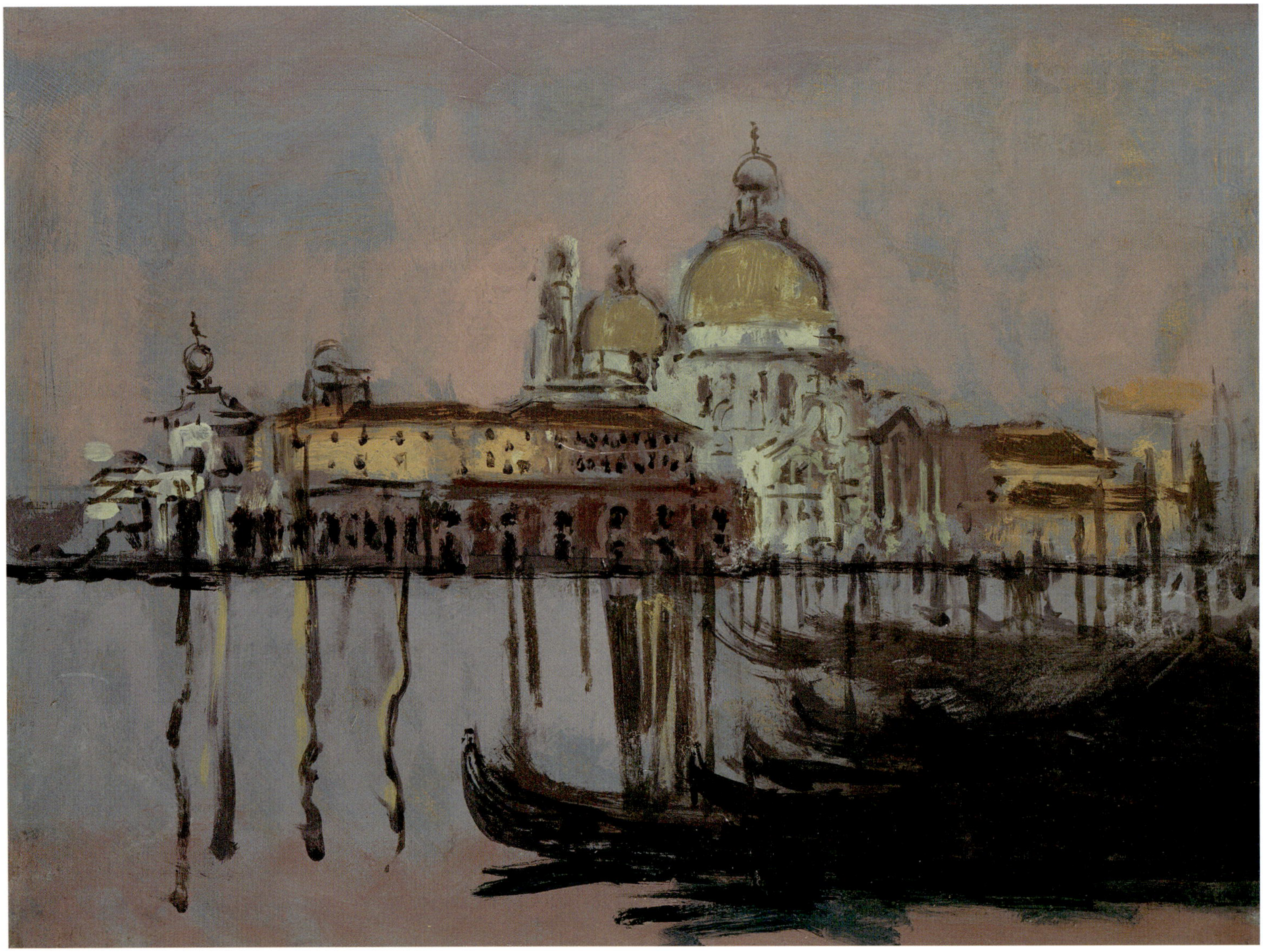

24
The Dogana and Santa Maria della Salute
*c.*1896
Oil on panel, 32 x 41 cm
Private Collection

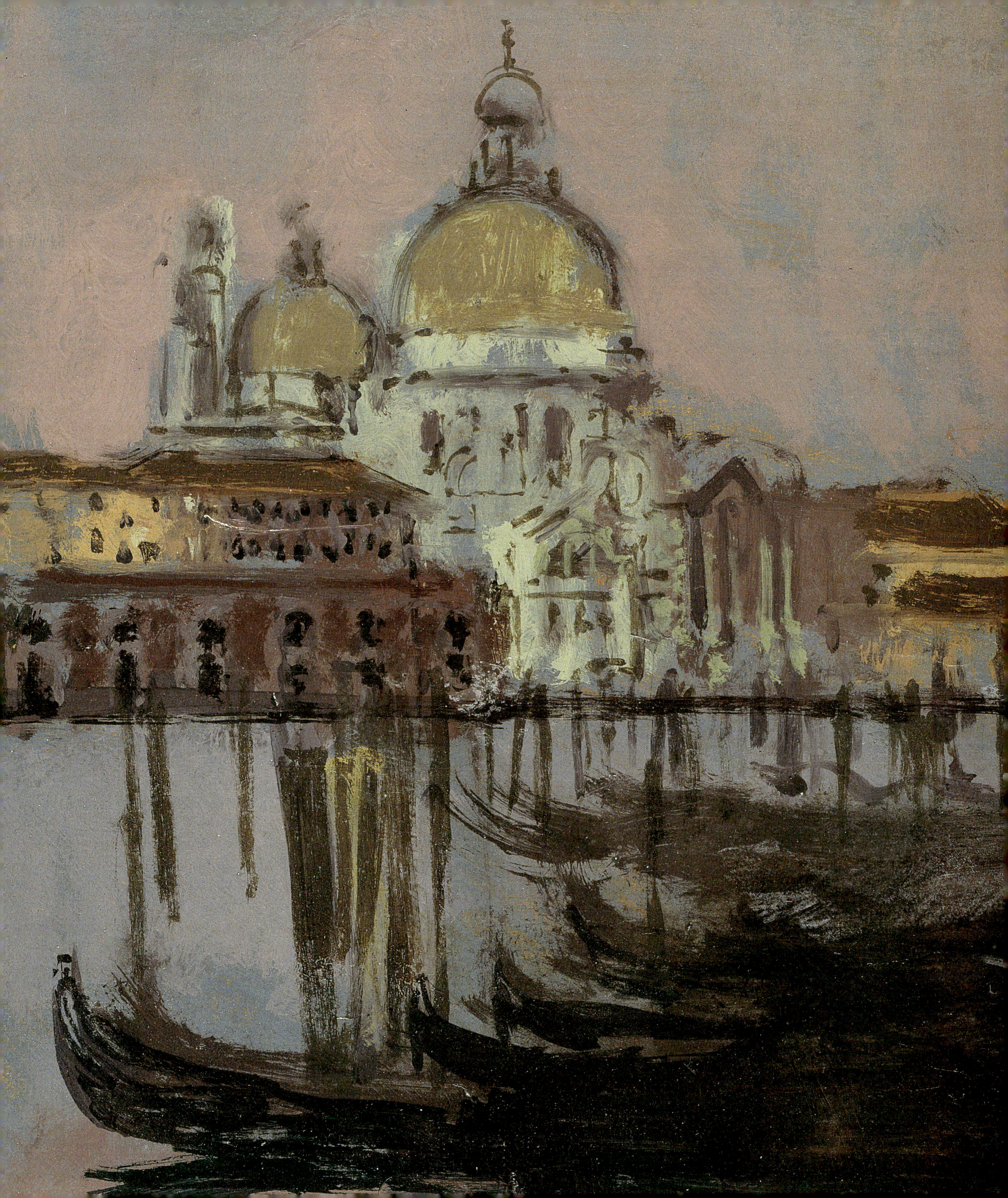

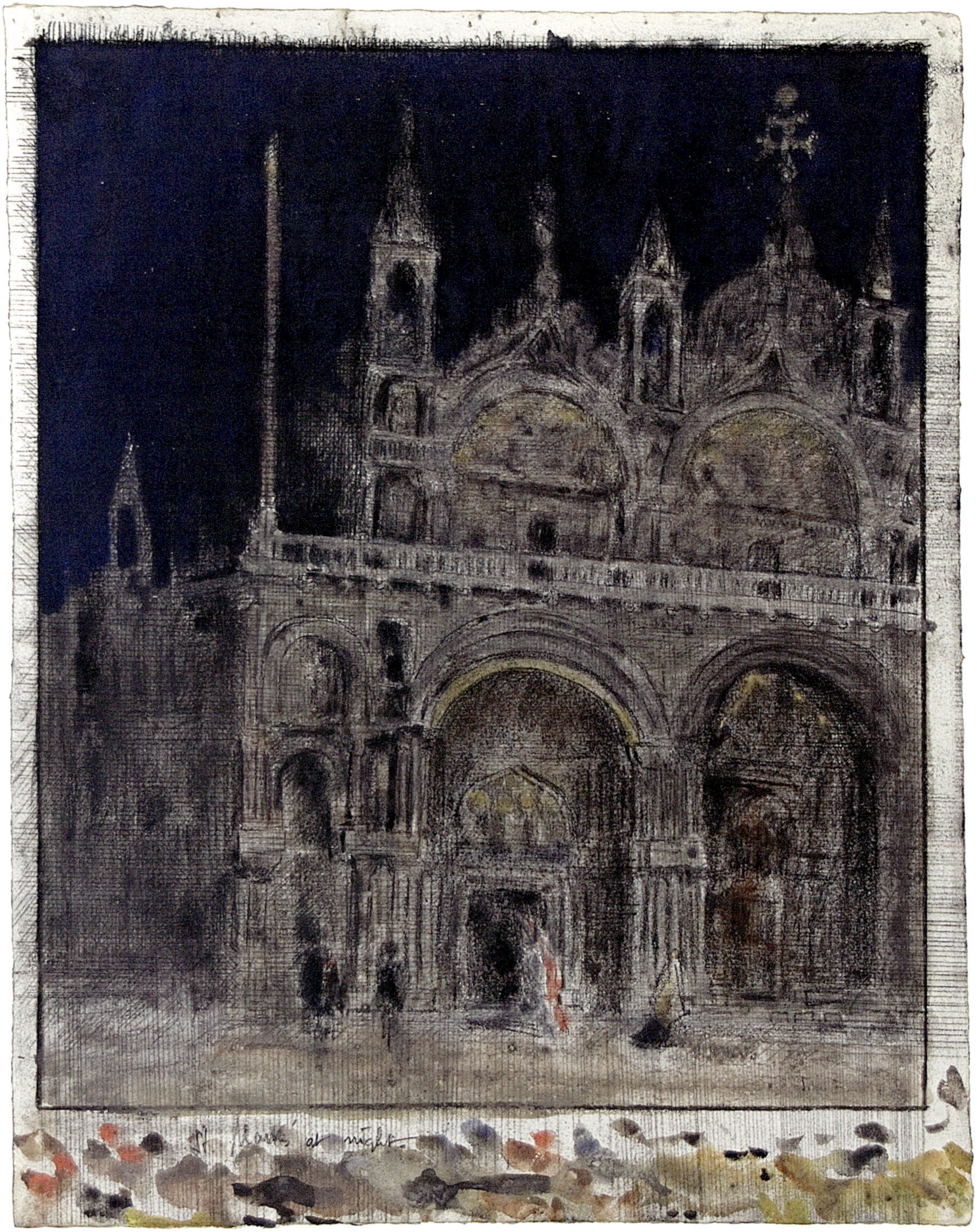

25
St Mark's at Night
1901
Black chalk, pencil and watercolour, 41.9 x 34.3 cm
New Walk Museum & Art Gallery, Leicester

26
San Marco by Night
1901
Oil on canvas, 78 x 66 cm
UK Government Art Collection, London

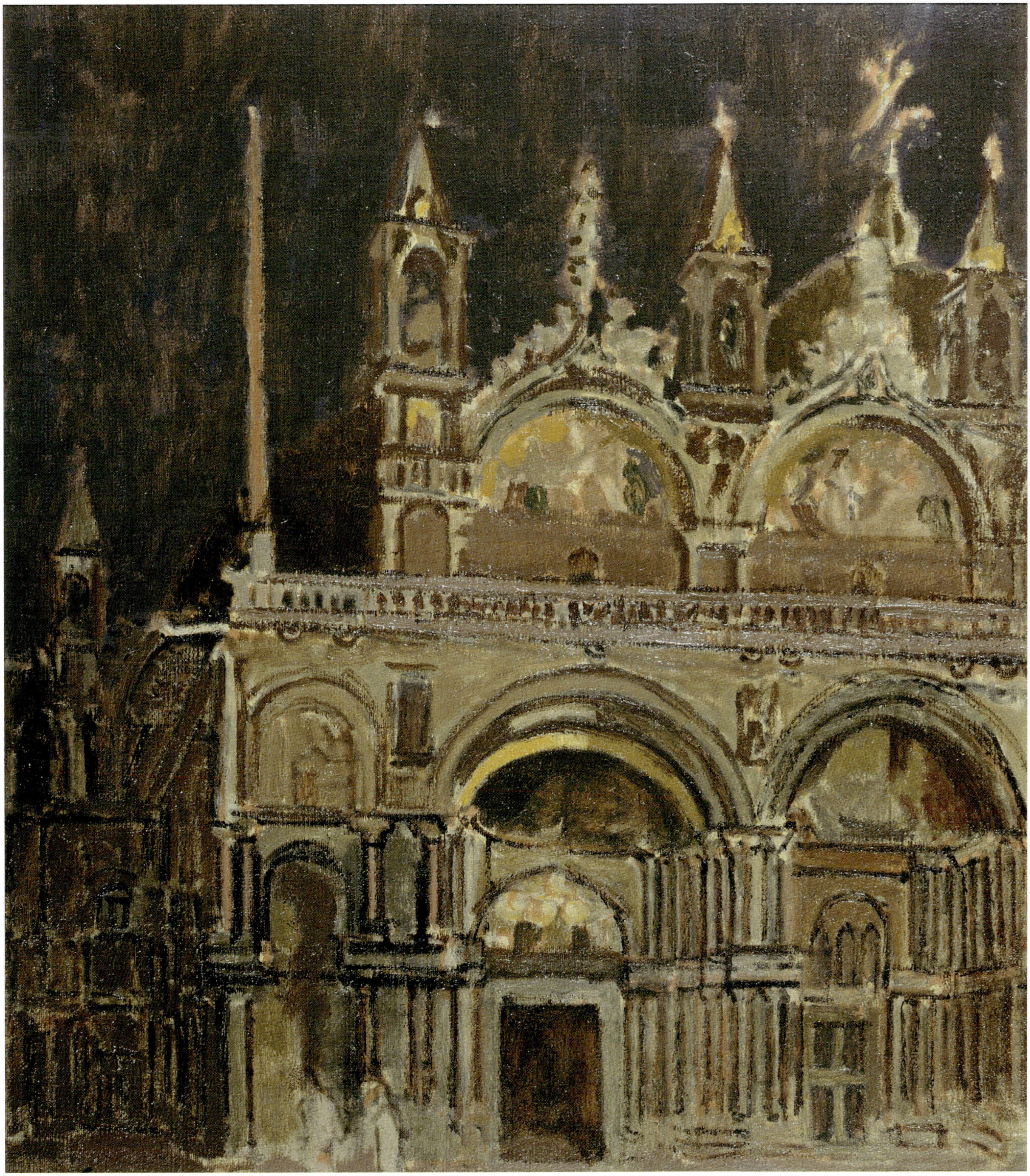

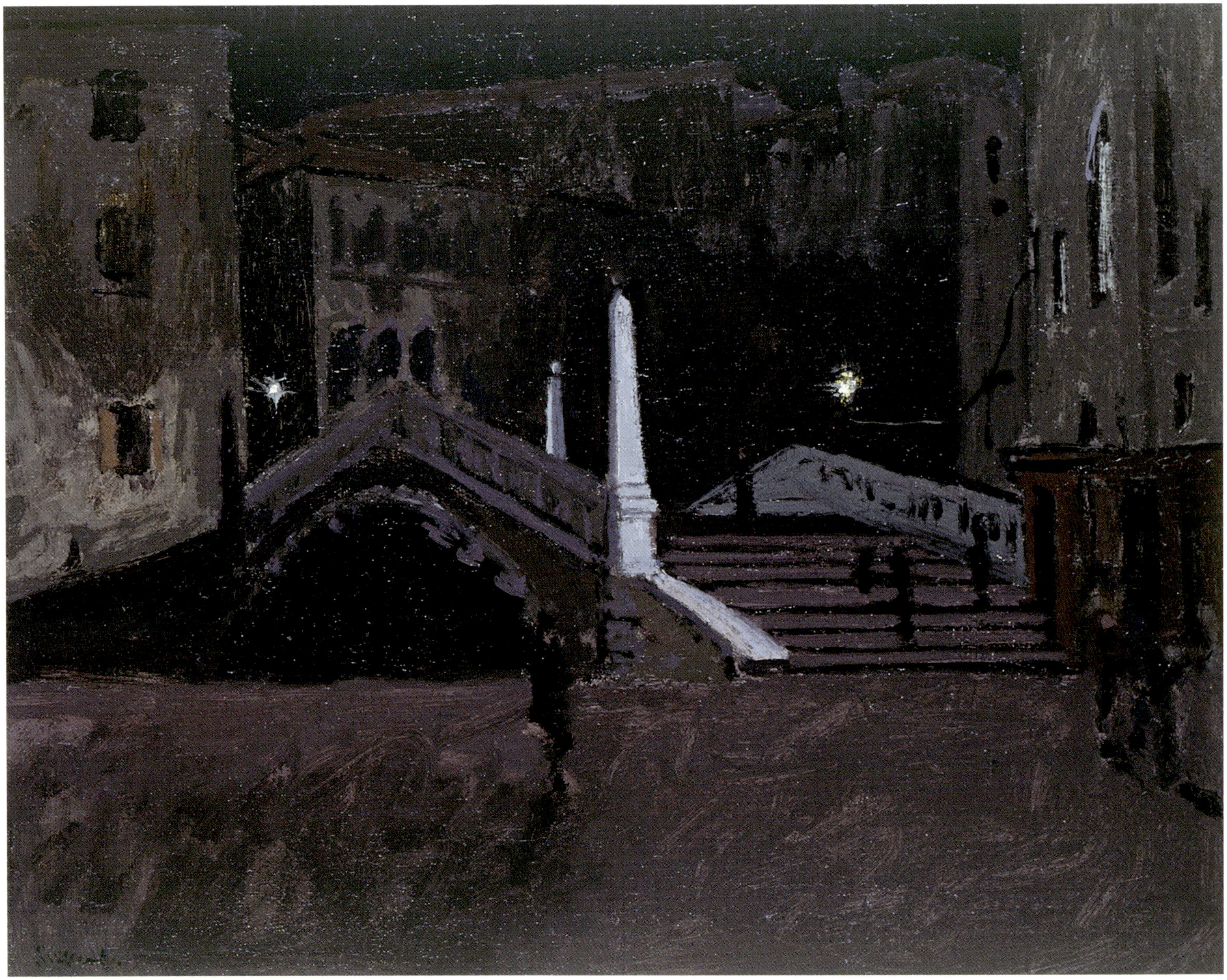

27
Ponte della Guglie sul Cannaregio
c.1896
Oil on canvas, 38 x 45.7 cm
Enrique Foster Gittes and Lois Severini

28
The Campanile, Venice
c.1901
Oil on canvas, 81.3 x 61 cm
Private Collection

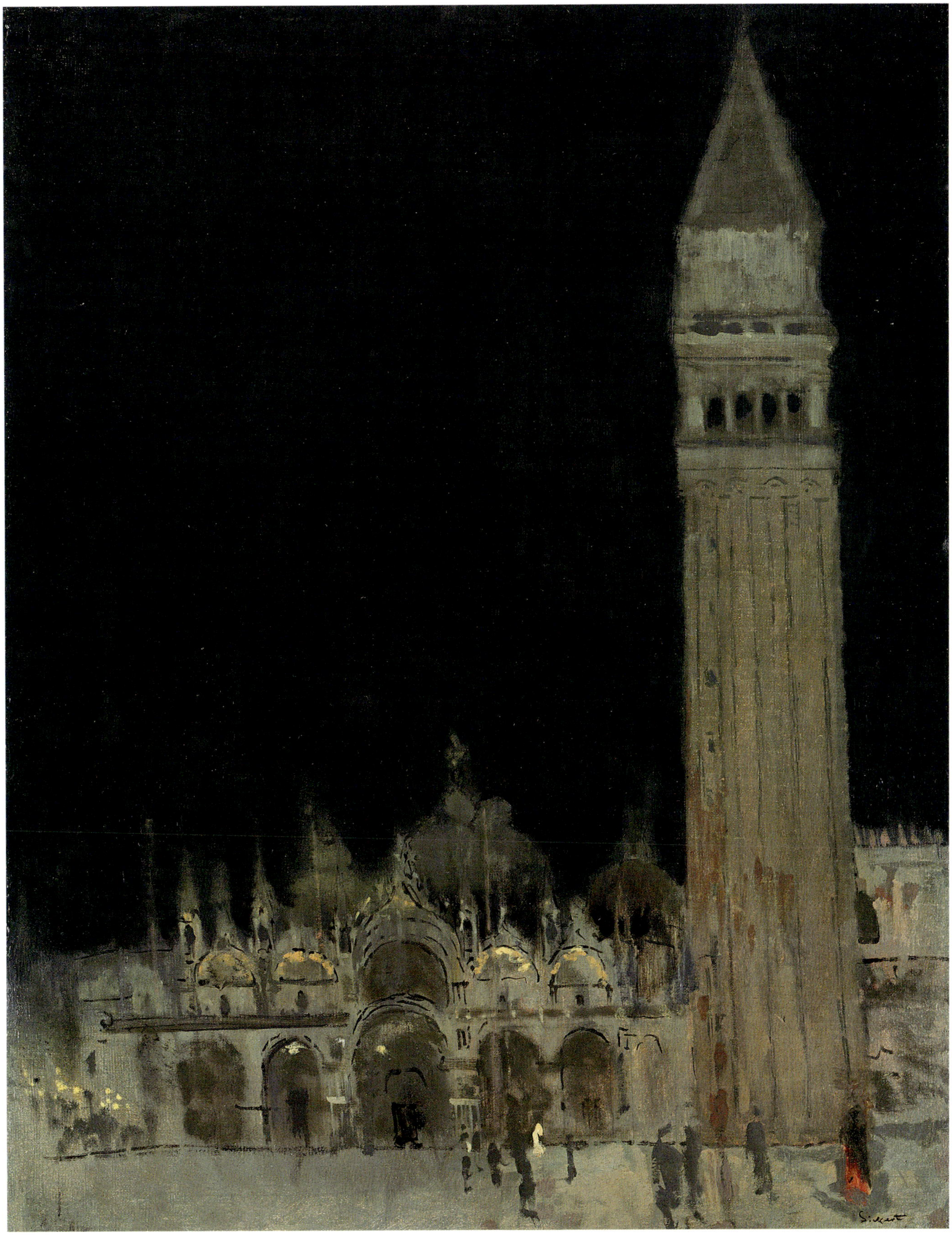

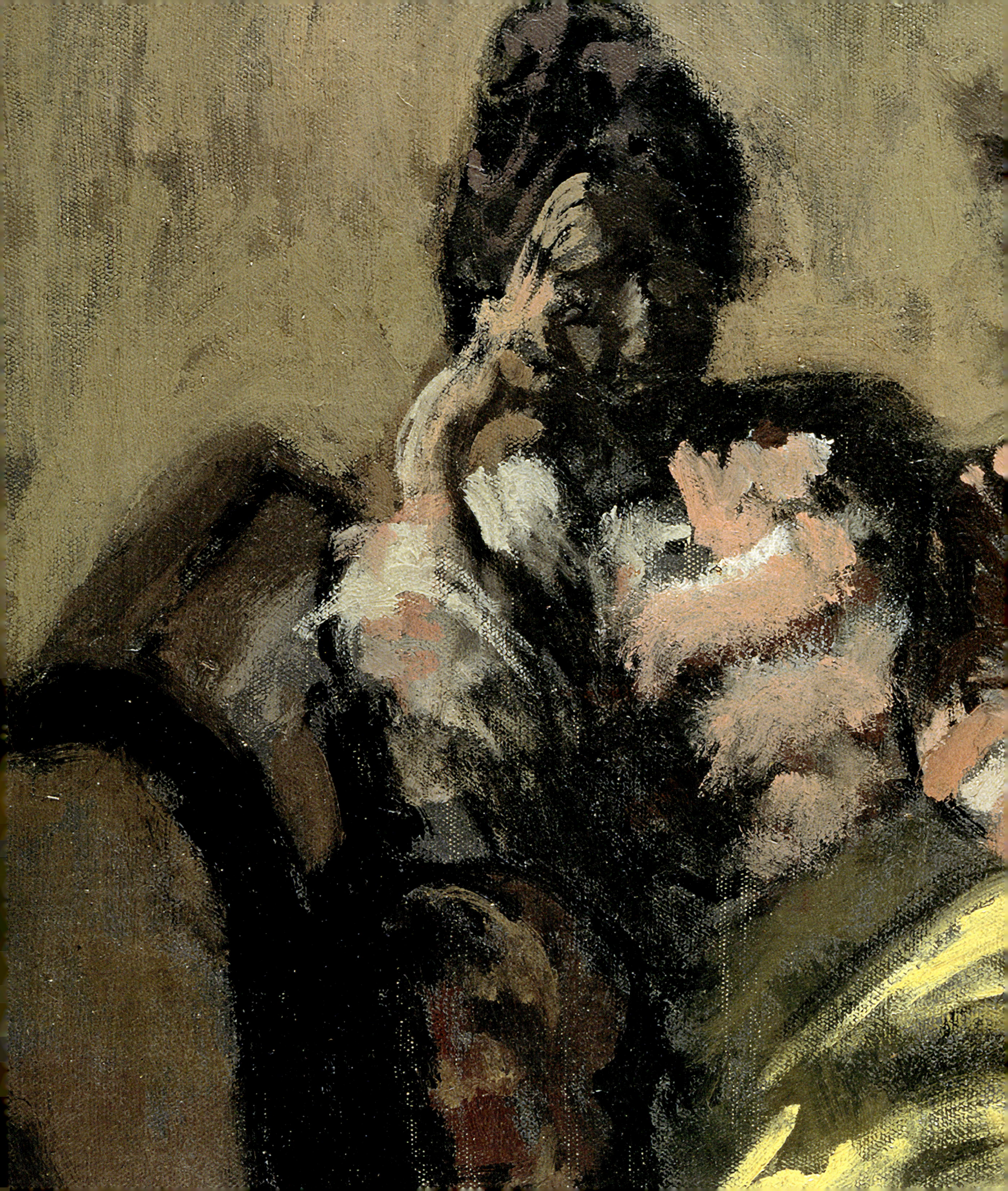

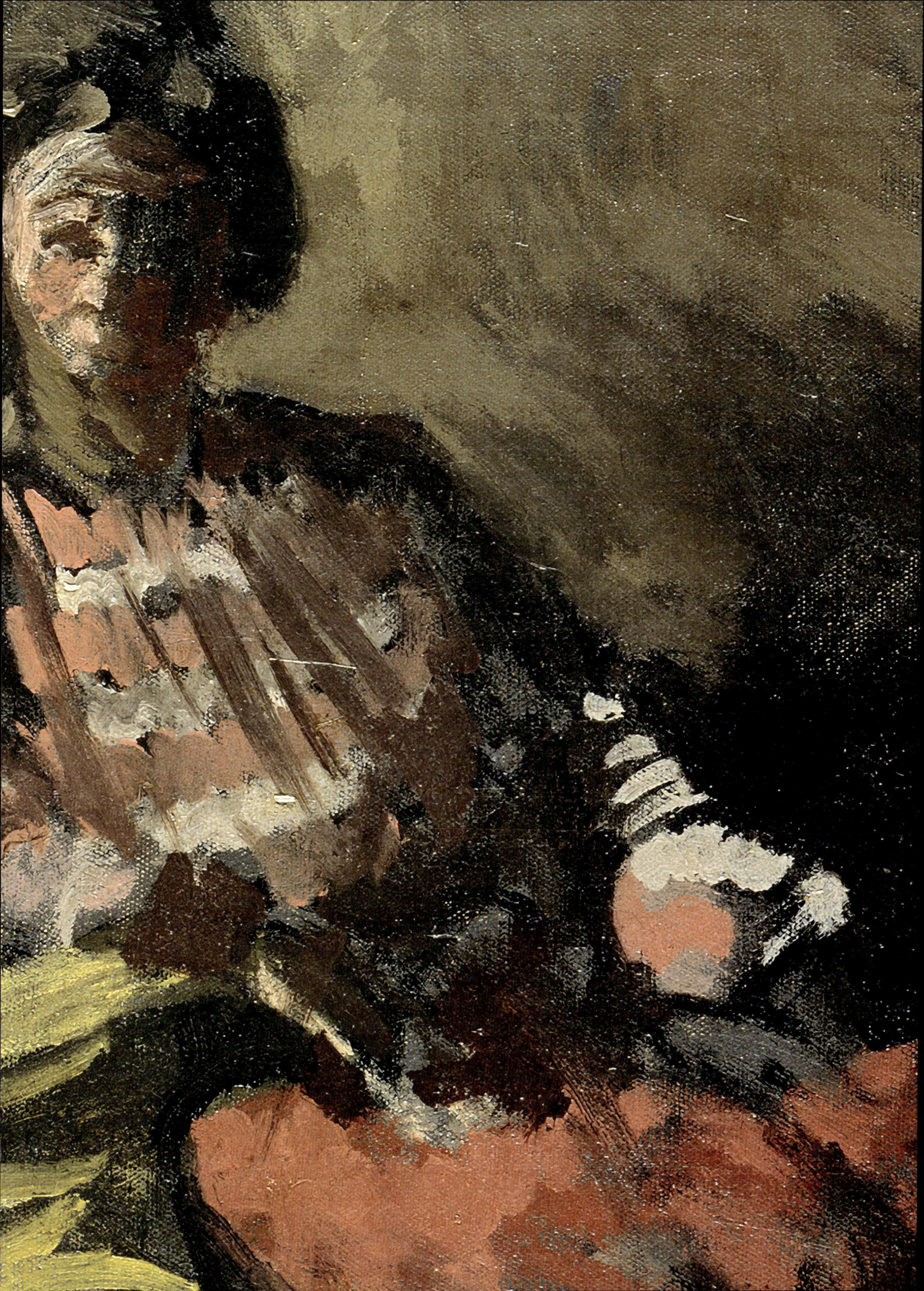

3

PORTRAITS AND FIGURES

Two Women on a Sofa – Le Tose
1903–04
(cat. 56, detail)

In all his visits to Venice up to 1903–04, Sickert had focussed on painting architecture. But November and December 1903 were the wettest months on record and the city flooded. Sickert tried to continue with a pair of fisherman's waders, but eventually accepted defeat and moved indoors. He switched the focus of his art to painting a pair of local working-class women, La Giuseppina and Carolina del'Acqua. There was strong interest among the picture-buying public not only in scenes of Venice itself, but in the people who inhabited it. In an age of bourgeois conformity, the Venetians' distinctive costume, dialect and customs were all rich sources of interest and attraction. The plethora of English guide books on the city that appeared around this time all drew attention to the picturesque nature of Venice's inhabitants. In this, there was a certain patronising quality that emphasised their exoticism and otherness, and turned them into objects of ethnographic comparison.

Sickert painted his female models directly, asking them to adopt relaxed, natural poses that they held for an hour. He delighted in their banter and vulgar stories, and enjoyed the rich vitality of their lives. The pictures were painted in Sickert's studio, in a top-floor flat above a bar. Although they look entirely natural, they are in fact heavily contrived, and Sickert used his models like actors on a stage. Any narrative is suppressed in favour simply of mood and atmosphere, and capturing the fall of light on the figure. Sickert painted the women both singly and together, developing scenes of them chatting or lounging together on the bed. We are offered snapshots of their lives, albeit contrived by Sickert himself.

In addition, Sickert painted more conventional straightforward portraits, such as that of Signor de Rossi (cat. 31), the proprietor of the trattoria Giorgione di San Silvestro in which he took his lunch; it was reputedly de Rossi who provided the female models. Sickert also made drawings of the other customers and of the restaurant itself. Other portraits were daring and highly innovative in their conception. Sickert's painting of his friend Israel Zangwill (cat. 30) showed him in profile hard up against the picture space. In the background is Venice's Jewish Ghetto, an allusion to Zangwill's novel *Children of the Ghetto* (1892) about life in the East End of London, which overnight turned him into a literary celebrity. Sickert based the background on his small Venetian oil sketch of the Jewish Ghetto (cat. 12). This use of a profile against an architectural background was repeated in the self-portrait drawing he made of himself (cat. 29), showing the artist standing on the Ponte della Paglia, the Bridge of Sighs visible above his head, perhaps symbolically locating himself between the Doge's Palace and the Republic's prison.

29
Self-Portrait
1897
Ink and wash on buff paper, 23.9 x 18.4 cm
Mark Samuels Lasner, on loan to the University of Delaware Library

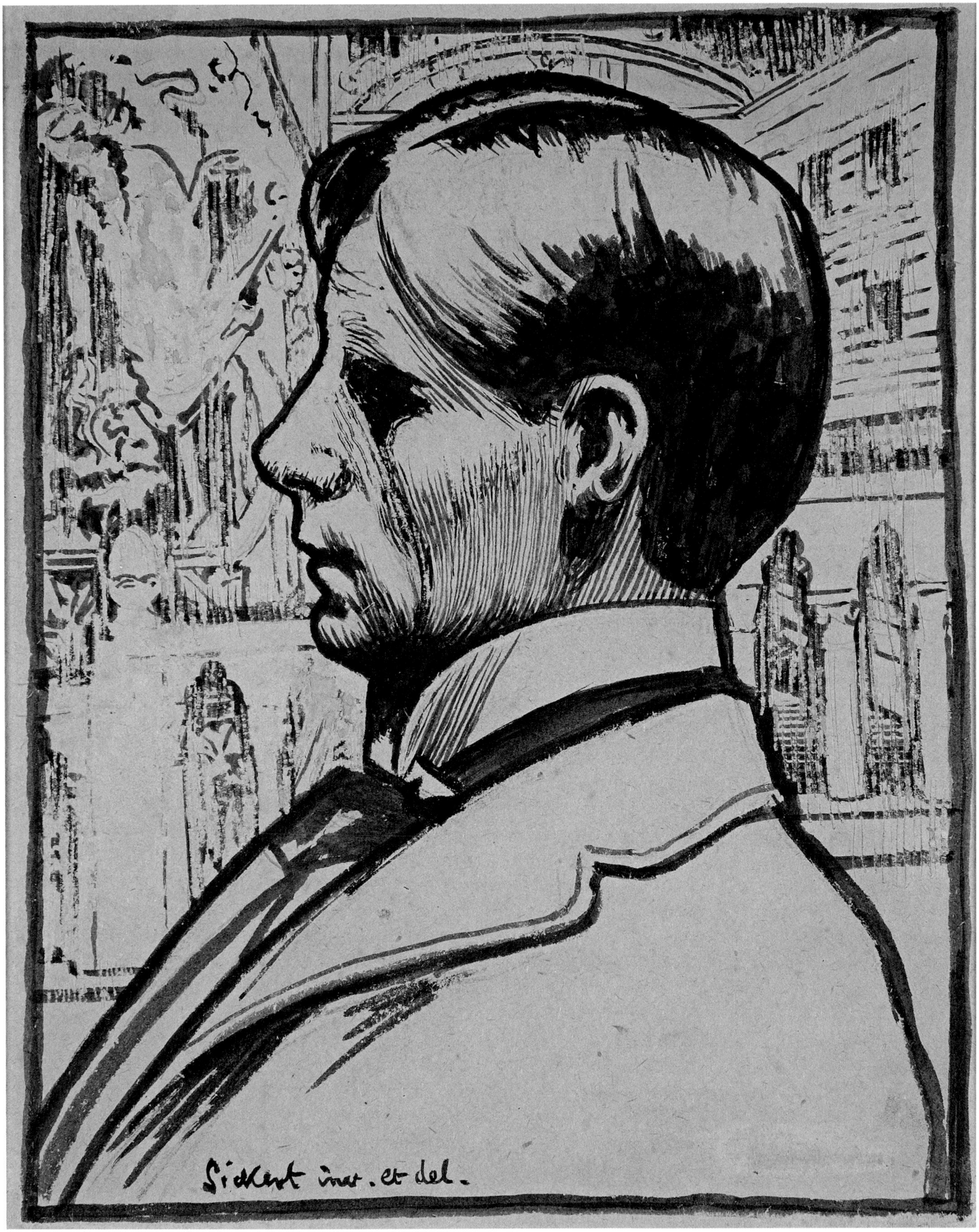
Sickert inv. et del.

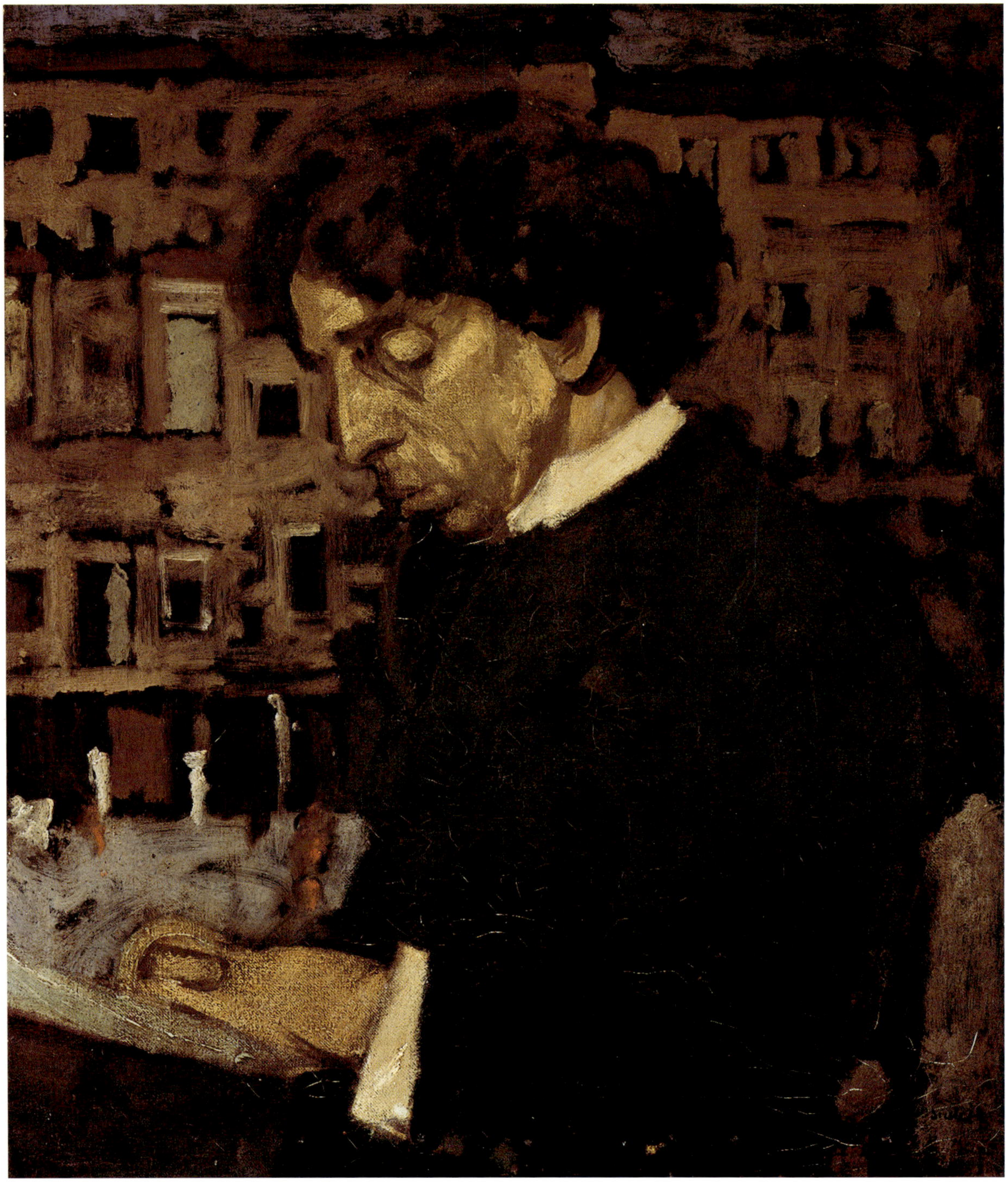

30
Israel Zangwill
*c.*1896–98
Oil on canvas, 59.7 x 50.8 cm
Scottish National Gallery of Modern Art, Edinburgh

31
Signor de Rossi
1901
Oil on canvas, 54 x 44.1 cm
Hastings Museum & Art Gallery

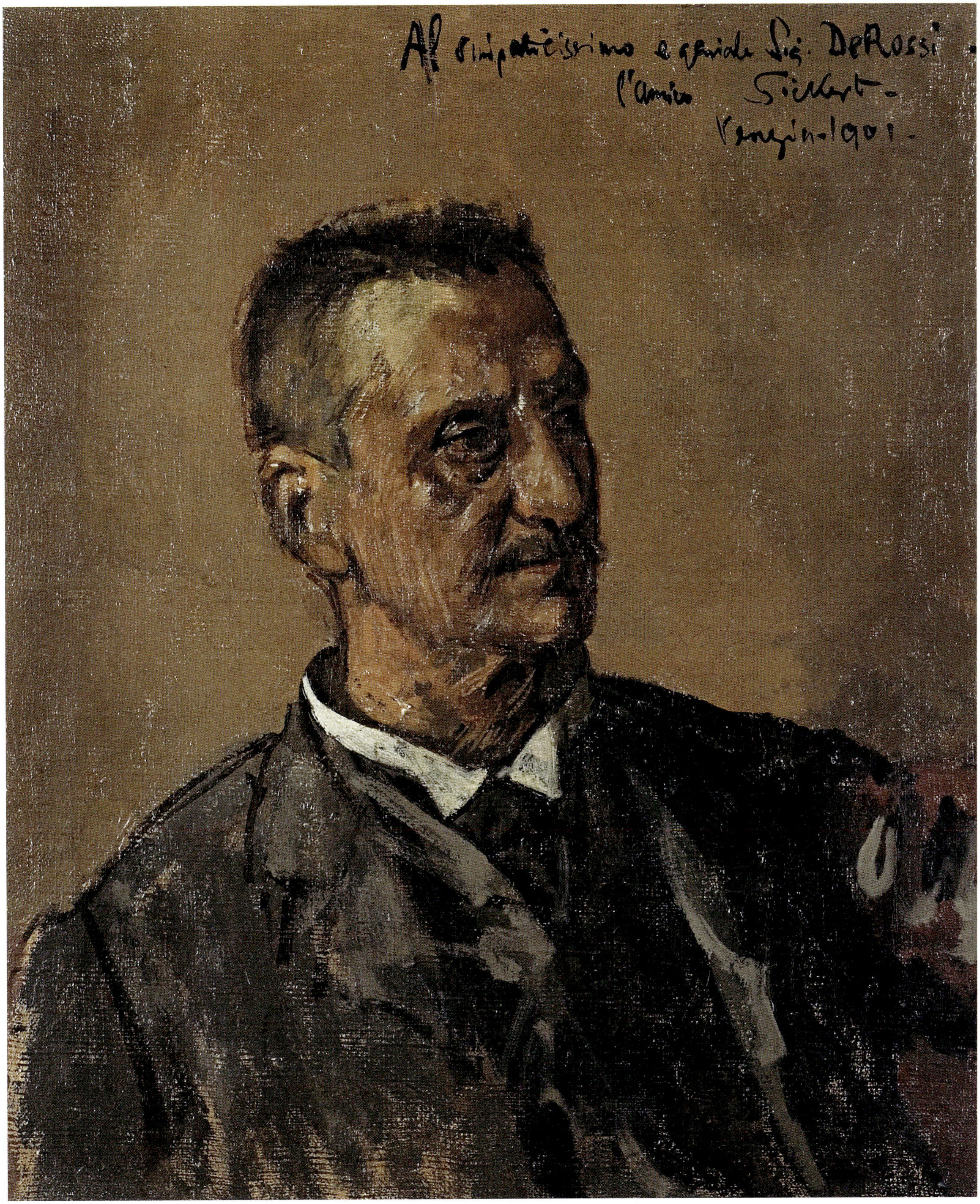

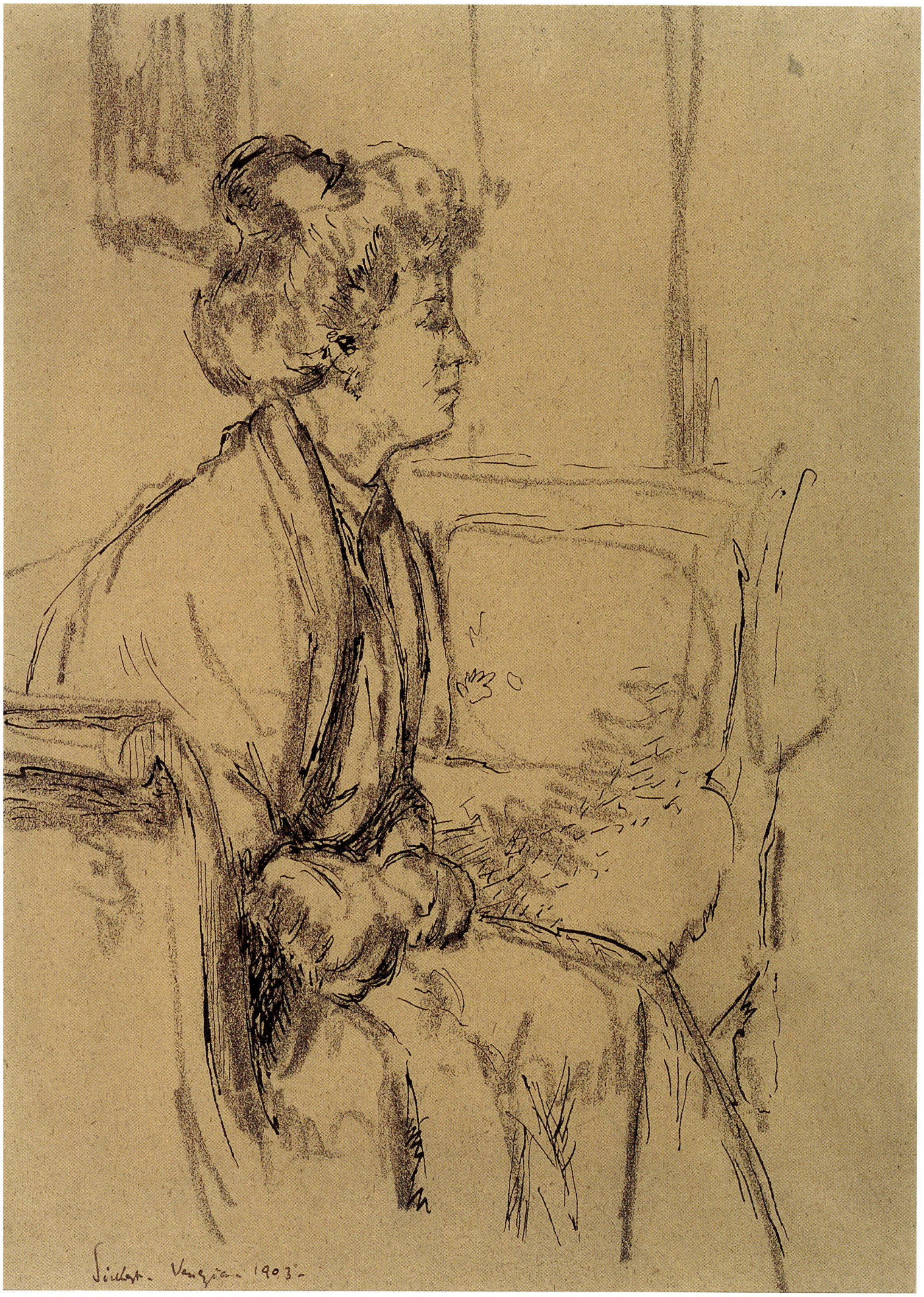

32
La Giuseppina
1903
Pen and blue ink, 29 x 20.9 cm
Manchester City Galleries

33
Four Drawings of
La Giuseppina
1903–04
Pencil on buff paper, 30 x 22 cm
Private Collection

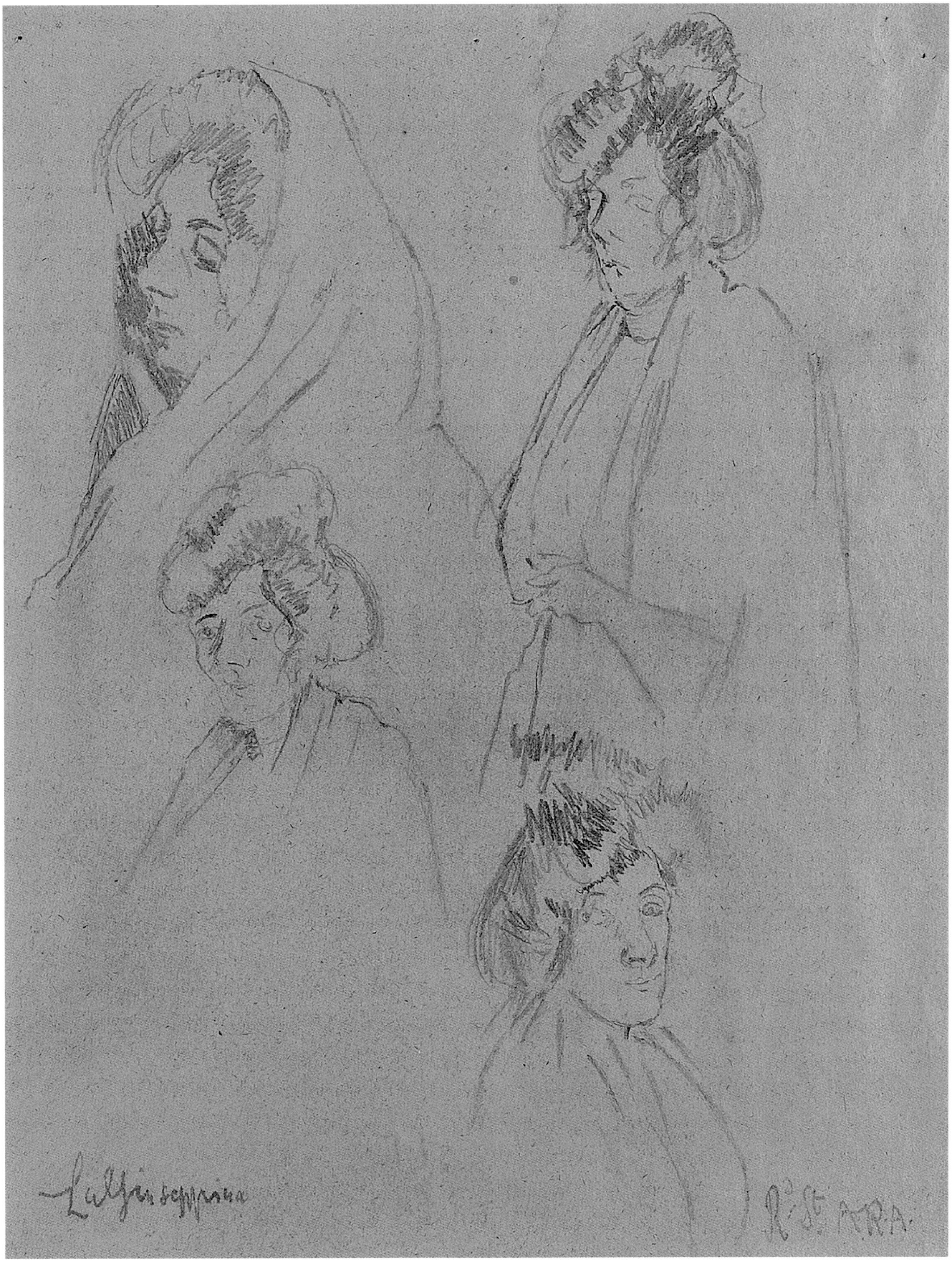

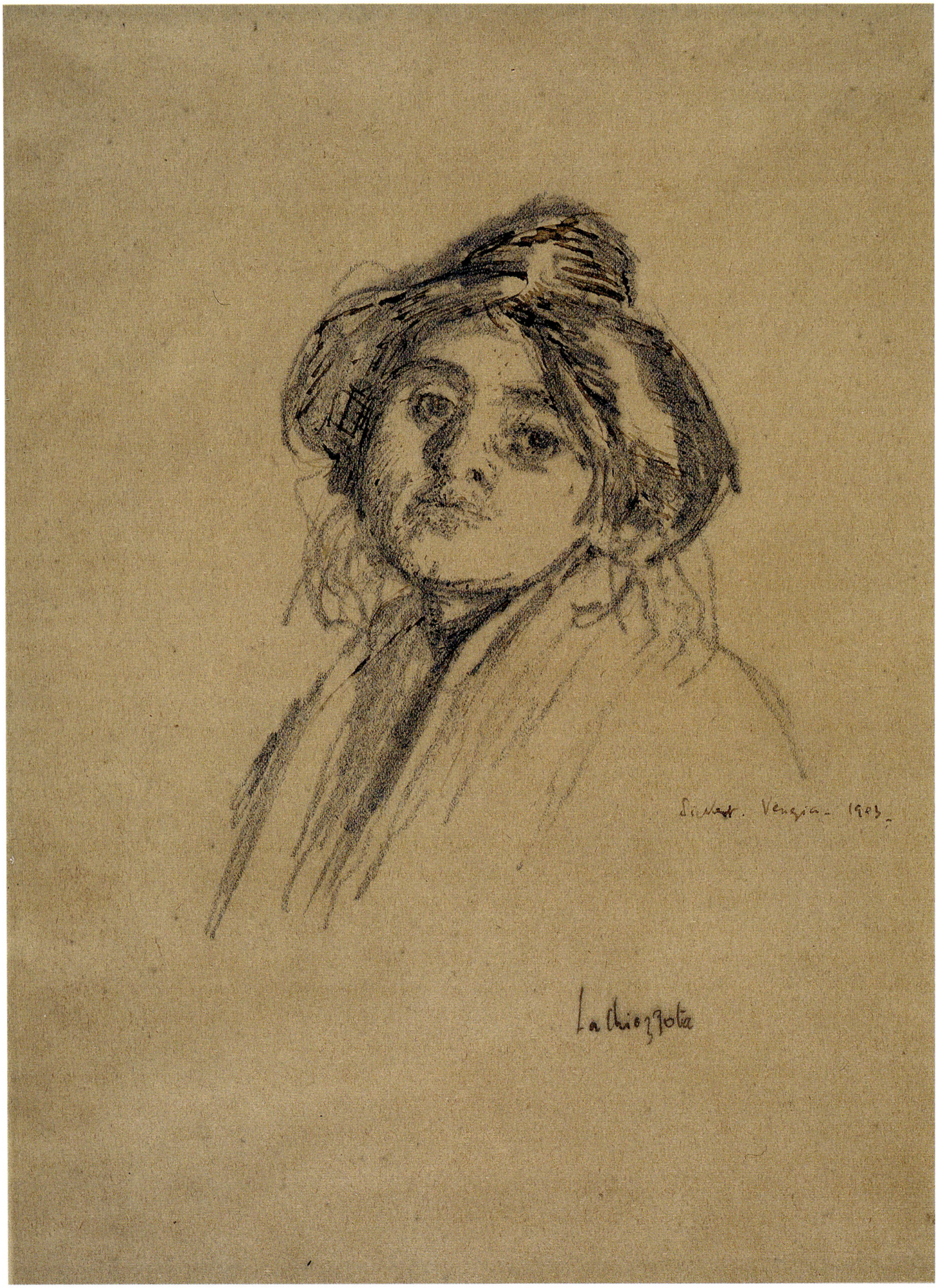

34
La Chiozzotta – Study for 'La Inez'
1903
Pencil, pen and ink,
31.8 x 22.8 cm
The Whitworth Art Gallery,
The University of Manchester

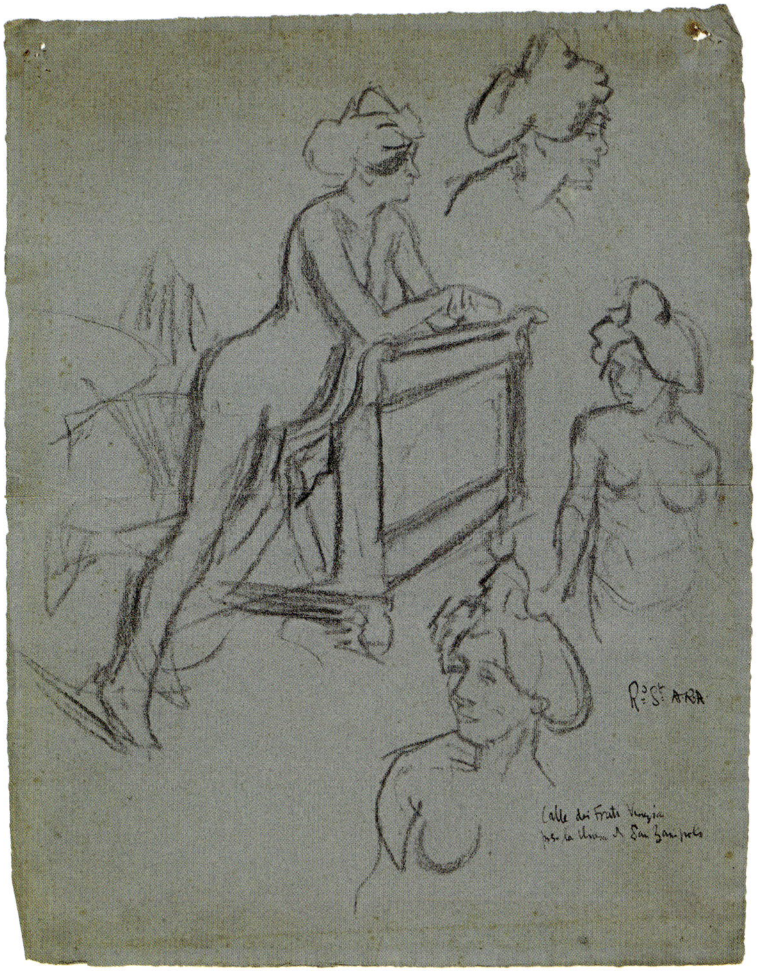

35
Nude Studies
1903–04
Charcoal on blue paper,
62 x 47.5 cm
Fitzwilliam Museum,
Cambridge

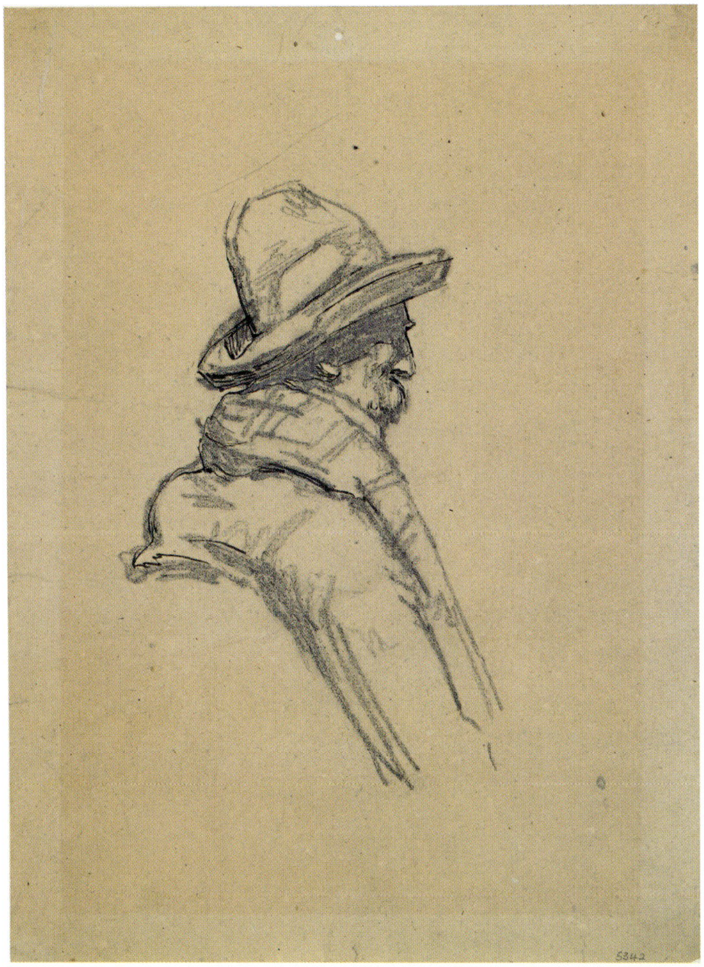

36
Man Wearing a Wide Brimmed Hat (The Candle Seller)
*c.*1903
Pencil on paper, 31.5 x 22.5 cm
National Museums Liverpool,
Walker Art Gallery

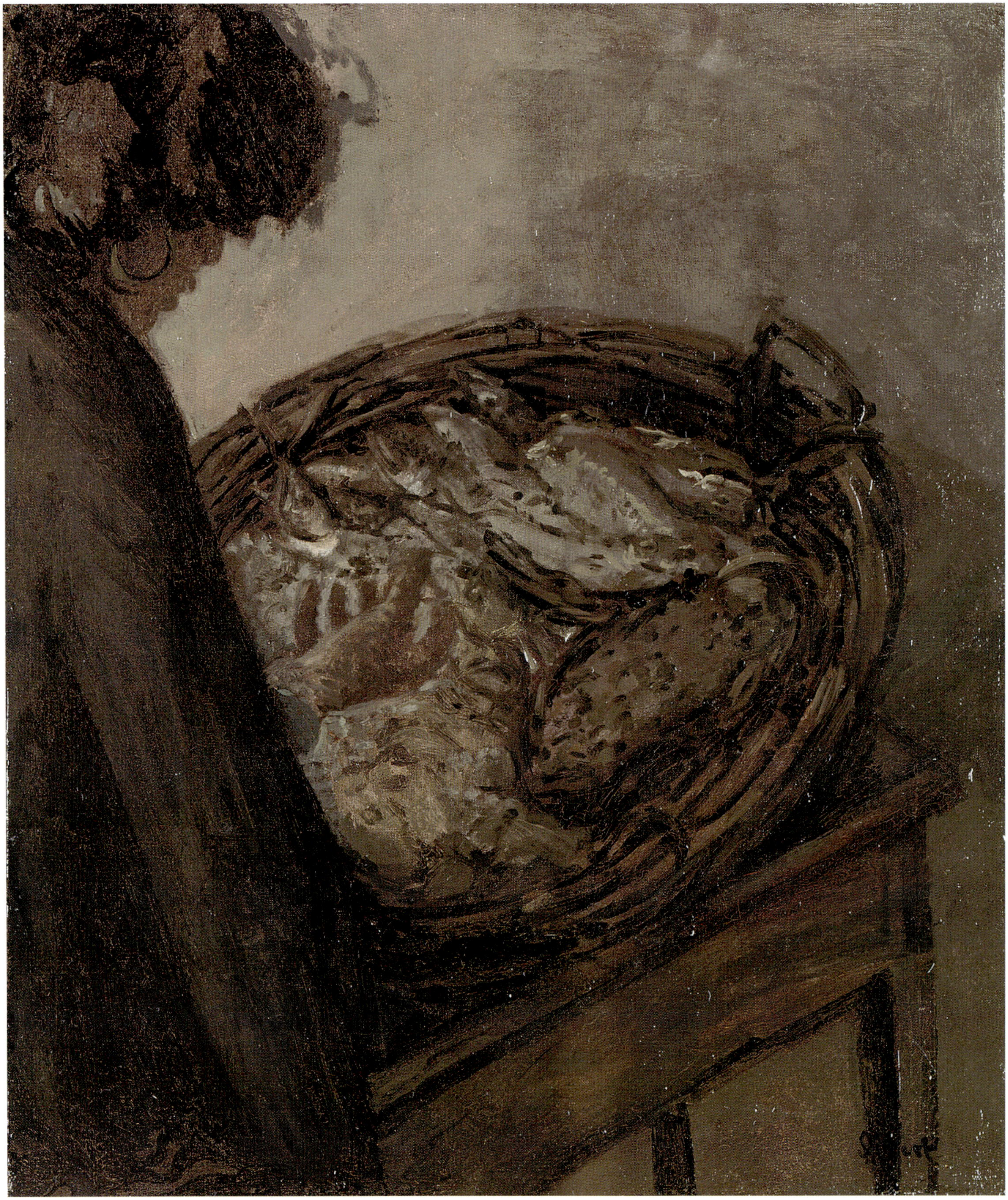

37
Alla Pescheria
1903–04
Oil on canvas,
55.2 x 46.4 cm
Private Collection

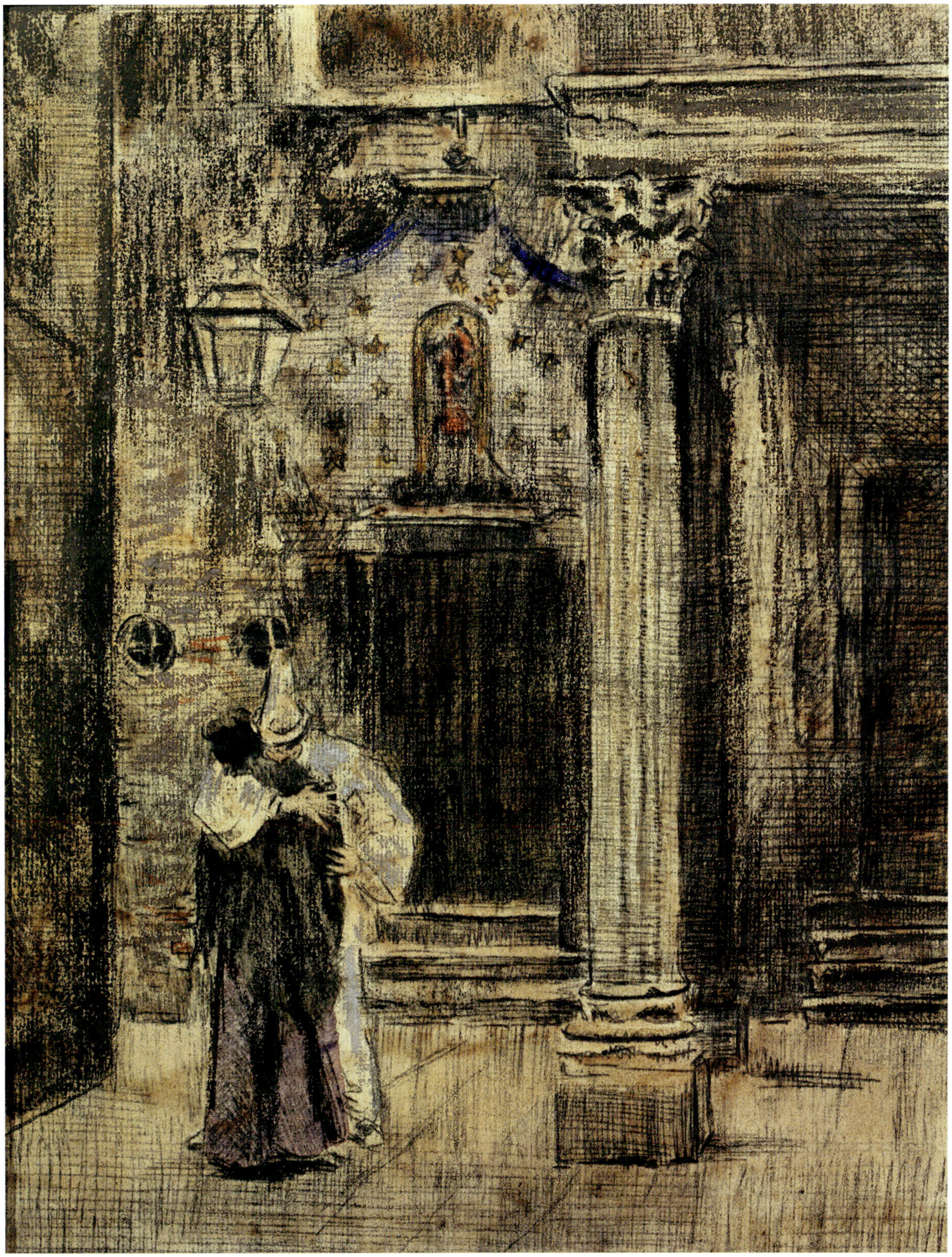

38
Pierrot and Woman Embracing
1903–04
Gouache and chalk on paper,
41 x 31 cm
Tate

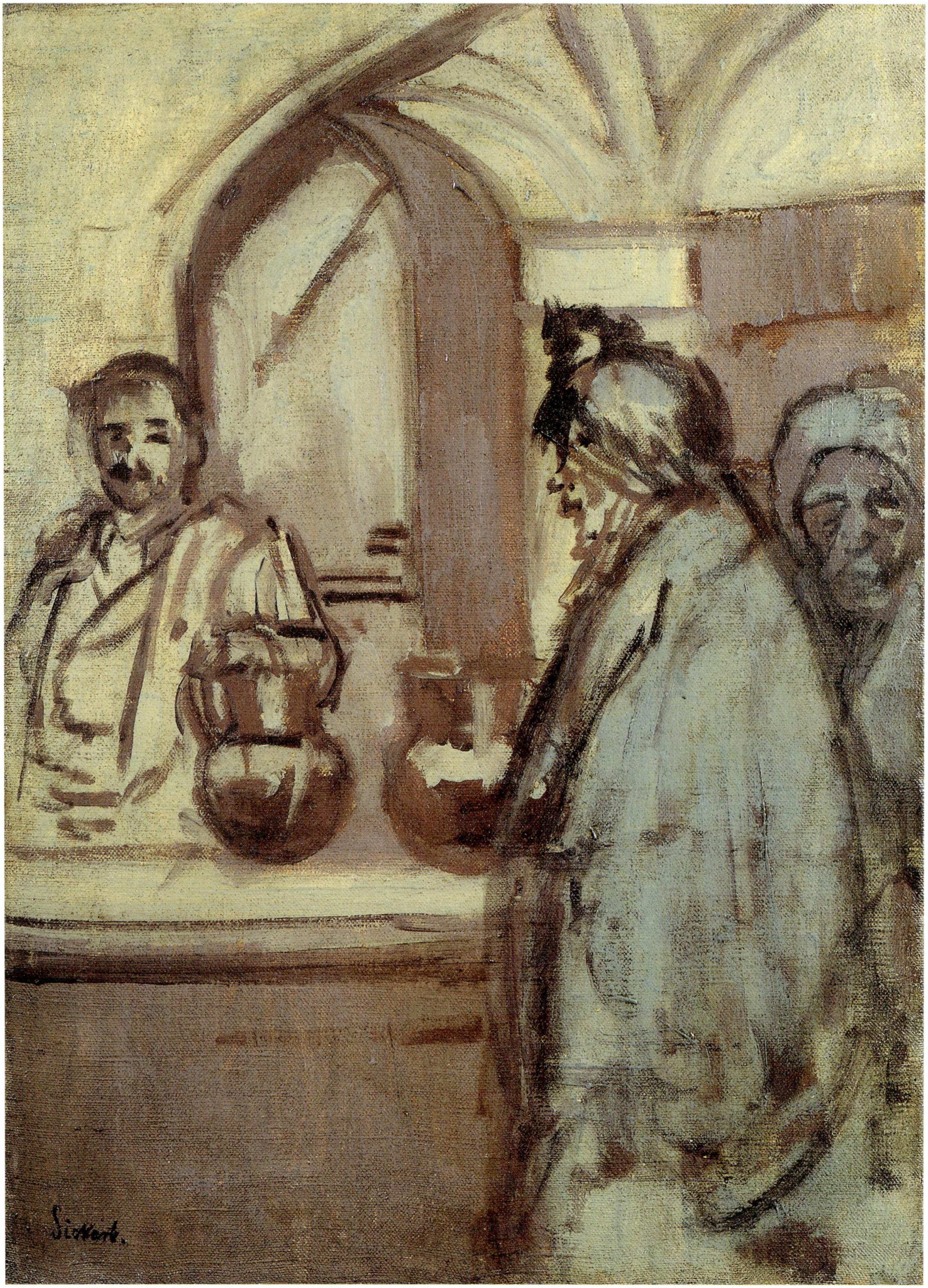

39
Ladies' Bar
c.1906
Oil on canvas,
45.7 x 40.6 cm
Private Collection

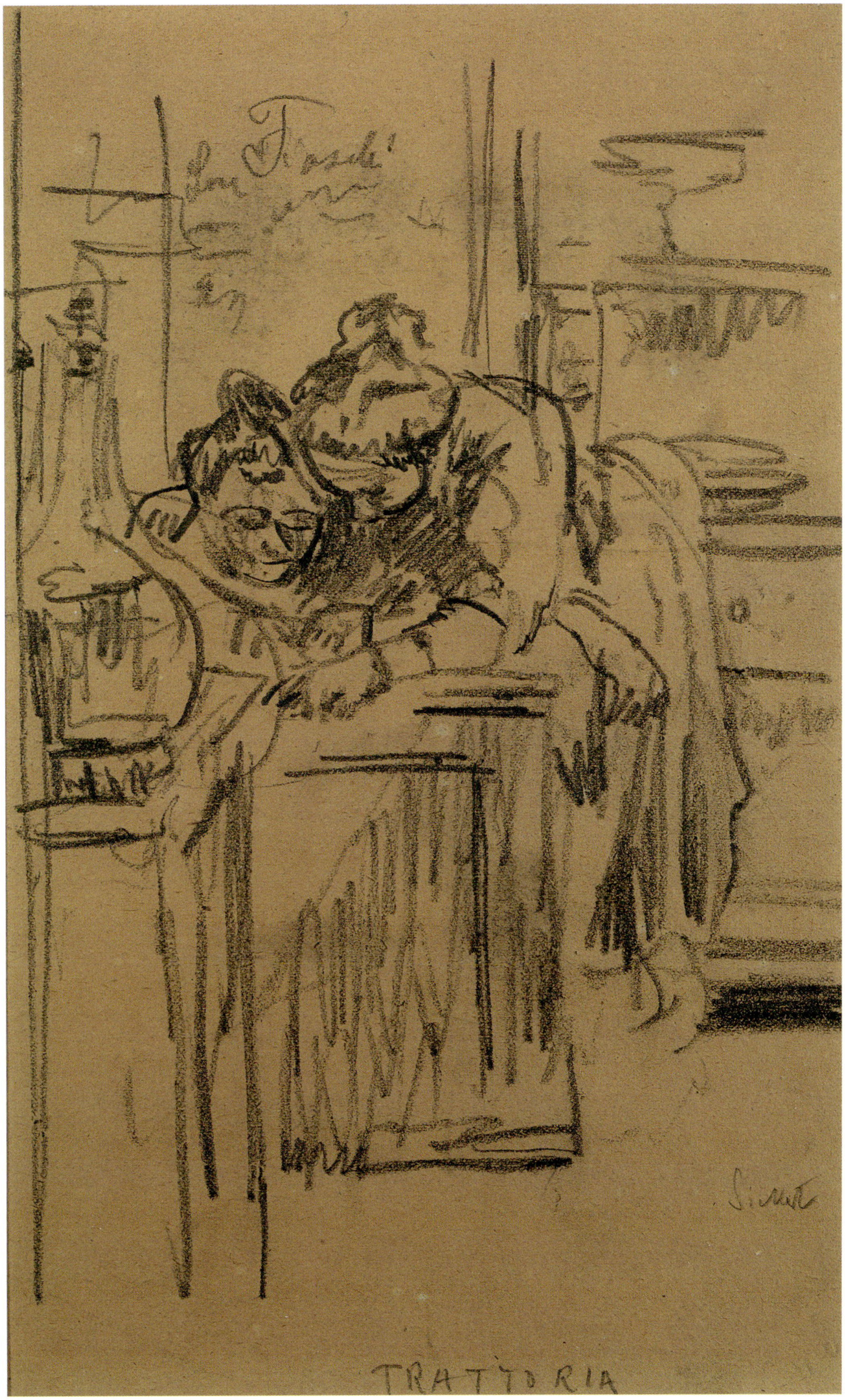

40
Trattoria
1903–04
Pencil, 50 x 41 cm
Private Collection

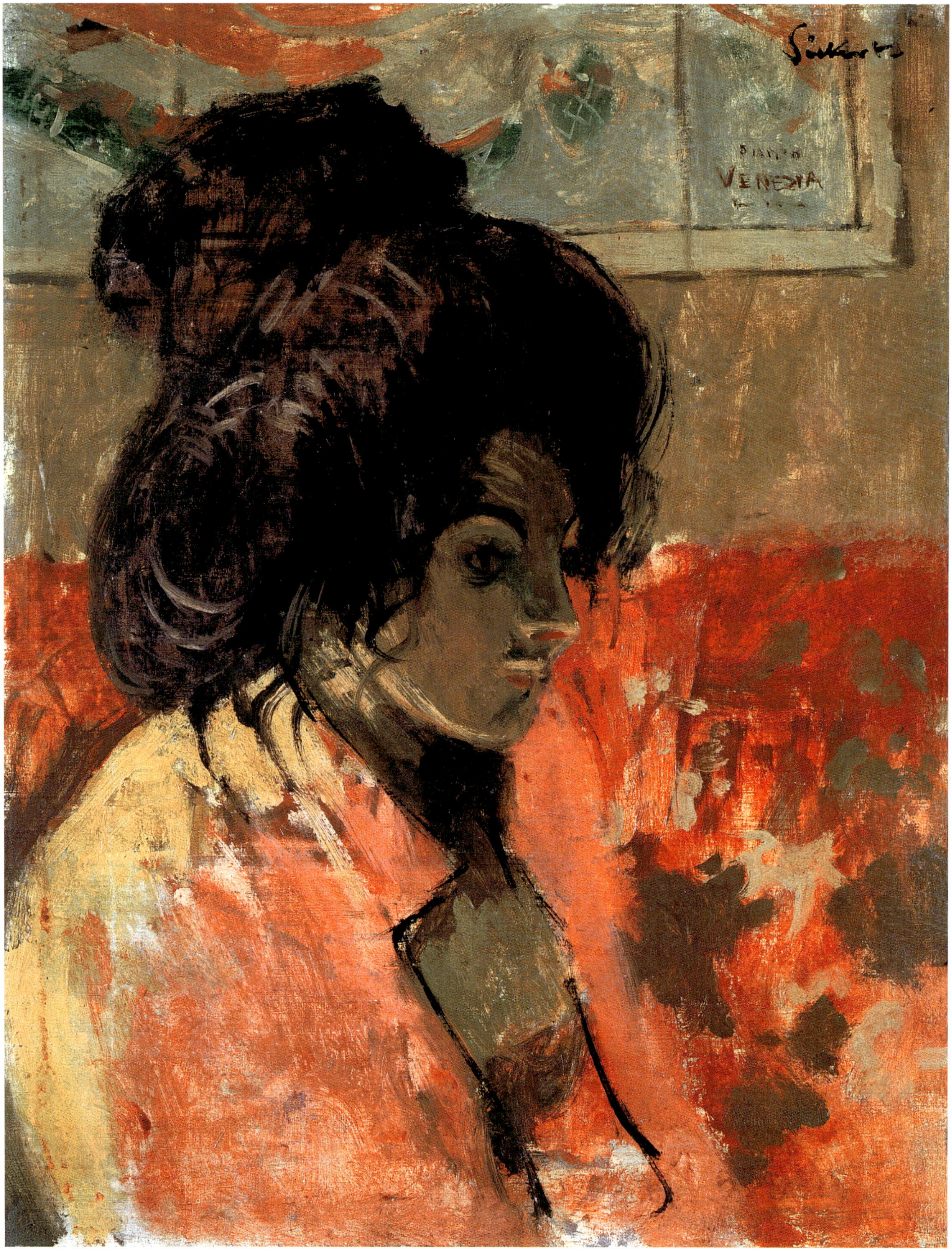
Sickert
VENEZIA

41
La Giuseppina against a Map of Venice
*c.*1903–04
Oil on canvas,
50.8 x 40.6 cm
Private Collection

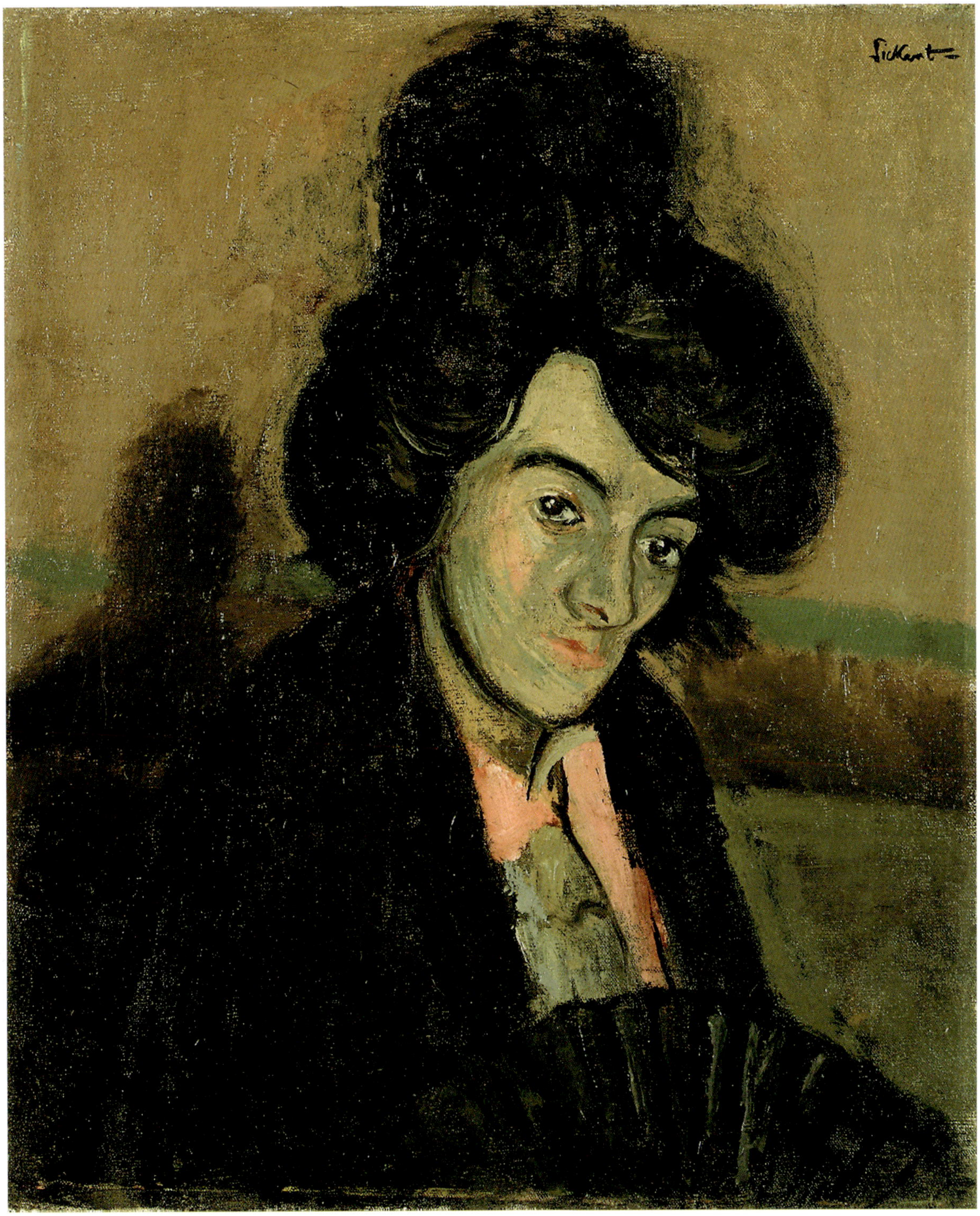

42
La Giuseppina: La Callera
1903–04
Oil on canvas,
49.5 x 39.4 cm
Private Collection

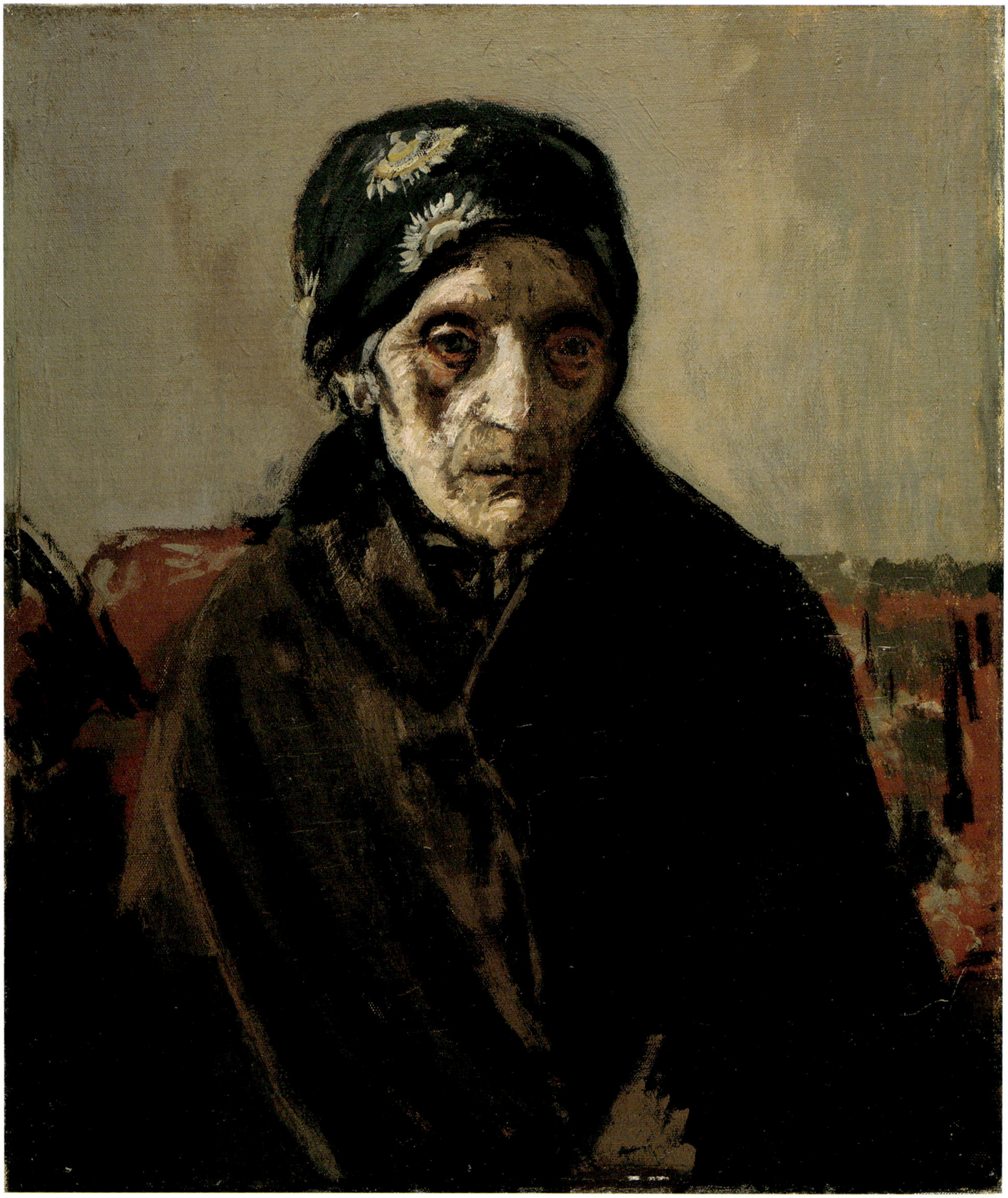

43
Mamma Mia Poveretta
1903–04
Oil on canvas, 46 x 38.1 cm
Manchester City Galleries

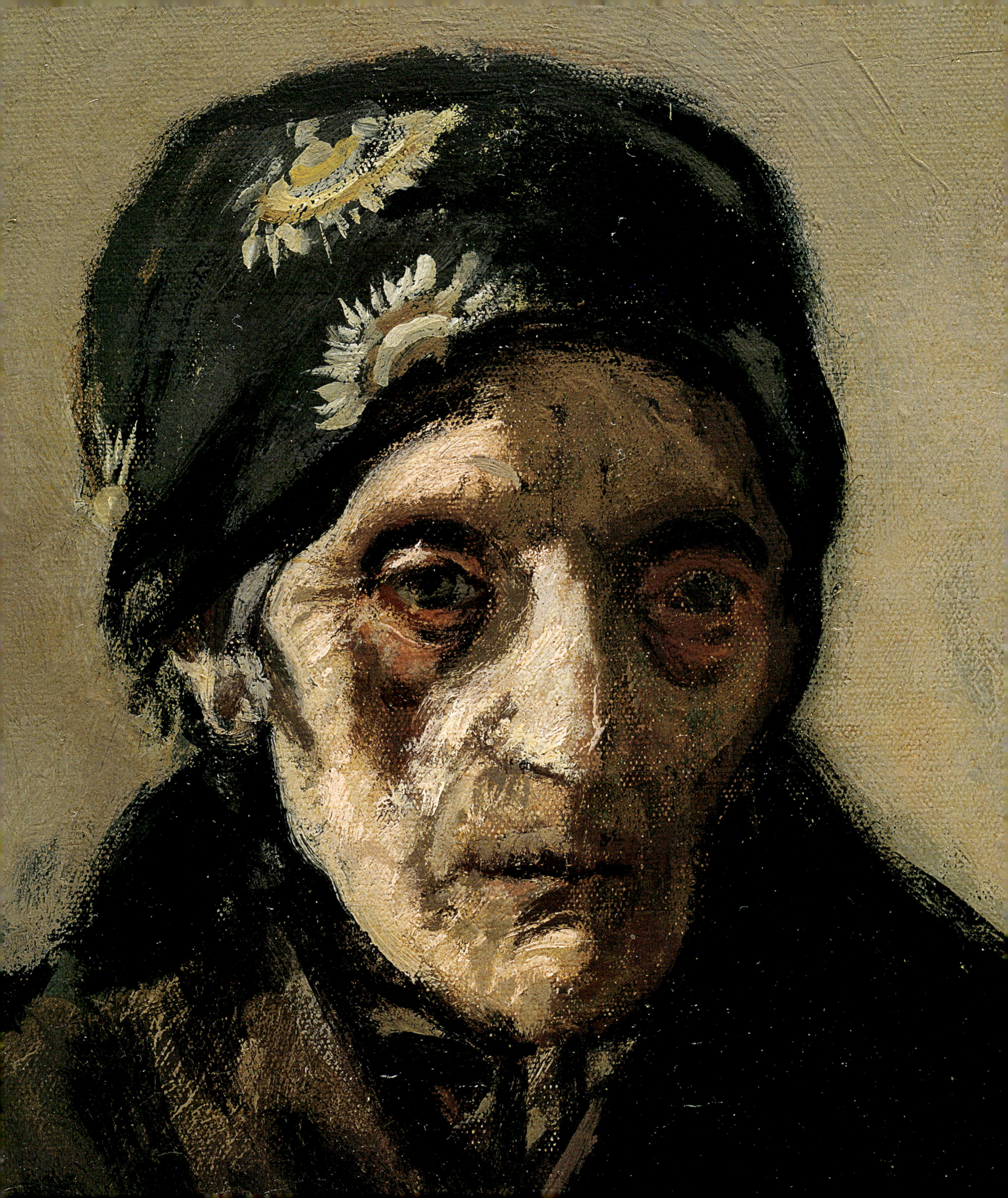

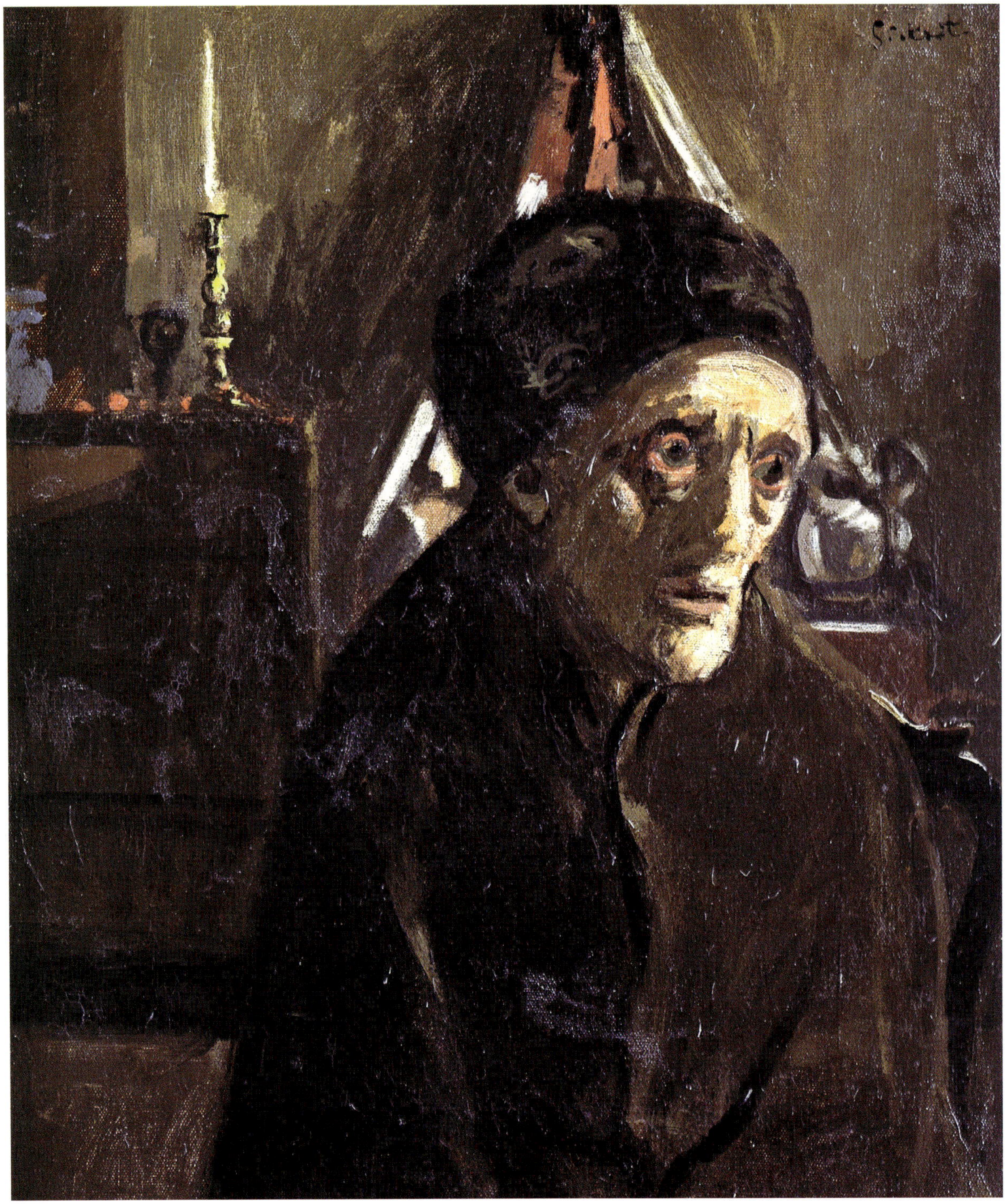

44
Mamma Mia Poveretta
1903–04
Oil on canvas, 45.7 x 38.1 cm
Private Collection, courtesy of Ivor Braka Ltd

45
La Carolina Standing in an Interior
1903–04
Oil on canvas, 54.6 x 46.4 cm
Private Collection

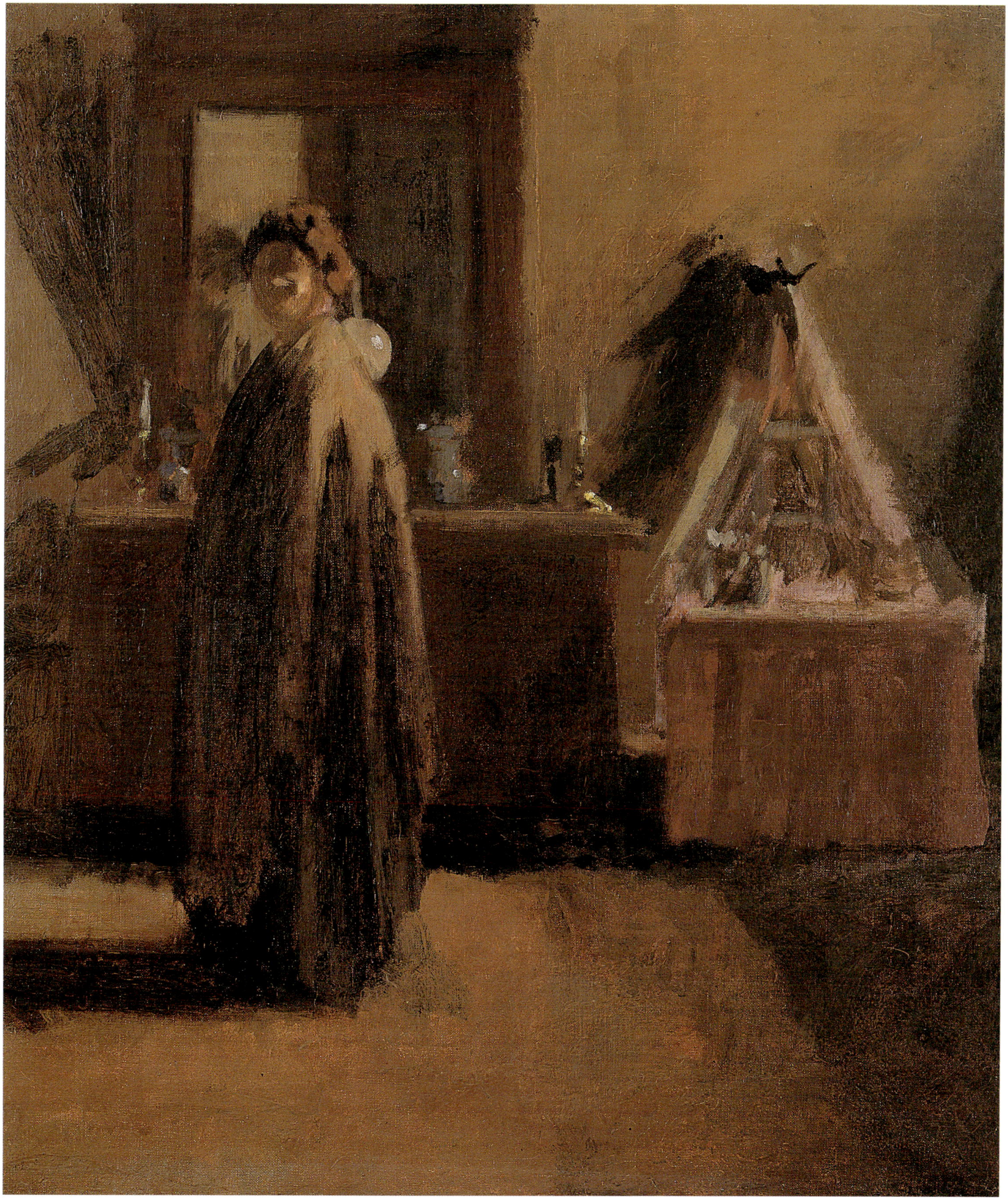

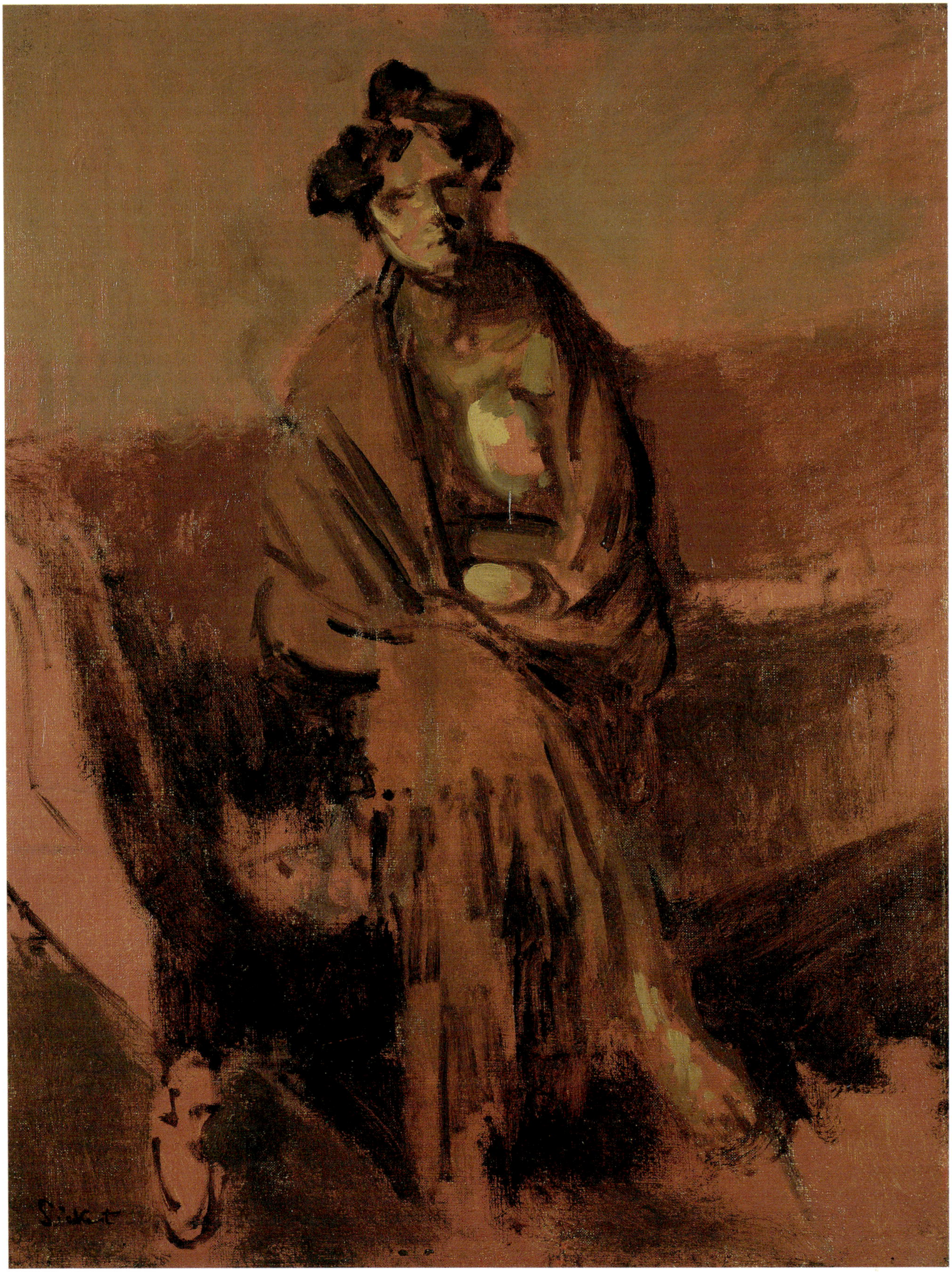

46
Study in Rose
1903–04
Oil on canvas,
54.6 x 40.6 cm
Private Collection

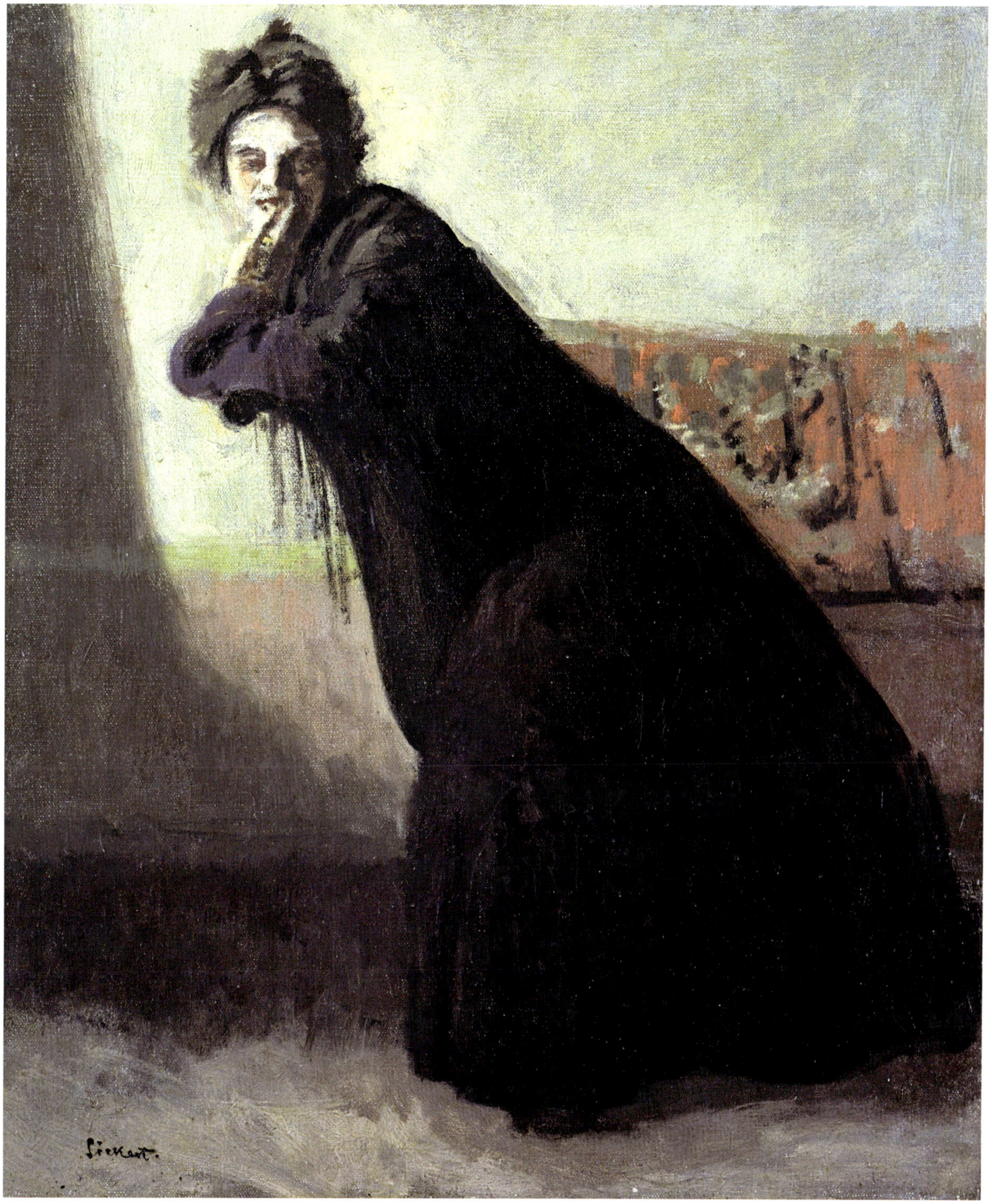

47
Le Châle Vénitien
1903–04
Oil on canvas, 45.7 x 38.1 cm
Ivor Braka Ltd

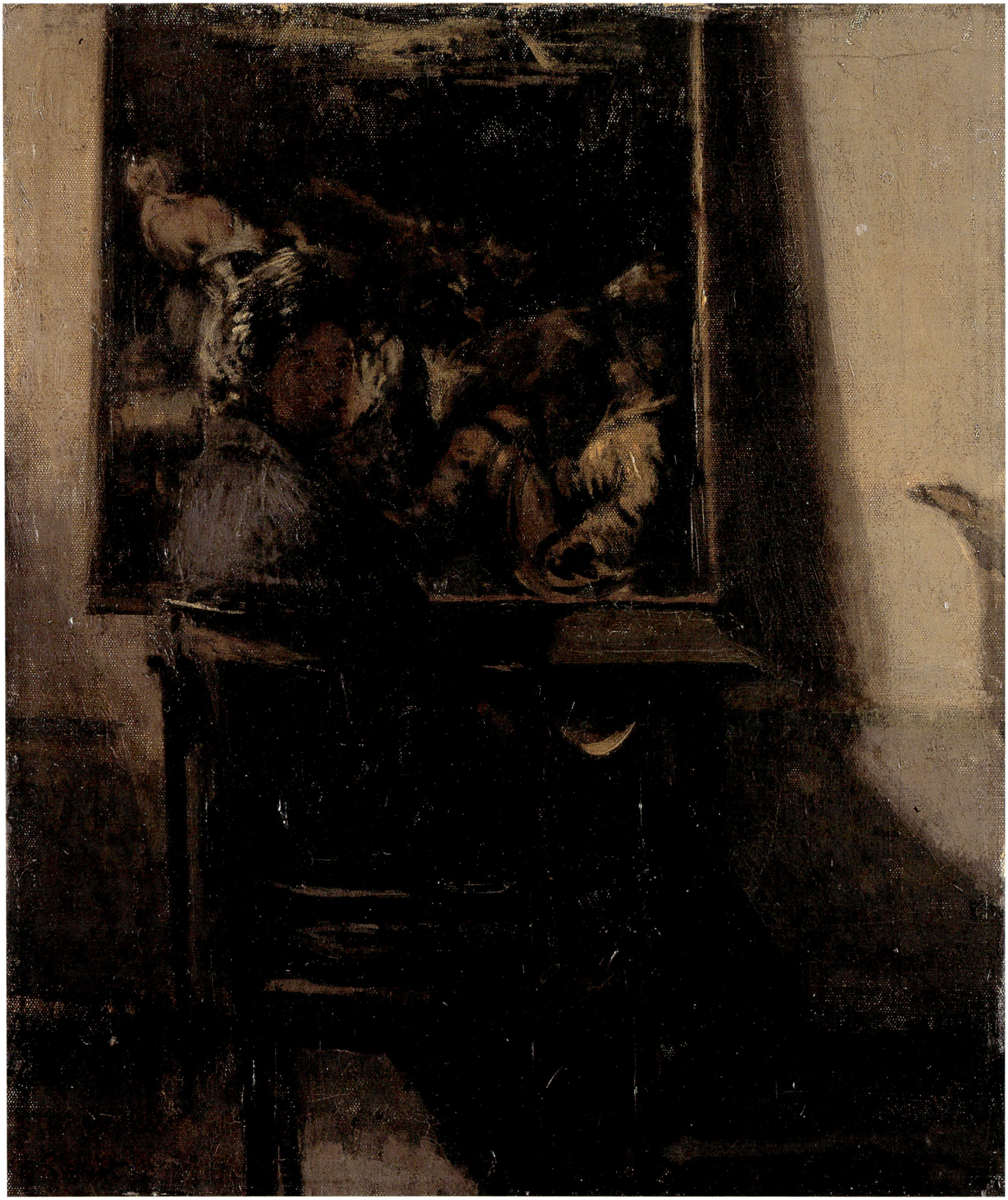

48
La Nera
1903–04
Oil on canvas, 45.7 x 38.1 cm
City & County of Swansea:
Glynn Vivian Art Gallery
Collection

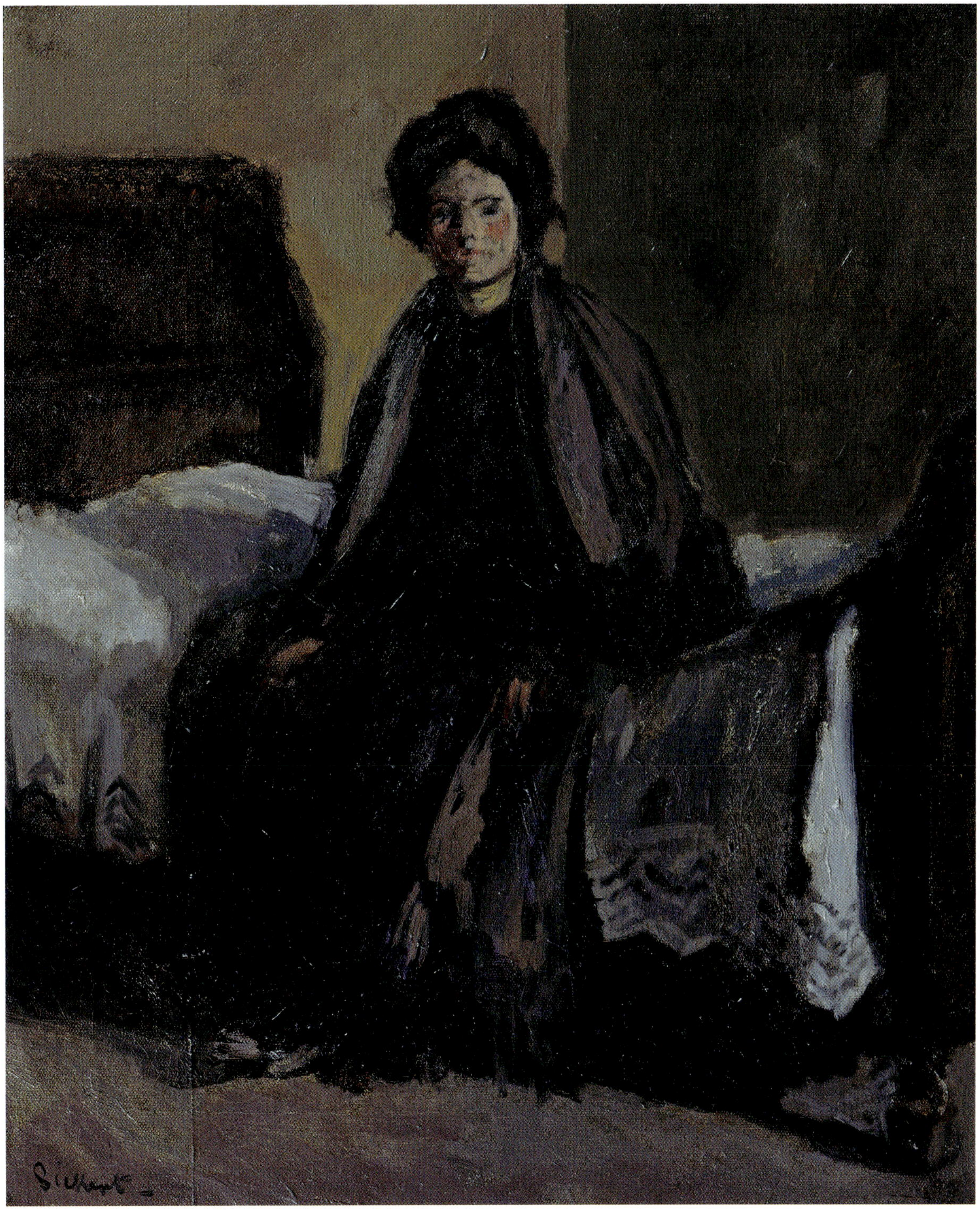

49
Carolina del'Acqua
1903–04
Oil on canvas, 47 x 38.5 cm
Daniel Katz Family Trust

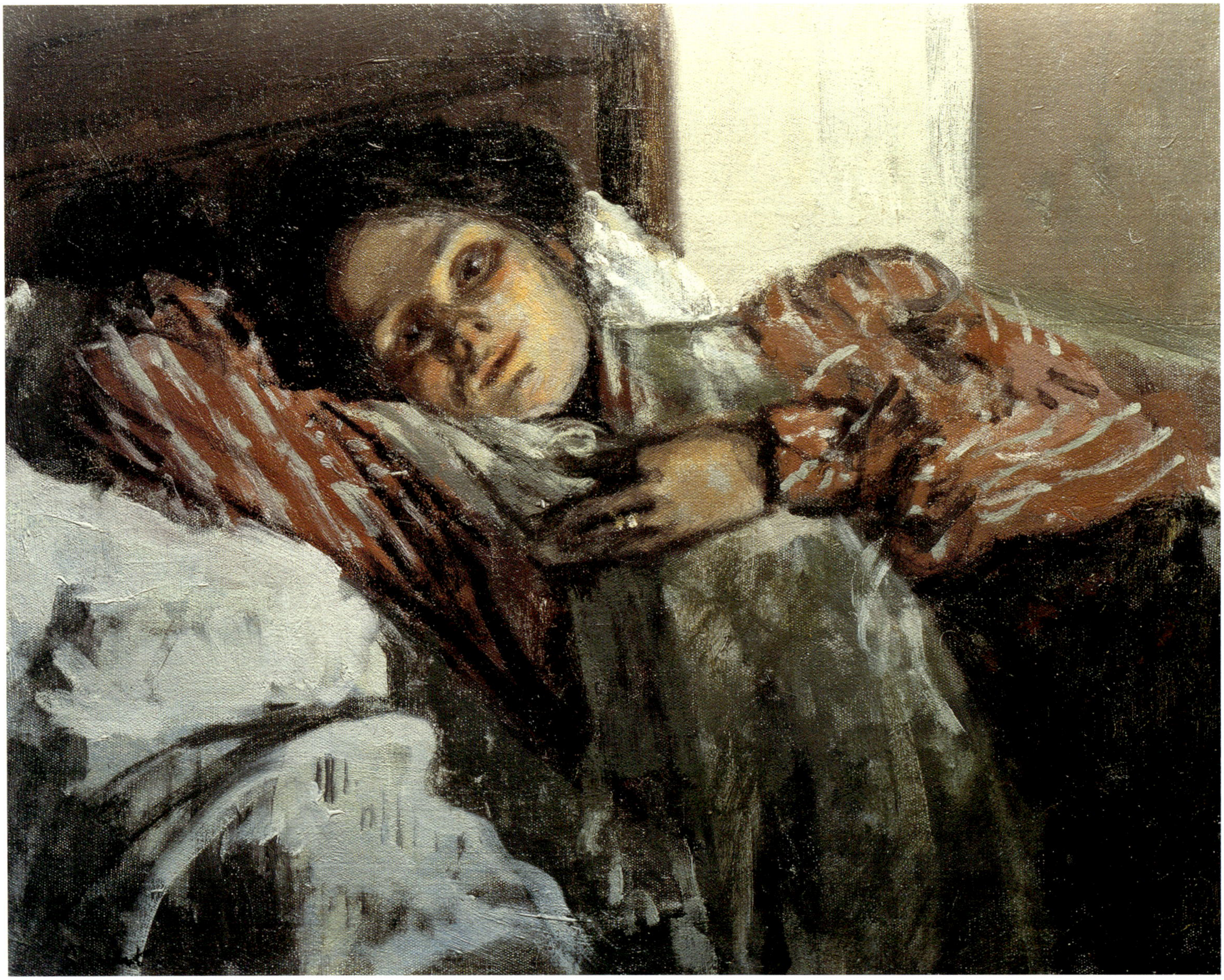

50
The Siesta
1903–04
Oil on canvas, 38.1 x 45.7 cm
Private Collection

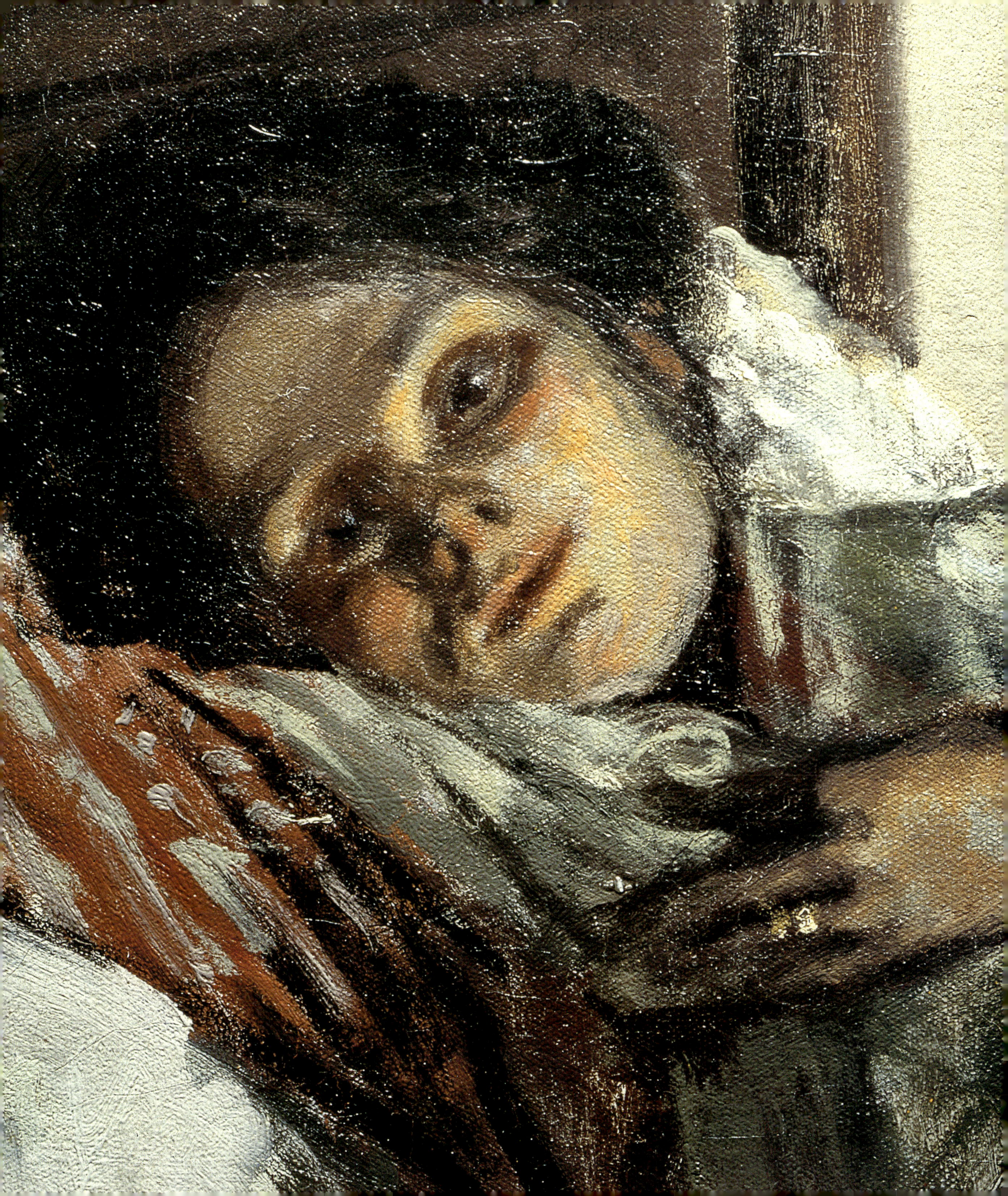

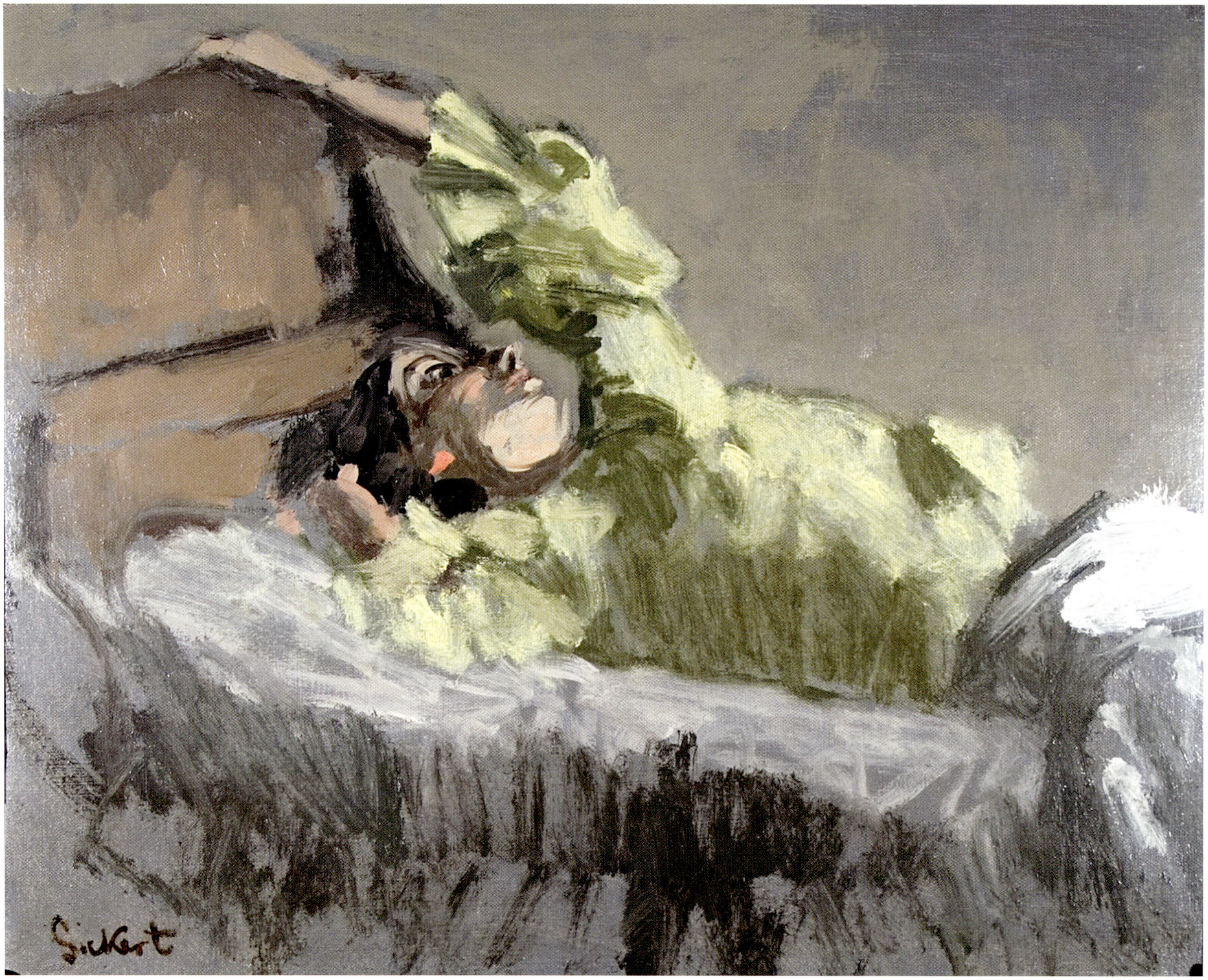

51
The Yellow Sleeve:
La Chiozzotta
1903–04
Oil on canvas, 38.1 x 45.7 cm
New Walk Museum & Art
Gallery, Leicester

52
Conversation
1903
Oil on canvas, 48.3 x 40.6 cm
Private Collection, courtesy
of Belgrave Gallery

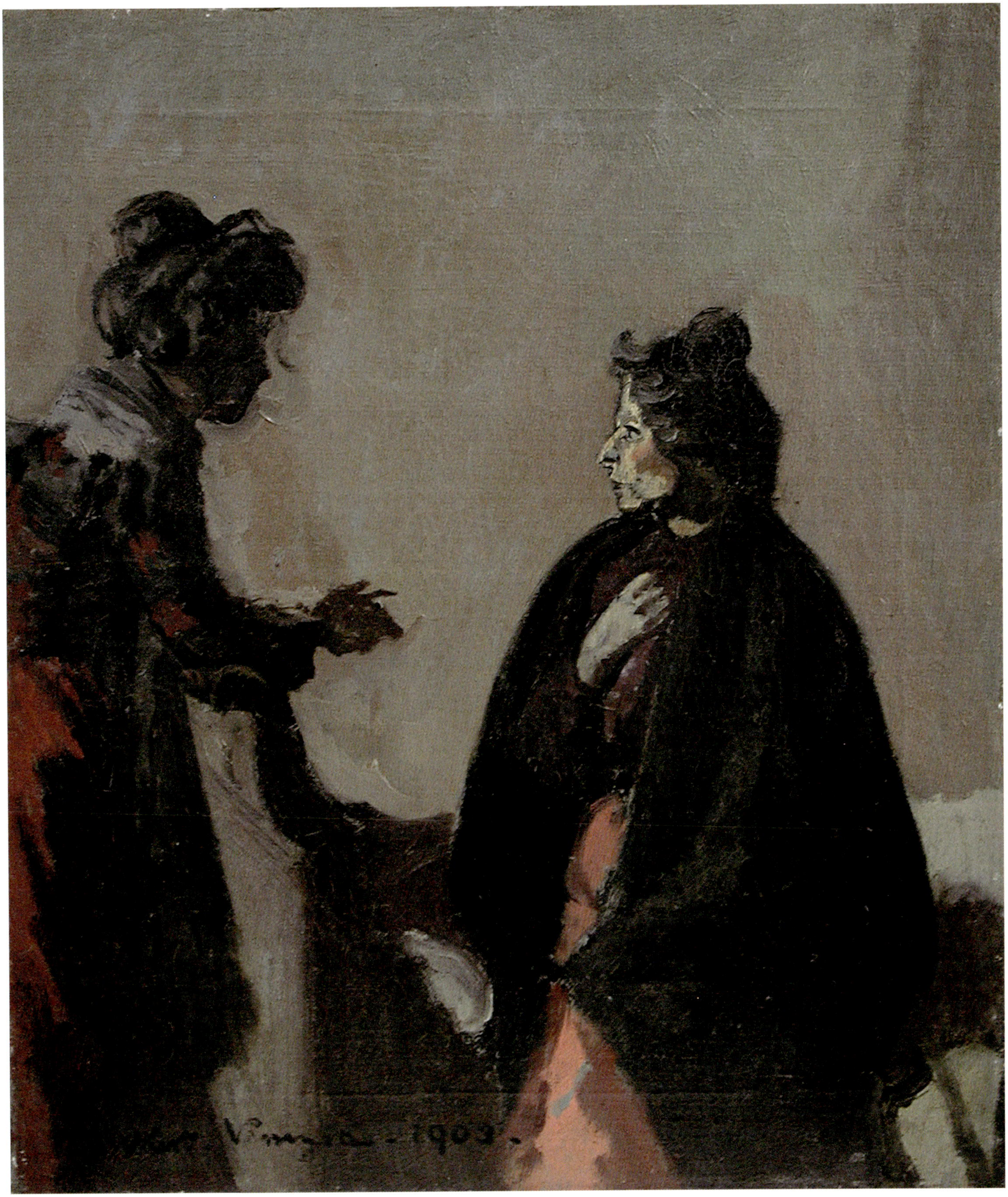

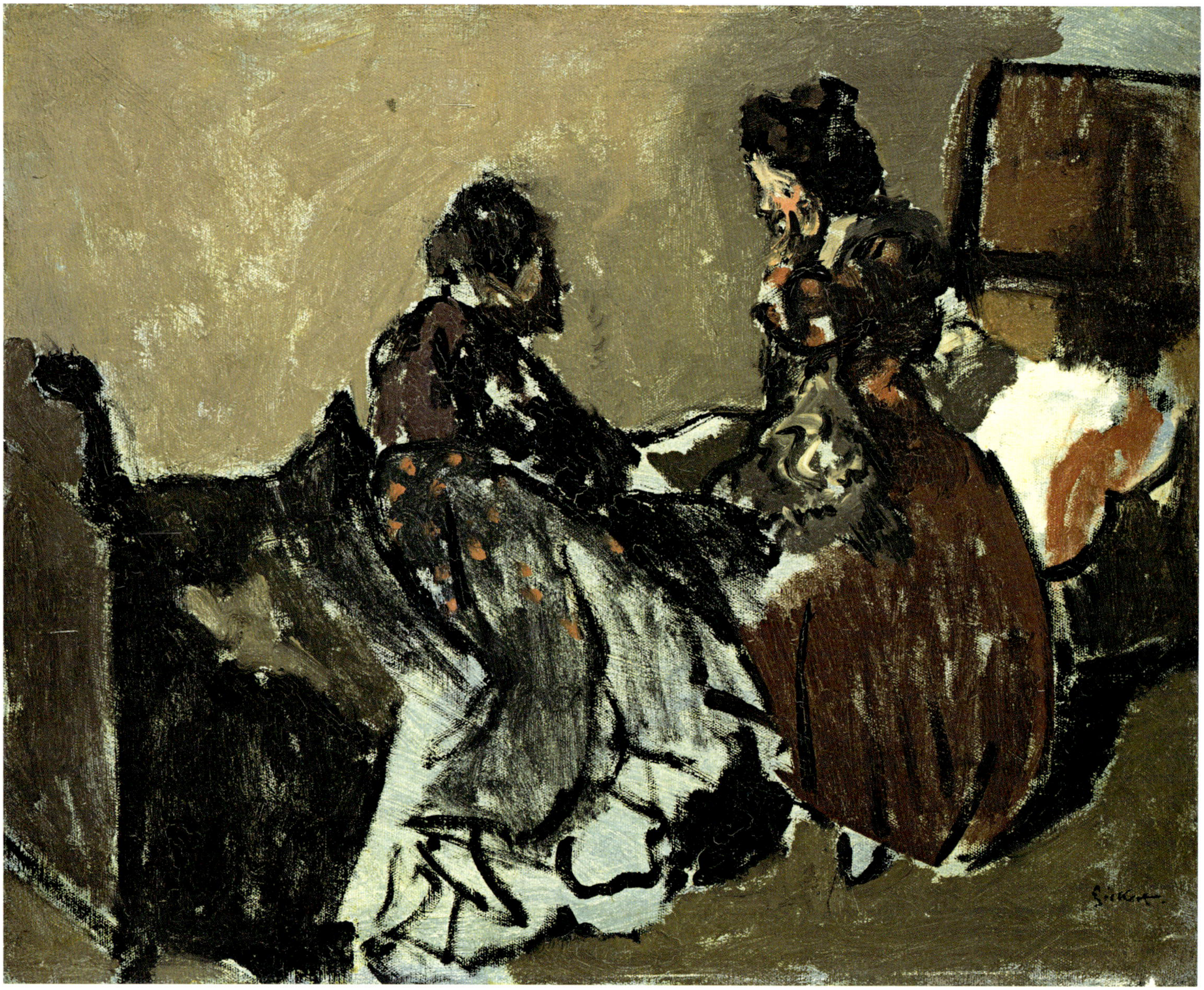

53
A Marengo
1903–04
Oil on canvas, 38.1 x 45.7 cm
Tate

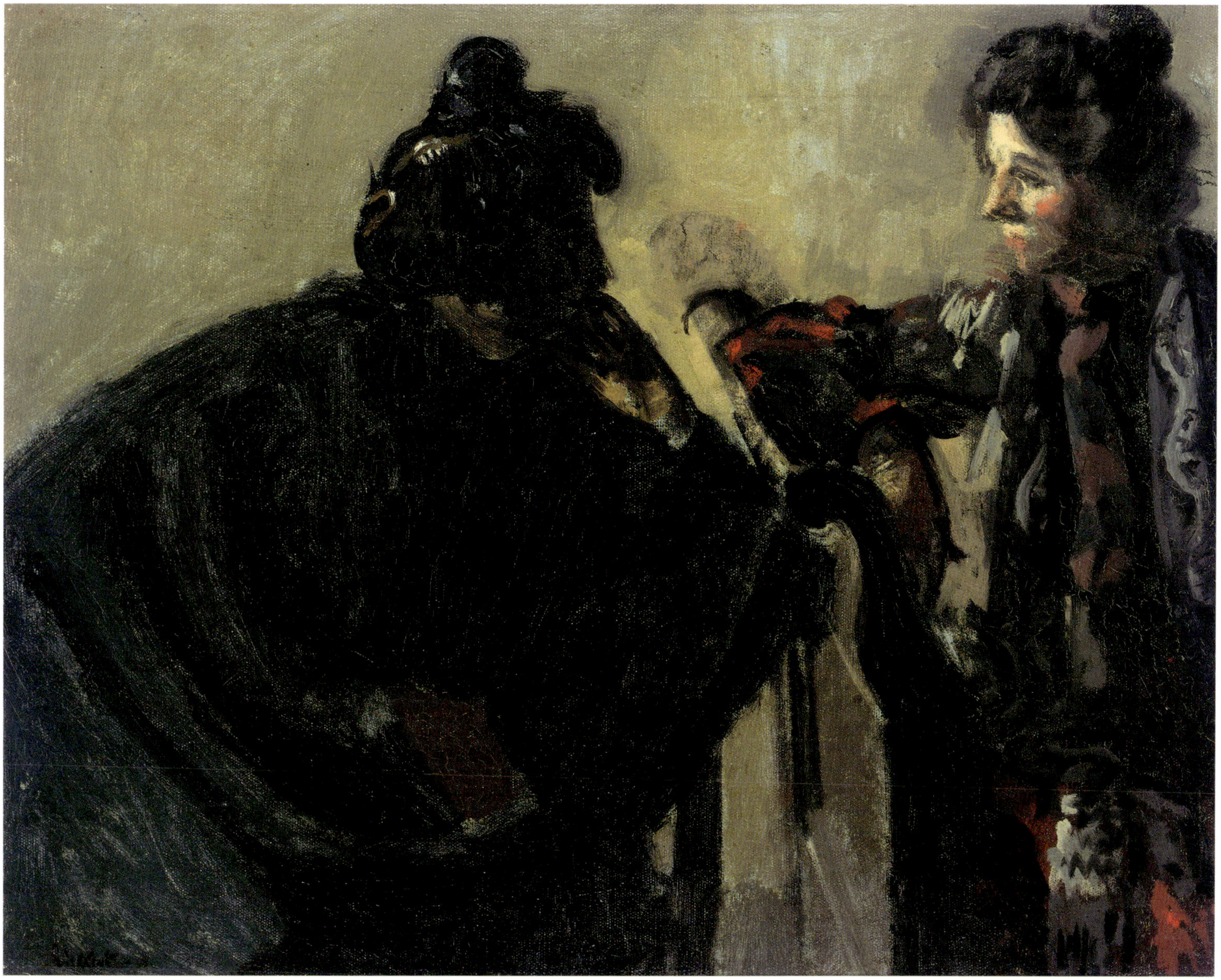

54
Caquetoeres
1903–04
Oil on canvas, 39.4 x 47 cm
Private Collection

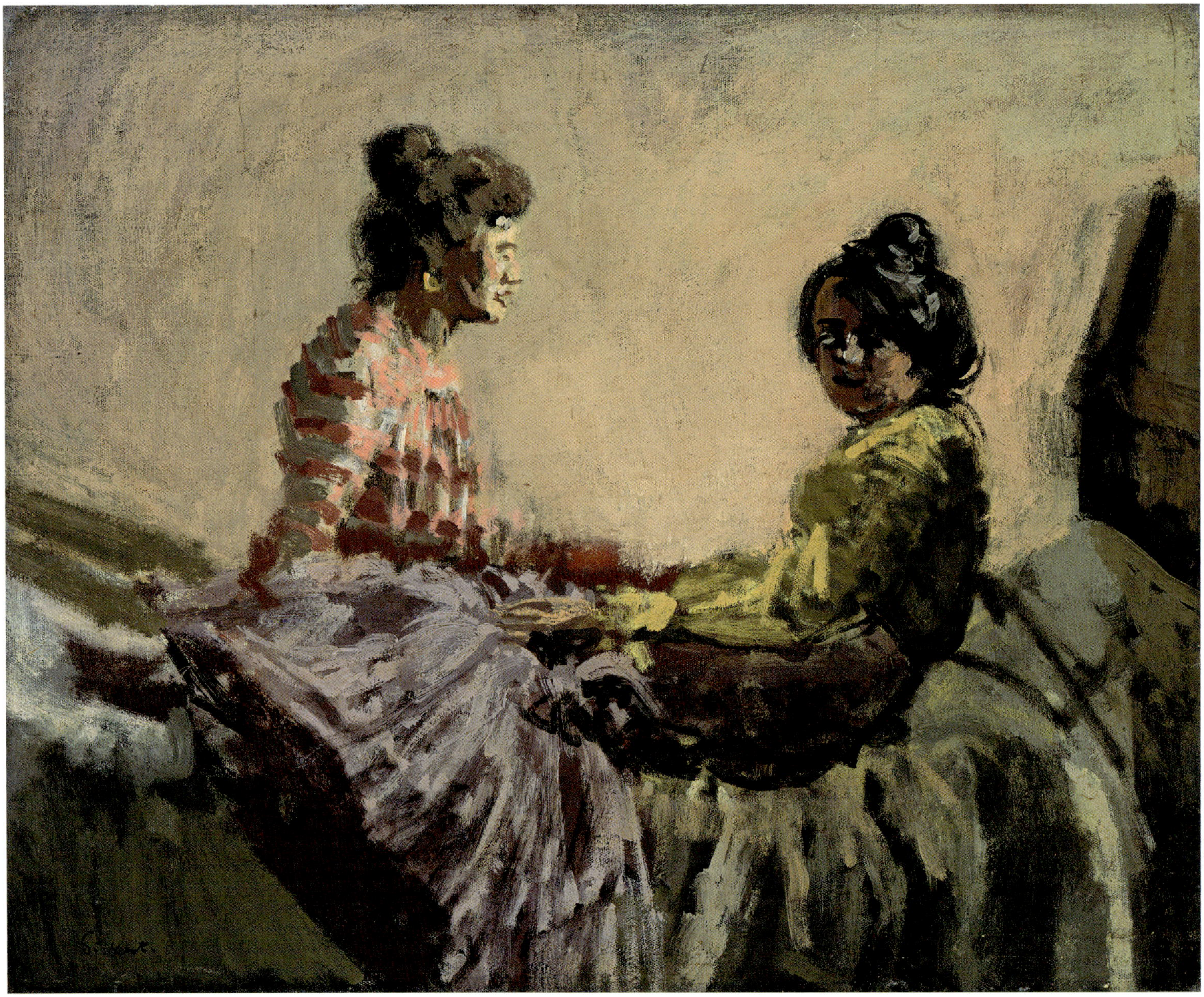

55
Les Vénitiennes (Venetian Women)
1903–04
Oil on canvas, 45.7 x 55.3 cm
Museum of Fine Arts, Boston

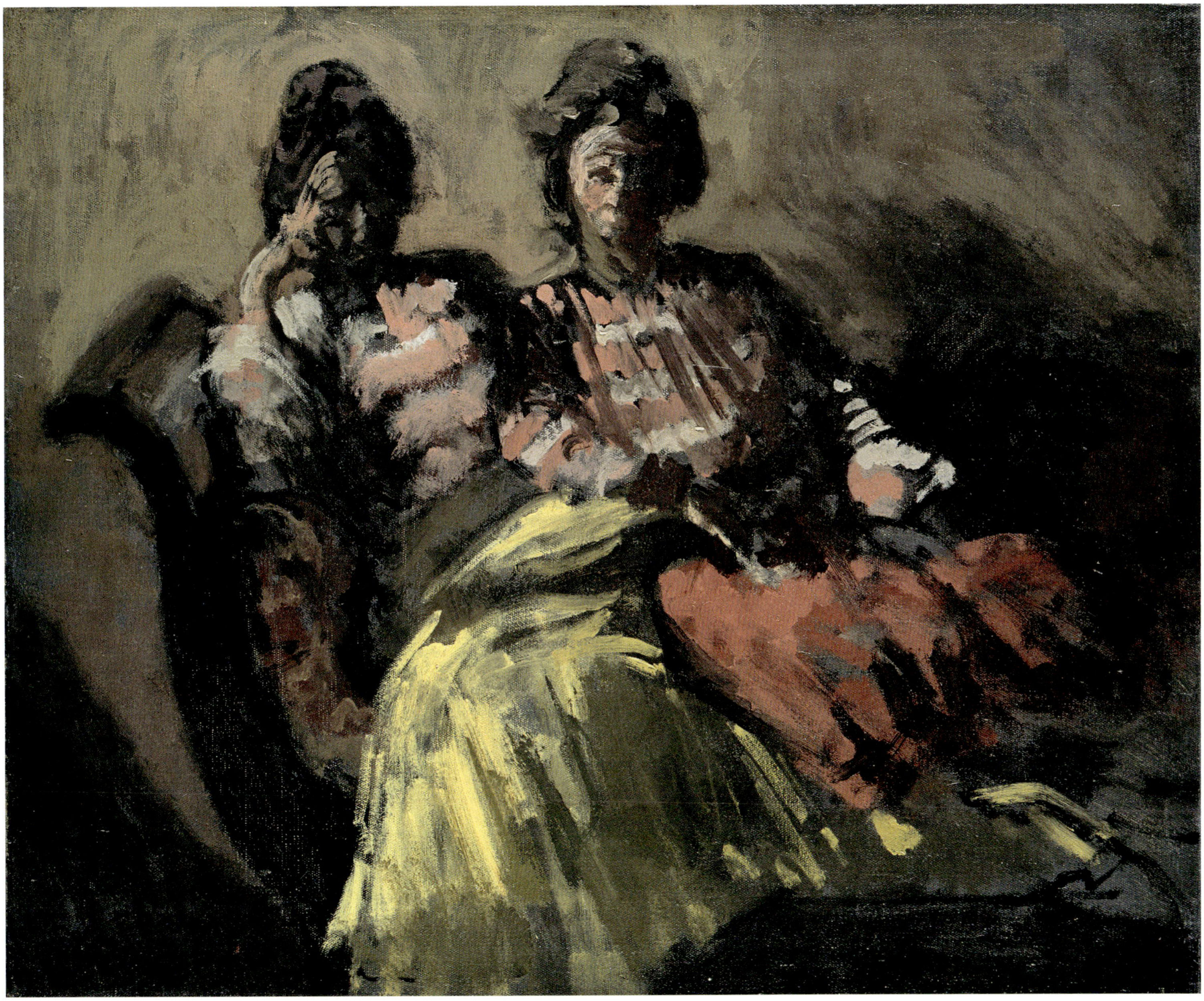

56
Two Women on a Sofa – Le Tose
*c.*1903–04
Oil on canvas, 45.7 x 53.3 cm
Tate

Selected Bibliography

Arts Council, *Late Sickert: Paintings 1927–1942*, exhibition catalogue (London: 1981–82)

Wendy Baron, *Perfect Moderns: The Camden Town Group* (Aldershot: 2000)

Wendy Baron, *Sickert: Paintings and Drawings* (New Haven and London: 2006)

Wendy Baron and Richard Shone (eds), *Sickert Paintings*, Royal Academy exhibition catalogue (London: 1992–93)

Ruth Bromberg, *Walter Sickert Prints: A Catalogue Raisonné* (New Haven and London: 2000)

Lillian Browse, *Sickert* (London: 1960)

Penelope Curtis (ed.), *Sickert Drawings and Paintings*, Tate Liverpool exhibition catalogue (1989)

Robert Emmons, *The Life and Opinions of Walter Richard Sickert* (London: 1941)

Marjorie Lilly, *Sickert: The Painter and his Circle* (London: 1971)

David Peters Corbett, *Walter Sickert* (London: 2001)

Anna Gruetzner Robins, *Walter Sickert Drawings: Theory and Practice: Word and Image* (Aldershot: 1996)

Anna Gruetzner Robins (ed.), *Walter Sickert: The Complete Writings on Art* (Oxford: 2000)

Richard Shone, *Walter Sickert* (Oxford: 1988)

Osbert Sitwell, *A Free House! Or The Artist as Craftsman Being the Writings of Walter Richard Sickert* (London: 1947)

Alistair Smith (ed.), *Walter Sickert: 'Drawing is the Thing'*, Whitworth Art Gallery exhibition catalogue (Manchester: 2004)

Matthew Sturgis, *Walter Sickert: A Life* (London: 2004)

Robert Upstone (ed.), *Modern Painters: The Camden Town Group*, Tate Britain exhibition catalogue (London: 2008)

Walter Sickert: The Human Canvas, Abbot Hall Art Gallery exhibition catalogue (Kendal: 2004)

Barnaby Wright (ed.), *Walter Sickert: The Camden Town Nudes*, exhibition catalogue (London: 2008)

Index

Numbers in *italics* indicate catalogue illustrations; those in **bold type** indicate figures in the essay.

Credits

Additional credits for works in the exhibition

cat. 1: Tate. Purchased 1923
cat. 4: Tate, London. Bequeathed by General Sir Ian Hamilton GCB, GCMG, DSO 1949
cat. 8: Tate. Purchased 1941
cats. 10, 12, 24, 40, 45: Photograph by Matthew Hollow
cat. 13: Photograph by Prudence Cuming Associates.
cat. 16: Tate, London. Bequeathed by Lady Henry Cavendish-Bentinck 1940
cat. 26: © Crown copyright: UK Government Art Collection
cat. 38: Tate, London. Bequeathed by Lady Henry Cavendish-Bentinck 1940
cat. 53: Tate. Purchased 1922
cat. 55: Museum of Fine Arts, Boston. Anonymous gift, 38.776. Photograph © 2009 Museum of Fine Arts Boston
cat. 56: Tate, London. Bequeathed by Sir Hugh Walpole 1941

Photography credits and other additional information for figure illustrations

fig. 1: National Portrait Gallery, London
figs. 2, 19, 23: © Fondo Fotografico Tomaso Filippi – I. R. E. Venezia
figs. 3, 8: Fitzwilliam Museum, Cambridge
fig. 4: © Tate, London 2009
fig. 5: Amgueddfa Genedlaethol Cymru, National Museums Wales
fig. 6: Collection of the Guild of St George, Museums Sheffield
fig. 7: Chester Dale Collection, Image courtesy of the Board of Trustees, National Gallery of Art, Washington
fig. 9: Tate, London. Presented by W. Graham Robertson, 1940
fig. 10: Musée Royaux des Beaux-Arts de Belgique, Bruxelles
fig. 11: © Tate, London 2009. Bequeathed by Arthur Studd 1919
fig. 12: Harvard Art Museum, Fogg Art Museum, Loan and Promised Gift of Patricia Cornwell, 1.2005.9. Photo: Katya Kallsen © President and Fellows of Harvard College
fig. 13: National Gallery of Victoria, Melbourne, Australia. Felton Bequest, 1905
fig. 14: Salomon R. Guggenheim Museum, New York. Thannhauser Collection, Gift, Justin K. Thannhauser, 1978. 78.2514.34
fig. 15: Albright-Knox Art Gallery, Buffalo, New York. Friends of the Albright Art Gallery Fund, 1916
fig. 16: Time and Life Pictures / Getty Images
fig. 17: National Museums Liverpool, Lady Lever Gallery
fig. 18: Birmingham Museums & Art Gallery
fig. 20: Book supplied courtesy of the author
fig. 21: Rouen, Musée des Beaux-Arts. Don Jacques-Emile Blanche, 1923. © Musées de la Ville de Rouen
fig. 22: Image courtesy of Daniel Katz Ltd
fig. 25: Image courtesy of Sotheby's
fig. 26: © Tate, London 2009. Bequeathed by Dame Peggy Ashcroft 1992

Acknowledgements

The idea for this exhibition grew out of writing catalogue entries for the Venetian Sickerts in Tate's collection. These will form part of the Camden Town Research Project, a major web-based initiative which will appear online in 2010. Venice was where Sickert reinvented himself, and the Venetian pictures, it seemed to me, unlocked those that followed them and shed light on his subsequent career. I am particularly grateful therefore to Dulwich Picture Gallery for giving me the opportunity to write more fully about this important aspect of Sickert's work, and for bringing together such a strong group of his Venice pictures.

Sickert studies offer new possibilities due to major recent publications by three scholars, each of whose books provided invaluable resources for this exhibition, and who also kindly gave me their time to discuss the subject. Wendy Baron's expanded catalogue of Sickert's oeuvre provides exhaustive information on every work; Matthew Sturgis's biography gives the most detailed account of Sickert's life ever available; and Anna Gruetzner Robins's collected volume of Sickert's writings allows us to understand fully his evolving opinions on contemporary and historic art. Similarly I am grateful to my colleagues in Tate Conservation, particularly Stephen Hackney, whose technical texts about Sickert's materials and techniques for the Camden Town Research Project provided unique insights and information.

Working with Dulwich has genuinely been a delight. Ian Dejardin was enthusiastic and supportive from the outset, appreciating the show's potential. Kate Knowles gave early encouragement and support, as well as securing publicity, and Dida Tait led fundraising to make the exhibition possible. I am particularly grateful to have worked with Sanne Klinge, who as well as being a perfect exhibition organiser has steered the project with patience, good humour and flair. Matthew Cowpe provided invaluable support with picture research. To all these and others at Dulwich I give heartfelt thanks. At Scala I have been similarly lucky in working with such a great team. Oliver Craske has been a source of calm and sound advice, and an excellent editor. I already admired Nigel Soper's previous book designs, so it was wonderful to have him work on this one. Tim Clarke provided exemplary colour proofing.

Finally – and most importantly – I should like particularly to thank the lenders. Without their kindness and support the exhibition simply would not have been possible and their generosity is greatly appreciated. I would like also to acknowledge those in the commercial art world who so generously gave their time contacting clients or helping with details about pictures: Julian Agnew, Ivor Braka, Will Darby, Richard Green, Irving Grose, Robert Holden, James Holland-Hibbert, Danny Katz, Peter and Renate Nahum, Elizabeth Oustinoff, Annabel Thomas and Offer Waterman.

Robert Upstone

This exhibition has been made possible with the assistance of the Government Indemnity Scheme which is provided by the Department for Culture, Media and Sport (administered by the MLA).